KU-202-045

Martin John Yate

Utimate
CV

Master the art of creating a winning CV with over 100 samples to help you get the job

FIFTH EDITION

KoganPage

Publisher's note

Every possible effort has been made to ensure that the information contained in this book is accurate at the time of going to press, and the publishers and author cannot accept responsibility for any errors or omissions, however caused. No responsibility for loss or damage occasioned to any person acting, or refraining from action, as a result of the material in this publication can be accepted by the editor, the publisher or the author.

First published in the United States in 1993 as *Knock 'em Dead* by Adams Media Corporation
First published in Great Britain in 2003 as *The Ultimate CV Book* by Kogan Page Limited
Reprinted in 2003, 2004, 2005, 2007
Second edition published in 2008 as *Ultimate CV*
Third edition 2012
Fourth edition 2015
Fifth edition 2018

Published by arrangement with Adams Media Corporation, 57 Littlefield Street, Avon, MA 02322, USA

Apart from any fair dealing for the purposes of research or private study, or criticism or review, as permitted under the Copyright, Designs and Patents Act 1988, this publication may only be reproduced, stored or transmitted, in any form or by any means, with the prior permission in writing of the publishers, or in the case of reprographic reproduction in accordance with the terms and licences issued by the CLA. Enquiries concerning reproduction outside these terms should be sent to the publishers at the undermentioned addresses:

2nd Floor, 45 Gee Street	c/o Martin P Hill Consulting	4737/23 Ansari Road
London EC1V 3RS	122 W 27th St, 10th floor	Daryaganj
United Kingdom	New York, NY 10001	New Delhi 110002
www.koganpage.com	USA	India

© Martin John Yate, 1993, 1995, 1998, 2001, 2003, 2008, 2012, 2015, 2018

The right of Martin John Yate to be identified as the author of this work has been asserted by him in accordance with the Copyright, Designs and Patents Act 1988.

ISBN   978 0 7494 8152 0
E-ISBN   978 0 7494 8153 7

British Library Cataloguing-in-Publication Data

A CIP record for this book is available from the British Library.

Typeset by Graphicraft Limited, Hong Kong
Print production managed by Jellyfish
Printed and bound by CPI Group (UK) Ltd, Croydon, CR0 4YY

CONTENTS

INTRODUCTION

The facts of life

On the list of things you want to do in life, working on your CV is right up there with hitting yourself in the head with a hammer. Yet having a brilliant CV is the foundation of every successful job search. Show me a stalled job search and I'll show you a flawed CV. What you learn in these pages will give you the best CV you have ever had, and if you pay close attention, you will learn how to change the trajectory of your career.

Your CV is the most financially important document you will ever have. When your CV works, you work; when it doesn't, you don't. It's the primary tool to introduce yourself to your professional world, and properly fashioned, it ensures that prospective employers and future colleagues see you as you want to be seen. Don't bother about your CV and you can say goodbye to that new job and career success.

No one likes writing a CV, but it's an essential part of presenting yourself. When it comes to a job search, you are a product, and your CV is the packaging that sells that product. This is critical in a world where your CV all too often disappears into CV databases with millions of others. When employers do find it, your CV will get a scan lasting five to forty-five seconds, and if a clearly defined and relevant employee doesn't jump out, they'll move on to the next one.

This book will give you control over these issues, delivering a CV that will consistently get picked from the databases and will resonate with employers on that first scan and also on deeper, more careful readings.

Remember: managers hate to interview; they just want to find someone who can do the job, so they can get back to work. This book shows you how to convince managers that you are a competent professional who can do the job. It will prepare you to talk about the job's big issues and answer the tough questions in ways you never thought possible . . . and it's all based on a common-sense approach you'll be able to grasp and apply to your future.

1

YOUR CV – THE MOST FINANCIALLY IMPORTANT DOCUMENT YOU'LL EVER HAVE

Read this book with a highlighter –
it will save time as you refer back to important passages.

Your CV is the most financially significant document you will ever have. When it works, the doors of opportunity open for you. When it doesn't work, they won't.

No one enjoys writing a CV, but it has such a major impact on the money you earn during your working life, and consequently on the quality of your life outside of work, that you know it needs to be done properly.

You didn't come to this book for a good read. You came because you are facing serious challenges in your professional life. The way the professional world works has changed dramatically in the past few years, and nothing has changed as much as recruitment. When employment practices have changed beyond recognition, your approach to getting hired needs to be re-evaluated from top to bottom.

In these pages, you are going to learn very quickly how to build a CV that works. But you're going to learn something more. Since my approach to CVs is part of a larger strategy for achieving long-term career and personal success, everything I teach you about developing a brilliant CV will apply to the broader challenges of the job search, interviewing, and career management.

In other words, not only will you leave this book with a CV, you'll leave it with critical job search and interview strategies, and even some amazing insights into winning raises and promotions.

Self-awareness: the key to professional survival and success

Understanding what employers want and need from a specific job, and how they express and prioritize those needs, will tell you what it takes to succeed in that job. It will also give you some hints about the story your CV needs to tell in order to get your foot in the door.

Employers just want to make money

Employees only get added to the payroll to enhance profitability in some way. Think about this: if you owned a company, there just isn't any other reason you would add workers to your payroll. So it is implicit in any employment contract that *your job contributes to profitability in some way*.

Depending on your job, you can help an employer by:

- Making money for the company
- Saving money for the company
- Saving time/increasing productivity

No matter what your job, no matter how impressive your title, at its very core, your position exists to help an employer maintain and increase profitability by:

- The *identification* of problems within your area of responsibility
- The *prevention* of problems within your area of responsibility
- The *solution* to problems within your area of responsibility

No CV gets read, no one gets interviewed, and no one gets hired unless someone somewhere is trying to solve a problem. That problem may be finding a quicker way to manufacture silicon chips, speed up the accounts receivable process, use social networking for brand management, or any one of a million other profit challenges.

The only reason your job exists is because your employer needed someone to identify, prevent, and solve the problems that regularly occur; it exists because not having someone like you is costing the company money.

Problem solving – the application of *analytical thinking* to the challenges within your area of expertise – is what you are paid to do. It is why every job opening exists, and why every job gets filled with the person who seems to have the firmest grip on how to identify, prevent, and solve the problems that make up the everyday activities of that job.

No one reads CVs unless they have to, so when your CV does get read, it means that a job exists: a job that has been carefully defined, budgeted, and titled, with a salary range that has been authorized and for which funds have been released. *Whenever an employer searches a CV database or reads a CV, she is doing it with a specific job and the language and priorities of that job description in mind.*

Why an employer may never get the chance to read your CV

The ongoing impact of technology on our world of work causes the nature of all jobs to change almost as rapidly as the pages on a calendar. CVs today rarely go straight to a manager's desk (though I'll show you how to make this happen); more often they go to a CV database.

This means that before anyone actually looks at your CV, it must first have been pulled from that database *by a recruiter with a specific job and the language and priorities of that job description in mind*. Keep in mind that some of those databases contain millions of CVs.

With this in mind, you can see that if your CV's just a jumble of everything you've ever done, or of everything that *you* happen to think is important (without reference to what your customers actually want), it is never going to work.

Understand your customer

"The customer is always right," "the customer comes first," and "understand your customer" are phrases that underlie all successful business stories. In the same way that companies tailor products to be appealing to *their* customers, you need to create a CV tailored to *your* customers' needs.

Your CV works when it matches your skills and experiences to the responsibilities of a specific target job. This requires that your CV focuses on how employers – your customers – think about, prioritize, and describe the job's deliverables: those things you are expected to deliver as you execute your assigned responsibilities.

A CV focused on a specific target job and built from the ground up with the customers' needs in mind will perform better in database searches, and it will resonate far more with human eyes.

This is not your last job change

In a world without job security, when job and even career changes are happening ever more frequently, being able to write a productive CV is one of life's critical survival skills.

This is probably not your first, and almost certainly won't be your last, job change. You are somewhere in the middle of a half-century work life, a span during which you are likely to have three or more distinct careers and are statistically likely to change jobs about every four years; where economic recessions come around every seven to ten years and age discrimination can begin to kick in around the age of fifty.

2

YOUR CUSTOMER KNOWS WHAT HE WANTS – HOW TO GET INSIDE HIS HEAD

"The customer is always right" is probably the first business lesson we ever learn. The customer knows exactly what he wants and when you accurately tailor your product to your customer's needs, you'll experience a success. This chapter is about how to customize your CV to your customers' needs.

Your CV is the primary marketing device for every job and career change throughout your career. In addition, it plays a role in subsequent internal promotions. In short, it is absolutely vital in determining your professional success. Yet when it comes to creating a CV, no one ever seems to think about what the customer wants! Instead, we just want to get it done as quickly as possible and with as little thought and effort as possible.

Your current CV is probably a simple recitation of all you have done: It lists everything that you *think* is important. I bet this CV isn't working. That's because a simple recitation of all your accomplishments and activities results in a hodge-podge of what you think is important, *not what your customers **know** is important. You need a CV that acknowledges the priorities of your customers,* because they won't make the time to struggle through an unfocused CV to see if you might have what they want. Why should they, when enough people have taken the time to learn what's needed?

Settle on a target job title

With just a few years' experience in the professional world, most people reach a point where they have experience that qualifies them for more than one job; still, this is not an argument for having a general CV as your primary marketing document. There are probably two or more jobs you can do, but the way recruitment works today, you have no choice but to go with a CV that focuses on a single target job. So your first task is to look at all the jobs you can do (they are all probably closely related in some way) and choose which one will represent the prime focus of your job search.

After your primary CV is completed, it is fairly easy to create a CV for any additional job you want to pursue. I'll explain exactly how you do this later in the book, but to set your mind at ease, that second CV will have a number of things in common with your primary CV. This means that you'll already have a template to start with, plus the dates, layout, chronology, contact information, and possibly even the list of employers you're going to contact.

But first you need to build a primary CV, so before going further, think through your options and decide on the job title that your *primary CV* will target.

You can base this decision on many criteria, but assuming your main goal is to get back to work, your best bet is to go with the job you can make the most convincing case for on paper. The job where, when you hit the ground running, you won't trip over your shoelaces. Once you've decided, build a primary CV around this target job.

To really understand your target job, deconstruct it

The most productive CVs start with a clear focus on the target job and its responsibilities. In other words, the customer comes first, so let's get inside the customer's head.

There's a practical and easy way to do this. It's called a Target Job Deconstruction (TJD). It's a way to get a tight focus on what your customers want before you even start writing your CV. Take half a day to do a TJD and your investment will yield:

- A template for the story your CV *must* tell to be successful
- An objective standard against which you can measure your CV's likely performance
- A complete understanding of where the focus will be during interviews
- A very good idea of the interview questions that will be heading your way and why
- Relevant examples with which to illustrate your answers
- A behavioural profile for getting hired and promoted, and therefore . . . greater professional success throughout your career

Target job deconstruction: the way into your customer's head

Step 1: Collect postings

Collect 6–10 job postings of *a single job* you can do and would enjoy. The most productive CVs focus on a single job. I'll show you a very fast and effective editing technique a little later in the chapter to develop a custom CV for different jobs you might be interested in.

Not sure where to start? Look on job sites, looking for jobs with your chosen keywords.

Step 2: Identify target job titles

What are the job titles used in your collection of job descriptions? Looking at them you can say, "When employers are hiring people like this, they tend to describe the job title with these words." From this, you can come up with a suitably generic target job title for your CV, which you will type after your name and contact information. This will help your CV's database performance and also act as a headline, giving the reader's eyes an immediate focus.

Step 3: Identify skills and responsibilities

Look through the job postings for a requirement that is common to all of your job postings. Take the most complete description and add additional words and phrases from the other job postings that describe this same requirement. Repeat this exercise for any other requirements common to all six of your job postings.

The greater the number of keywords in your CV that are directly relevant to your target job, the higher the ranking your CV will achieve in database searches. *And the higher your ranking, the greater the likelihood that your CV will be rescued from the avalanche and passed along to human eyes for further screening.* This database search has led directly to the increasing prevalence of Core Competency sections that capture all relevant keywords in one place. (More about Core Competency sections later.)

Repeat the exercise for requirements common to five of the jobs, then four, and so on, all the way down to those requirements mentioned in only one job posting.

Step 4: Identify problems to solve

At their most elemental level, all jobs are the same – all jobs focus on problem identification, prevention, and solution in that particular area of expertise; this is what we all get paid for, no matter what we do for a living.

Go back to your TJD and start with the first requirement. Think about the problems you will typically need to identify, solve, and/or prevent in the course of a normal workday as you deliver this requirement of the job. List specific examples, big and small, of your successful identification, prevention, and/or solution to the problems. Quantify your results when possible.

Repeat this with each of the TJD's other requirements. Some examples may appear in your CV as significant professional achievements, while others will provide you with the ammunition to answer interview questions. Interviewers are concerned with your practical problem identification and solution abilities, and they want to see them in action. That's why some questions at job interviews begin, "Tell me about a time when . . ." So at the same time that you're working on your CV you're also beginning to collect the illustrations you will use in response to those interview questions.

Step 5: Identify the behavioural profile of success

Think of the *best* person you have ever known doing this job and what made her stand out. Describe her performance, professional behaviour, interaction with others, and appearance: "That would be Carole Jenkins, superior communication skills, a fine analytical mind, great professional appearance, and a nice person to work with." Do this for each and every requirement listed on your TJD, and you are describing the person all employers want to hire. *This is your behavioural profile for professional success*. Apply what you learn from this exercise to your professional life.

Now you know your customers' needs

Once you complete your TJD, you will have a clear idea of now employers think about, prioritize, and express their needs when they hire someone for the job you want.

Now you know the story your CV needs to tell to be retrieved from the database for human review. You now have the proper focus for a first-rate CV.

When doing the TJD, you'll come across some skills that you possess or even excel at, but there will be other skills that you don't have, or that need polishing. As a rule of thumb, you need about 70 percent of a job's requirements to pursue that job with reasonable hope of landing interviews. If you complete the TJD process and realize you don't make the grade, you have probably saved yourself a good deal of frustration pursuing a job you had no real chance of landing. What you need to do is pull your goals back one level. Use this TJD and the missing skills it identifies as a professional development tool: to warrant that next promotion, you'll need to develop these abilities.

Here is a simple before-and-after example that will illustrate how powerful this process can be. The CV is for a young graduate with a computer science degree looking for her first position. When we first spoke, she had a couple of telephone interviews and one face-to-face interview. The first CV is the one she was using; the second she created after completing the Target Job Deconstruction.

Before

> ## JUAP EP EÑMKGQAA
>
> 11 ANY AVENUE
> ANYTOWN AA0 0AA
> jmokube@anyisp.com
> 01234 567890
>
> ### Education
>
> - University of the North
> - MSc. Computer Science 2007
> - University of Technology, Kingston, Jamaica
> - BSc. Computing & Information Technology, 2005
>
> ### Key Skills
>
> - Programming
> - Programming Languages: C, C++, Java, VB.Net
> - Database Programming: SQL
> - Website Design
> - Design Languages/Tools: HTML, CSS, JavaScript, Dreamweaver.
> - Problem Solving and Leadership
> - Honed an analytical, logical, and determined approach to problem solving and applied this as group leader for my final year (undergraduate) research project.
> - Team Player
> - Demonstrated the ability to work effectively within a team while developing a Point-of-Sale system over the course of three terms.
> - Communication
> - Demonstrated excellent written and oral communication skills through reports and presentations while pursuing my degrees, and as Public Relations Officer for the University of Technology's Association of Student Computer Engineers (UTASCE).
>
> ### Work Experience
>
> **January 2006–December 2007**
> - University of the North
> - Graduate Research Assistant, School of Computing
> - Developed a haptic application to demonstrate human-computer interaction using Python and H3D API.
> - Developed an application to organize text documents using the Self-Organizing Map algorithm and MATLAB.
>
> **July–November 2005**
> - Cable & Wireless Jamaica Ltd, Kingston, Jamaica
> - Internet Helpdesk Analyst
> - Assisted customers with installing and troubleshooting modems and internet service-related issues via telephone.
>
> **July–August 2003**
> - National Commercial Bank Ja. Ltd, Kingston, Jamaica
> - Change Management Team Member
> - Generated process diagrams and documentation for systems under development using MS Visio, MS Word, and MS Excel.

JYATITI MOKUBE   Page 2

Awards/Honours

- Foundation Award for Academic Excellence   March 2005
- Nominated School of Computing student of the year   March 2005
- Recognized by Jamaica Gleaner as top student in School of Computing & IT February 2005
- Nominated for Derrick Dunn (community service) Award   March 2004

Languages

- French (fluent), Italian (basic)

Extracurricular Activities

- Singing, acting, chess, reading
- Member of Association for Computing Machinery

References

- Available upon request.

After

JYATITI MOKUBE

11 Any Avenue
Anytown AA0.0AA
jmokube@anyisp.com
01234 567890

Talented, analytical, and dedicated Software Engineer with strong academic background in object-orientated analysis and design, comfortable with a variety of technologies, and interested in learning new ones.

SUMMARY OF QUALIFICATIONS

- Excellent academic record; BSc Computing & Information Technology; MSc Computer Science.
- Familiarity with the software development lifecycle, from identifying requirements to design, implementation, integration, and testing.
- Familiarity with agile software development processes.
- Strong technical skills in Java development and Object-Oriented Analysis and Design (OOA/D).
- Strong understanding of multiple programming languages, including C, C++, JavaScript, Visual Basic, and HTML.
- Familiar with CVS version control software.
- Excellent communications skills with an aptitude for building strong working relationships with teammates.
- Proven background leading teams in stressful, deadline-oriented environments.

TECHNICAL SKILLS

Languages:	Java, JavaScript, C, C++, Visual Basic, HTML, SQL, VB.Net, ASP.Net, CSS
Software:	Eclipse, NetBeans, JBuilder, Microsoft Visual Studio, Microsoft Office Suite (Word, PowerPoint, Excel, Access), MATLAB
Databases:	MySQL, Oracle
Operating Systems:	Windows (NT/2000/XP Professional)
Servers:	Apache Server

EDUCATION

MSc Computer Science, University of the North 2007
- Completed a thesis in the area of Computer Security (Digital Forensics: Forensic Analysis of an iPod Shuffle)

MSc Computing & IT, University of Technology, Kingston, Jamaica, November 2005

LANGUAGES

Fluent in English, French, and Italian

PROFESSIONAL EXPERIENCE

University of the North   01/2006–12/2007

Graduate Research Assistant, School of Computing

- Developed a haptic application to demonstrate human-computer interaction using Python and H3D API.
- Developed an application to organize text documents using the Self-Organizing Map algorithm and MATLAB.

Cable & Wireless Jamaica Ltd, Kingston, Jamaica   07/2005–11/2005

Internet Helpdesk Analyst

- Assisted customers with installing and troubleshooting modems and internet service-related issues via telephone.

National Commercial Bank Ja. Ltd, Kingston, Jamaica   07/2003–08/2003

Change Management Team Member

- Generated process diagrams and documentation for systems under development using MS Visio, MS Word, and MS Excel.

AWARDS/HONOURS

- Foundation Award for Academic Excellence   03/2005
- Nominated School of Computing student of the year   03/2005
- Recognized by Jamaica Gleaner as top student in School of Computing & IT   02/2005
- Nominated for Derrick Dunn (community service) Award   03/2004

PROFESSIONAL AFFILIATIONS

Association for Computing Machinery (ACM)

REFERENCES

Available upon request.

Without the research that defines exactly what your customers want to buy, you cannot hope to develop an effective CV that will stand out in database searches, and your lack of insight into what the customer wants and what you can offer in response will also hinder your interview performance. I have taken professionals from entry level to executives through this process. They all say a couple of things: it was a pain but it was also a logical, sensible, and valuable exercise that pays back your time and effort in many ways and situations, as you will see.

Now, what was the result of this CV revamp? She started using the new CV and almost immediately got an invitation to an interview. She subsequently started work for that company; she has been promoted and is still with the company today.

The target-job-focused CV opened doors, positioned her professionally, told her what the employer would want to talk about, and was a powerful spokesperson after she left the interview. The end result was a great start to a new career. It all came about because she took the time to understand how her customer – the employer – was thinking about and expressing the job she wanted to do!

3

HOW TO DEFINE AND BUILD A DESIRABLE PROFESSIONAL IMAGE

A CV is the primary tool that all professionals use to define and disseminate their *professional image* to an ever-expanding world of contacts. Long-term success – rewarding work, and professional growth – is much easier to achieve when you are credible and visible within your profession. Creating and nurturing a *professional image* as part of your overall career management strategy will help you achieve credibility and visibility throughout your profession, because it gives *you* focus and *motivation*, and *others* a way to recognize you.

Components of a desirable professional image

A viable *professional image* must be built on firm foundations. This means you must understand what employers look for when they employ (and subsequently promote) someone in your profession, at your level, and with your job title. Understanding how your employers think is critical for the success of this job search and for your career going forward; it's why you spent Chapter 2 learning how employers deconstruct your job into its component parts, and how they then prioritize those parts and, most importantly, the words they use to express these judgments . . . and by extension how they will reward those who give them what they want.

In this chapter, we'll examine a couple of additional and equally important dimensions of the *professional you*, which will influence your CV, your interviews, and your success in that next job on your career path. Specifically, we'll look at the *transferable skills and professional values* that underlie all professional success, no matter what you do.

Over the years, I've read a lot of books about finding jobs, winning promotions, and managing your career. A few were insightful and many were innocuous, but one theme that runs through them all is the absurd and harmful advice to "Just be yourself."

"Who you are is fine. Be yourself and you'll be fine." Wrong. Remember that first day in your first job, when you went to get your first cup of coffee? You found the coffee machine, and there, stuck on the wall behind it, was a handwritten sign reading:

YOUR MOTHER DOESN'T WORK HERE TIDY UP AFTER YOURSELF

You thought, "Tidy up after myself? That means I can't behave like I do at home and get away with it." And so you started to observe and emulate the more successful professionals around you. You behaved in a way that was appropriate to the environment, and in doing so demonstrated *emotional intelligence*. Over time you developed many new ways of conducting yourself at work in order to be accepted as a professional in your field. You weren't born this way. You developed a behavioural profile, a *professional persona* that enabled you to survive in the professional world.

There is a specific set of *transferable skills and professional values* that underlies professional success: skills and values that employers all over the world in every industry and profession are anxious to find in applicants from entry level to the boardroom. Why this isn't taught in schools and universities is unfathomable, because these skills and values are the foundation of every successful career. They break down into these groups:

1 *The Technical Skills of Your Current Profession.* These are the technical competencies that give you the *ability* to do your job. The skills needed to complete a task and the know-how to use them productively and efficiently. These *technical skills* are mandatory if you want to land a job within your profession. *Technical skills,* while transferable, vary from profession to profession, so many of your current *technical skills* will only be transferable within your current profession.

2 *Transferable Skills That Apply in All Professions.* The set of skills that underlies your ability to execute the *technical skills* of your job effectively, whatever your job might be. They are the foundation of the professional success you will experience in this and any other career that you pursue over the years.

3 *Professional Values.* These are an interconnected set of core beliefs that enable professionals to determine the right decision for any given situation.

The importance of the whole series of *transferable skills and professional values* led to an entirely new approach to interviewing and the science of employee selection: behavioural interviewing. These behavioural interviewing techniques predominate in the selection process because of their ability to determine whether you possess those *transferable skills and professional values*.

A review of transferable skills and professional values

As you read through the following breakdown of each *transferable skill and professional value* you may, for example, read about *communication*, and think, "Yes, I can see how communication skills are important in all jobs and at all levels of the promotional ladder, and, hallelujah, I have good communication skills." Take time to recall examples of your *communication skills* and the role they play in the success of your work.

You might also read about *multitasking skills* and realize that you need to improve in that area. Whenever you identify a *transferable skill* that needs work, you have found a *professional development project:* improving that skill. Your attention to those areas will repay you for the rest of your working life, no matter how you make a living.

Here are the *transferable skills and professional values* that will help with this job search and your long-term professional success. You'll find that you already have some of them to a greater or lesser degree, and if you are committed to making a success of your life, you'll commit to developing of all of them.

Transferable Skills	**Professional Values**
Technical	*Motivation and Energy*
Analytical Thinking	*Commitment and Reliability*
Communication	*Determination*
Multitasking	*Pride and Integrity*
Teamwork	*Productivity*
Leadership	*Systems and Procedures*
Creativity	

Transferable Skills

Technical Skills

The *technical skills* of your job are the foundation of success within your current profession; without them you won't even land a job, much less keep it for long or win a promotion. They show your *ability* to do the job, the skills necessary for the day-to-day execution of your duties. These *technical skills* vary from job to job and profession to profession.

Technology constantly changes so, if you want to stay employable, you need to keep up to date with the skills most prized in your profession.

In addition to the technical skills that are specific to your job alone, there is also a body of skills that are as desirable in other jobs and other professions, just as much as they are in yours. Possession of these *transferable skills* will not only enhance your employability in your current profession, it is also likely to help you should you ever change your career; something that the statistics say you will do three or more times over the span of your working life.

Any employer would welcome an employee who, as well as the must-haves of the job, possesses the *written communication skills* to create a PR piece or a training manual; who knows how to structure and format a proposal; who is able to stand up and make presentations; or who knows how to research, analyze, and assimilate hard-to-access data.

Some of the *transferable technical skills* sought across a wide spectrum of jobs include:

- Selling skills – even in nonsales jobs, the art of persuasive *communication* is always appreciated, because no matter what the job . . . you are always selling something to someone.
- Project management skills
- Management skills
- Quantitative analysis skills
- Theory development and conceptual thinking skills
- Counselling and mentoring skills
- Writing skills for PR, technical, or training needs
- Customer Resource Management (CRM) skills
- Research skills
- Social networking skills

While the *technical skills* of your job are not necessarily technological in nature, it is a given that one of the *technical skills* essential to almost every job is technological competence. You must be proficient in all the technology and internet-based applications relevant to your work. Even when you are not working in a technology field, strong *technology skills* will enhance your stability and help your professional growth.

Some of your *technology skills* will only be relevant within your current profession, while others (Word, Excel, PowerPoint, to name the obvious) will be transferable across all industry and professional lines. Knowing the essential *technical* and *technology skills* of your chosen career path is key to your professional stability and growth.

There are also *technology skills* that have application within all professions in our technology-driven world. It is pretty much a given that you need to be computer literate to hold down any job today. Just about every job expects competency with Microsoft Word, email, Excel, PowerPoint, and a host of other communication tools.

Any employer is going to welcome a staff member who knows his or her way around spreadsheets and databases, who can update a webpage, or who is knowledgeable in CRM. Some of the *technology skills* that enhance employability on nontechnology jobs include:

- Database management
- Spreadsheet creation
- Word processing
- Building and designing of presentations
- Email and social media communication

Eventually, more and more of these skills will become specific requirements of the jobs of the future.

Analytical thinking skills

As I noted earlier, your job, whatever it is, exists to solve problems and to prevent problems from arising within your area of expertise. *Analytical*, or *problem-solving* skills represent a systematic approach to dealing with the challenges presented by your work. *Analytical thinking skills* allow you to think through a problem, define the challenge and its possible solutions, and then evaluate and implement the best solution from all available options.

Fifty percent of the success of any project is in the preparation; *analytical thinking* is at the heart of that preparation. In addition, using *analytical thinking* to properly define a problem always leads to a better solution.

Communication skills

As George Bernard Shaw said: "The greatest problem in communication is the illusion that it has been accomplished." Every professional job today demands good *communication skills*, but what are they?

When the professional world talks about *communication skills*, it is referring not just to *listening* and speaking but to four primary skills and four supportive skills.

The primary *communication skills* are:

- Verbal skills – what you say and how you say it.
- Listening skills – listening to understand, rather than just waiting your turn to talk.
- Writing skills – clear written communication creates a lasting impression of who you are and is essential for success in any professional career.
- Technological communication skills – your ability to evaluate the strengths, and weaknesses of alternative communication media, and then to choose the one appropriate to your audience and message.

The four supportive *communication skills* are:

- Grooming and dress – these tell others who you are and how you feel about yourself.
- Social skills – how you behave toward others in all situations; this defines your professionalism.
- Body language – this displays how you're feeling deep inside, a form of communication that precedes your speech. For truly effective communication, what your mouth says must be in harmony with what your body says.
- Emotional IQ – your emotional self-awareness, your maturity in dealing with others in the full range of human interaction.

All the *transferable skills* are interconnected – for example, good *verbal skills* require both *listening* and *analytical thinking skills* to process incoming information accurately and enable you to present your outgoing verbal messaging persuasively in light of the interests and sophistication of your audience so that it is understood and accepted. Develop effective skills in all eight of the subsets that together comprise *communication skills* and you'll gain enormous control over what you can achieve, how you are perceived, and what happens in your life.

Multitasking

This is one of the most desirable skills of the new era. According to numerous studies, however, the *multitasking* demands of modern professional life are causing massive frustration for professionals everywhere. The problem is NOT *multitasking*, the problem is the assumption that *multitasking* means being reactive to *all* incoming stimuli and therefore jumping around from one task to another as the emergency of the moment dictates. Such a definition of *multi-tasking* would of course leave you feeling that wild horses are attached to your extremities and tearing you limb from limb.

Few people understand what *multitasking* abilities are really built on: sound *time management* and *organizational skills*. Here are the basics:

Establish priorities

Multitasking is based on three things:

1 Being organized

2 Establishing priorities

3 Managing your time

The Plan, Do, Review Cycle

At the end of every day, review your day:

- What happened: ı .u. and x.u.?
- What went well? Do more of it.
- What went wrong? How do I fix it?
- What projects do I need to move forward tomorrow?
- Rank each project. A= Must be completed tomorrow. B= Good to be completed tomorrow. C= If there is spare time from A and B priorities.
- Make a prioritized To Do list.
- Stick to it.

Doing this at the end of the day keeps you informed about what you have achieved, and lets you know that you have invested your time in the most important activities today and will do so again tomorrow. That peace of mind helps you feel better, sleep better, and come in tomorrow focused and ready to rock.

Teamwork

Companies depend on teams because the professional world revolves around the complex challenges of making money, and such complexities require teams of people to provide ongoing solutions. This means that you must work efficiently and cooperatively with other people who have totally different responsibilities, backgrounds, objectives, and areas of expertise. It's true that individual initiative is important, but as a professional, much of the really important work you do is done as a member of a group. Your long-term stability and success require that you learn the arts of cooperation, team-based decision making, and team *communication*.

Teamwork demands that a *commitment* to the team and its success comes first. This means you take on a task because it needs to be done, not because it makes you look good.

As a *team player* you:

- Always cooperate.
- Always make decisions based on team goals.
- Always keep team members informed.
- Always keep commitments.
- Always share credit, never blame.

If you become a successful leader in your professional life, it's a given that you were first a reliable *team player*, because a leader must understand the dynamics of *teamwork*. When *teamwork* is coupled with the other *transferable skills and professional values*, *it results in greater responsibility and promotions*.

Leadership skills

Leadership is the most complex of all the *transferable skills* and combines all the others. As you develop *teamwork skills*, notice how you are willing to follow true leaders, but not people who don't respect you and who don't have your best interests at heart. When others believe in your competence, and believe you have everyone's success as your goal, they will follow you. When your actions inspire others to think more, learn more, do more, and become more, you are becoming a leader. This will ultimately be recognized and rewarded with promotion.

- Your job as a leader is to help your team succeed, and your *teamwork skills* give you the ability to pull a team together as a cohesive unit.
- Your *technical* expertise, *analytical thinking*, and *creative skills* help you correctly define the challenges your team faces and give you the wisdom to guide them toward solutions.
- Your *communication skills* enable your team to *understand* your directives and goals. There's nothing more demoralizing than a leader who can't clearly articulate why you're doing what you're doing.
- Your *creativity* (discussed next) comes from the wide frame of reference you have for your work and the profession and industry in which you work, enabling you to come up with solutions that others might not have seen.
- Your *multitasking skills*, based on sound *time management* and *organizational* abilities, enable you to create a practical blueprint for success. They also allow your team to take ownership of the task and deliver the expected results on time.

Leadership is a combination of all the *transferable skills* plus the clear presence of all the *professional values* we are about to discuss. Leaders aren't born; they are self-made. And just like anything else, it takes hard work.

Creativity

Your *creativity* comes from the frame of reference you have for your work, profession, and industry. This wide frame of reference enables you to see the *patterns* that lie behind challenges, and so connect the dots and come up with solutions that others might not have seen. Others might be too closely focused on the specifics of the issue – thus, they don't have that holistic frame of reference that enables them to step back and view the issue in its larger context.

There's a big difference between *creativity* and just having ideas. Ideas are like headaches: we all get them once in a while, and like headaches, they disappear as mysteriously as they arrived. *Creativity*, on the other hand, is the ability to develop those ideas with the strategic and tactical know-how that brings them to life. Someone is seen as creative when his ideas produce tangible results. *Creativity* also demands that you harness other *transferable skills* to bring those ideas to life. *Creativity* springs from:

- Your *analytical thinking skills*, applied within an area of *technical expertise* (the area where your *technical skills* give you a frame of reference for what works and what doesn't).

- Your *multitasking skills*, which in combination with your *analytical thinking* and *technical skills* allow you to break your challenge down into specific steps and determine which approach is best.

- Your *communication skills*, which allow you to explain your approach and its building blocks persuasively to your target audience.

- Your *teamwork* and *leadership skills*, which enable you to enlist others and bring the idea to fruition.

Creative approaches to challenges can take time or can come fully formed in a flash, but the longer you work on developing the supporting skills that bring *creativity* to life, the more often they *will* come fully formed and in a flash. Here are five rules for building *creative skills* in your professional life:

1 **Whatever you do in life, engage in it fully.** Commit to developing competence in everything you do, because the wider your frame of reference for the world around you, the more you will see the patterns and connectivity in your professional world, delivering the high-octane fuel you need to propel your ideas to acceptance and reality.

2 **Learn something new every day.** Treat the pursuit of knowledge as a way of life. Absorb as much as you can about everything. Information exercises your brain, filling your mind and contributing to that ever-widening frame of reference that allows you to see those patterns behind a specific challenge. The result is that you will make connections others won't and develop solutions that are seen as magically creative.

3 **Catch ideas as they occur.** Note them in your smartphone or on a scrap of paper. Anything will do, as long as you capture the idea.

4 **Welcome restrictions in your world.** They make you think, they test the limits of your skills and the depth of your frame of reference; they truly encourage *creativity*. Ask any successful business leader, entrepreneur, writer, artist, or musician.

5 **Don't spend your life glued to YouTube or the TV.** You need to live life, not watch it go by out of the corner of your eye. If you do watch television, try to learn something or motivate yourself with science, history, or documentaries. If you surf the internet, do it with purpose.

Building *creative skills* enables you to bring your ideas to life; and the development of each of these seven interconnected *transferable skills* will help you bring your dreams to life.

Professional values

Professional values are an interconnected set of core beliefs that enable professionals to determine the right decision for any given situation. Highly prized by employers, this value system also complements and is integral to the *transferable skills*.

Motivation and energy

Motivation and *energy* express themselves in your engagement with and enthusiasm for your work and profession. They involve an eagerness to learn and grow professionally, and a willingness to take the rough with the smooth in pursuit of meaningful goals. *Motivation* is invariably expressed by the *energy* you demonstrate in your work. You always give that extra effort to get the job done.

Commitment and reliability

This means dedication to your profession, and the empowerment that comes from knowing how your part contributes to the whole. Your *commitment* expresses itself in your *reliability*. The *committed* professional is willing to do whatever it takes to get a job done, whenever and for however long it takes.

Doing so might include duties that might not appear in a job description and that might be perceived by less enlightened colleagues as "beneath them."

Determination

The *determination* you display with the travails of your work shows a resilient professional who does not back off when a problem or situation gets tough. It's a *professional value* that marks you as someone who chooses to be part of the solution.

The *determined* professional has decided to make a difference with her presence every day, because it is the *right* thing to do.

She is willing to do whatever it takes to get a job done, and she will demonstrate that determination on behalf of colleagues who share the same values.

Pride and integrity

If a job's worth doing, it's worth doing well. That's what *pride* in your work really means: attention to detail and a *commitment* to doing your very best. *Integrity* applies to all your dealings, whether with co-workers, management, customers, or suppliers. Honesty really *is* the best policy.

Productivity

Always work toward *productivity* in your areas of responsibility, through efficiencies of time, resources, money, and effort.

Economy

Remember the word "frugal"? It doesn't mean poverty or shortages. It means making the most of what you've got, using everything with the greatest efficiency. Companies that know how to be frugal with their resources will prosper in good times and in bad, and if you know how to be frugal, you'll do the same.

Systems and procedures

This is a natural outgrowth of all the other *transferable skills and professional values.* Your *commitment* to your profession in all these ways gives you an appreciation of the need for *systems and procedures* and their implementation only after careful thought. You understand and always follow the chain of command. You don't implement your own "improved" procedures or encourage others to do so. If ways of doing things don't make sense or are interfering with efficiency and profitability, you work through the system to get them changed.

Development of *transferable skills and professional values* supports your enlightened self-interest, because it will be repaid with better job security and improved professional horizons.

Transferable skills, professional values, and the secret language of job postings

There are six keywords and phrases that you see in almost every job posting: *communication skills, multitasking, teamwork, creativity, problem solving*, and leadership. They are so commonly used that they are often dismissed as meaningless.

Far from being meaningless, they represent a secret language that few job hunters understand. The ones who do "get it" are also the ones who get the job offers. Understanding the secret language of job postings can supercharge your CV and your cover letters and will help you turn job interviews into job offers. That is because these six key phrases represent the very skills that power success; they represent the specific *transferable skills* that enable you to do your job well, whatever your job may be. You know them as *transferable skills* because no matter what the job, your possession of these skills can make the difference between success and failure.

Decoding made easy

For example, when problem-solving skills are mentioned in a job posting, it means the employer is looking for someone who knows his or her area of responsibility well enough to identify, prevent where possible, and solve the problems that the job generates on a daily basis. The employer wants someone who has thought through and can discuss the challenges that lie at the heart of that job and who has developed intelligent strategies and tactics in response.

Think about how a job-posting requirement for "teamwork" applies to your job. Consider which aspects of your work require you to interact with other people and other departments to get your work done. For example, an accountant working in Accounts Receivable will think about problem accounts and how such accounts can require working with sales and the nonpaying customer, as well as working laterally and upward within the Accounting Department.

Teamwork also embraces other *transferable skills* – for instance, the *communication skills* you need to work effectively with others. You understand that talk of *communication* always refers to verbal, written, and *listening skills*, and you also know that, to an employer, it also refers to the supporting *communication skills* of:

1 Digital communication literacy

2 Dress

3 Body language

4 Social skills

5 Emotional maturity

Together, these five components of effective *communication* impact the power and persuasiveness of all your interactions with others.

When you relate each of the *transferable skills* to each of your professional responsibilities, you'll discover the secrets to success in your profession. When you express your possession of them in your CV and cover letters, you can dramatically increase interviews. When you understand how these skills impact every action you take with every responsibility you hold, and you can explain to interviewers how you integrate these skills into all you do, you become a more desirable employee and colleague.

In your CV

You might decide to highlight special achievements with a *Performance Highlights* or a *Career Highlights* section. This is usually a short sequence of bulleted statements, each addressing one of the company's stated requirements and thereby emphasizing the fit between employer needs and your capabilities. Illustrate with an example if you can do so succinctly:

Performance Highlights

35% increase in on-time delivery + 20% reduction in client complaints

Effective Operations Management demands understanding every department's unique problems and timelines. Building these considerations into daily activities helped:

- Finance & Supply Chain, saved £55,000 in last three quarters
- Increased productivity, with a 35% increase in on-time delivery

---

> These on-time delivery increases were achieved with improved communica-
> tions, connecting Purchasing, Supply Chain, Customers, and Customer Service:
>
> - Delivered 20% reduction in client complaints

In a cover letter

Where there is more space, these same achievements might appear with the company's requirement above:

"Problem-solving skills"
- Thorough knowledge of the problems that impact productivity in Operations enabled a 35% increase in on-time delivery.

"Work closely with others"
- Improvements in on-time delivery made possible by improved communications with Purchasing, Supply Chain, Customers, and Customer Service. This delivered a 20% reduction in client complaints.

"Multitasking"
- Effective Operations Management demands understanding of every department's critical functions and timelines. Building these considerations into daily activities helped Finance & Supply Chain save £55,000 in last three quarters.

In your life

Every time you see a job posting that mentions any of the *transferable skills or professional values*, think how *that skill or value is applied in each aspect of your work*. Then recall examples that illustrate how you used that skill in the identification, prevention, and solution of the daily problems that get in the way of the smooth functioning of your job.

4

THE SIMPLEST, SMARTEST, FASTEST WAY TO WRITE YOUR CV – KEEP IT SIMPLE

The most effective way to get a premium, powerful CV for a professional job in the shortest time with the least amount of hassle.

No one likes writing a CV, but you have to trust me when I tell you that there is no easier way than the way I am showing you. That shortcut you're thinking of? It won't work. If it did, I'd be telling you about it. This is the most streamlined way I know to give you a premium, powerful CV in the shortest time with the least amount of hassle.

Five steps to a great CV

Your CV is a concise document that captures your professional life in a couple of pages. A great finished product usually takes four steps:

1 A first draft to capture all the essentials on a basic CV template.

2 Two, three, five, or more gradually improving versions built over a time, as you tweak words and phrases; add and subtract; and cut, move, and paste until you cannot possibly improve it further.

During this time, you should work on your CV for a couple of hours every day as you simultaneously organize, your job search.

3 A third draft, where you paste your work into different templates and choose the best one(s) for you. As you do this, it is quite likely that you will still be tweaking a word here and there.

4 A final draft of your formatted CV where you do a grammatical edit and complete the polishing process.

Putting together your first draft

With your completed TJD, you know both *what the customer wants* and what you have to offer. Now you need to start assembling the pieces in a way that tells your story effectively.

To help you do this most efficiently, I've created a CV *Layout Template* for you. It is *not* intended as a template for your finished CV; it's just a gathering place for all the components of a cutting-edge CV. By using it, you'll become familiar with all the building blocks, and when the time comes to decide on a layout, everything will be ready to cut and paste.

Name

Address   **Telephone**   **Email address**

Target Job Title

A target job title, perhaps followed by an *optional* statement, as in the following example, helps database visibility and gives focus to the reader. The brief statement suggests what you bring to the job, example:

Pharmaceutical Sales

Experienced professional in pharmaceutical software sales: a record
of achievement with major pharmaceutical companies

Performance Profile/Performance Summary

What goes here? Take the most common requirements from your TJD and rewrite them as a performance profile/performance summary. Helps database visibility and creates immediate resonance with reader's eyes. A maximum five lines of text can be followed by a second paragraph or list of bullets.

Core Competencies

A list of all the skills you identified in your TJD. Repeat each skill listed here in context of the jobs where it was applied. This increases database visibility and gives reader immediate focus, "Oh s/he can talk about all of these things . . ." Example:

4-Handed Dentistry	Infection Control	Preventative Care
Oral Surgery/Extraction	Casts/Impressions	Emergency Treatment
Root Canals	Diagnostic X-Rays	Instrument Sterilization
Prosthetics/Restorations	Teeth Whitening	Radiology

Technical Competencies

An optional category depending on professional relevance.

Performance Highlights

An optional category depending on your experience.

(continued)

Professional Experience

Employer's name	Dates
The company's focus	
Job Title	

If you are going to bold/caps anything, draw attention to what is most important: your job title.

Contact information at the top of each page. Keep your CV tightly edited but do not worry about page count. Reason: jobs are more complex than they used to be, the additional info increases database performance, and readers won't mind as long as the CV is telling a relevant story.

Employer's name	Dates
The company's focus	
Job title	

Repeat employment history as necessary.

Education
May come earlier if these are critical professional credentials (as in medicine, law, etc) that are especially relevant to job requirements, or highlight an important strength.

Licences/Professional Accreditations
May come earlier if these credentials are critical, especially relevant, or highlight an important strength.

Ongoing Professional Education

Professional Organizations/Affiliations

Publications, Patents

Languages
Add them to the end of performance profile/performance summary and repeat them here.

(continued)

Extracurricular Interests

Add them here, if they relate to the job. Sports demonstrate fitness; chess, etc, denotes analytical skills; they can all be relevant.

(References)

Never list references on your CV. Employers *assume* that your references are available, but it certainly doesn't hurt to end with a statement if you have empty space at the end of the page and nothing else to add:

References Available on Request

Or

Excellent references available on request.

The layout template is *not* intended as a final CV template, but as a tool to help you learn the component parts your CV needs.

How to build your CV

Name

Give your first and last name because that is the way you introduce yourself to someone in person. It isn't necessary to include your middle name(s), and unless you are known by your initials, don't use them on your CV.

It is not necessary to place Mr, Ms, Miss, or Mrs before your name, unless yours is a unisex name like Jamie, Carroll, or Leslie; if you feel it necessary, it is acceptable to write Mr Jamie Jones or Ms Jamie Jackson.

Address

The accepted format for laying out your address looks like this:
Maxwell Krieger
11 Any Avenue
Anytown
County, AA0 0AA

With a CV, if space is an issue, you can put your contact information on a single line:

11 Any Avenue, Anytown, County, AA0 0AA

Telephone number

Always include your area code and never use a work telephone number.

You should include your mobile number, and if you might decide to use the mobile number as your primary contact. Because we tend to answer our mobile phones at all times, if a job call comes at a bad time, you should be prepared to say that you'd like to talk but will need to call back.

Email as a marketing tool

In an internet-based job search, your email address is a powerful marketing tool, but for most job hunters it's a lost opportunity. Since it's the first thing any potential employer sees, it's a perfect opportunity for immediately positioning your credentials.

This might be a good time to retire those addresses like binkypoo@yahoo. com, bigboy@hotmail.com, or DDdoll@live.com, or at least restrict them to exclusively nonprofessional activities where they won't detract from your professional reputation.

Most email hosts allow you to register a number of different email addresses, so simply add an email account devoted exclusively to your job search and career-management affairs.

Create an account name that reveals something about your professional profile, such as *SystemAnalyst@hotmail.com* or *Accountant@yahoo.com*.

This type of email address acts as a headline to tell the reader who is writing, and to give some idea of what the *communication* is about.

Using a profession-orientated email address does double duty: it introduces the *professional you*, and it protects your identity. In a competitive job search, the little things can make a big difference; the way you introduce yourself is one of them. Finally, your email address is an integral part of your contact information, and should always be hyperlinked on your CV so that the reader can respond easily.

The contact information on your CV can also include a link to your LinkedIn profile.

We are just entering the world where a link on your CV to a social media profile is becoming a contribution to creating a powerful CV and you can add the link immediately under the email address.

Target job title

Eighty percent of CVs lack a target job title, and this makes a CV less accessible to a harried employer who might spend as little as five seconds reviewing it before moving on to another CV where the writer has better focus and *communication skills*.

Target job titles are used in database searches, so using one at the start of your CV helps it get picked. Once it is in front of human eyes, having a target job title gives a manager immediate visual focus.

A target job title comes immediately after your contact information, at the top of your CV, and is most often centered on the page, is in a larger font than body copy, and is often in bold.

A target job title explains what the CV is about. Decide on a target job title by taking all the title variations you collected in the TJD process. You should choose a common or generic target job title, something to widen your appeal. Here are some examples taken from finished CVs:

- **Certified Occupational Health Nurse Specialist**
- **Global Operations Executive**
- **Campaign Field Director**
- **Marketing Management**

- **Operations/Human Resources/Labour Relations/Staff Development**
- **Career Services Professional**
- **Operations Management**
- **Healthcare Review—Clinical Consultant**
- **Agricultural/Environmental Manager**
- **Horticultural Buying—International Experience**

Integrating a professional image into your CV

Your *professional image* is communicated throughout your CV, but never more so than with your opening statement. The first place you begin to establish a *professional image* is with your target job title, where you consciously decide on the job that best allows you to package your skill sets and create a *professional focus*.

A target job title followed by a considered statement gives the reader a fast focus on the CV's purpose and the type of person it represents. Your opening statement is a short phrase following the target job title that defines what you will bring to the job. It says, "These are the benefits my presence on your payroll will bring to your team and your company."

Opening statement

Notice how the following statements focus on the benefits brought to the job, but do not take up space identifying the specifics of how this was done. *Professional* statements often start with an action verb such as "Delivering," "Dedicated to," " Bringing," "Positioned to," or "Constructing":

Senior operations/plant management professional

Dedicated to continuous improvement ~ Lean Six Sigma ~ Startup & turnaround operations ~ Mergers & change management ~ Process & productivity optimization ~ Logistics & supply chain

Bank collections management

Equipped to excell in loss mitigation/collections/recovery management.

Mechanical/design/structural engineer

Delivering high volume of complex structural and design projects for global companies in Manufacturing / Construction / Power Generation.

Account management/client communications manager

Reliably achieving performance improvement and compliance within the Financial Services Industry.

Marketing communications

Consistently delivering successful strategic marketing, media relations, & special events.

Administrative/office support professional

Ready, willing, and competent; detail-oriented problem solver; consistently forges effective working relationships.

Senior engineering executive

Bringing sound technical skills, strong business acumen, and real management skills to technical projects and personnel in a fast-paced environment.

Use headlines to guide the reader

Headlines act like signposts, guiding a jaded and distracted reader through your CV. Your CV's job is to open as many doors for you as it can. It does this by making the information as accessible as possible. Using headlines in your CV is both a visual and textual aid to comprehension, helping that tired-eyed, distracted reader absorb your message. Here are the headlines you will usually use and the way they guide the reader:

Target job title
(Here's the job I'm after)

Performance profile or performance/career/executive summary
(This is what I can do for you)

Core/professional competencies
(Here are all the key professional skills that help me do my job well)

Technology competencies
(Here are the *technology skills* that help me do my job well)

Performance highlights
(Here are some examples of my performance using the expertise you are interested in)

Professional experience
(Where and when everything happened)

In little more than half a page, these headlines help the reader grasp what you bring to the table. Once you have an employer's attention, she will read your whole CV with serious interest.

A professional message

Integrate your professional strengths, into the CV as you write it. As you revise and polish your CV monitor and tweak your work to ensure that it supports your professional image, especially in these sections of your resume:

- Performance Profile
- Professional Competencies
- Performance/Career Highlights
- Professional Experience

Performance profile

After your target job title and opening statement comes the performance profile. The essence of every manager's job is performance management, and they spend a portion of every year thinking about and giving performance reviews. For that reason, this new and powerful headline will resonate with every manager. It demonstates your grasp of the job and your goal orientation. It also encourages you to stay with the issues you know to be important to your target readers.

Take the major requirements from your TJD and turn them into 3–5 sentences, or no more than five lines without a paragraph break. The Performance Profile should clearly convey your understanding of the customer's priorities.

You can use headlines like Career/Professional/Executive Summary, but be aware that these traditional headlines encourage you to think about everything *you've* done rather than focus on customer needs.

Never use job objective

Stay away from Job Objective (or Career Objective) if you can, for these reasons:

1 At this stage, no one cares what you want. The only issue is whether you can do the job.

2 Job Objective as a headline will not help your performance in database searches or resonate with employers, so you are wasting valuable selling space.

If you must use a Job Objective because you are at the start of your career and have no experience, that's okay—your competitors are in the same boat. Tilt the game in your favour by starting your objective with "The opportunity to" and then, referring to your TJD exercise, rewrite the target job's major priorities as your job objective. This will make a big difference to your CV's *productivity*.

Of the three traditional options for this important section of your CV—Career Summary, Job Objective, and Performance Profile—you will find the "Performance Profile" headline most productive. Managers respond because it succinctly captures what you bring to the job.

How to create a performance profile

The Performance Profile or Performance Summary section of your CV comes right after the Target Job Title. Its intent is to capture your skills as they relate to the job's requirements; this gets the critical skills of the job and its most relevant keywords right at the top of the CV. This gives the document focus for the reader and helps make the CV more discoverable in database searches. To create a powerful Performance Profile:

1 Take the 3–6 most important/common requirements identified in your TJD exercise and write 3–6 bulleted statements that capture your skills as they relate to the priorities identified in your TJD.

2 Combine all this information into just 3–5 short sentences. Together they will clearly show what you bring to the target job.

3 Check against your TJD to see that, wherever possible, you use the same words employers are using.

4 Dense blocks of text are hard on the eyes. If you have more than five lines, break the text into two paragraphs.

Your goal with a performance profile is to demonstrate that you possess exactly the kinds of skills employers seek when hiring this type of person. It's a powerful way to open your CV both for its impact with search engines and because it gives the readers the information they need: you're explaining what you bring to the table, based on their own prioritization of needs.

The finished product will be a performance profile that captures the *professional you* in words most likely to be used in database searches and have a familiar ring to managers' ears.

Using keywords in a performance profile

The words that employers use in job postings will be used by recruiters as search terms when they are searching the CV databases; so *using the same words in your CV as employers do in their job postings—words you know are important—will help your CV get picked from the databases into which you load it.* Use them immediately, because search engine algorithms give weight to placement of words nearer the top of a document. Use as many keywords as you reasonably can in your performance profile.

Here's a performance profile for a Corporate Communications Management professional:

PERFORMANCE PROFILE

9 years' strategic communications experience, developing high-impact and cost-efficient media outreach plans for consumer and business audiences in media, entertainment, and technology practice areas. Experienced in managing corporate and personal crisis communications. Goal and deadline orientated, with five years' experience managing internal and external communications. Adept at working with multiple teams and stakeholders.

Professional competencies

A Professional/Core Competencies section is designed to capture all the skills you bring to your work in a succinct and easily accessible format, usually single words or short phrases in three or four columns. *Think of your core competencies section as an electronic business card that allows you to network with computers.* The positioning of likely keywords at the top of a document is favoured by the search engines, and will help your cv's ranking in database searches; each one acts as an interest generator for the employer.

Employers appreciate a Professional Competencies section as a summary of the CV's focus. Each keyword or phrase acts as an affirmation of a skill area and possible topic of conversation. Confirming lots of topics to talk about so early in the CV is a bonus. It acts as a preface to the body copy, in effect saying,

"Hey, here are all the headlines. The stories behind them are immediately below," so the reader will pay closer attention.

There's no need to use articles or conjunctions. Just list the word, starting with a capital—"Forecasting," for example—or a phrase, such as "Financial Modelling."

Here's an example of a Competencies section for a PR professional:

Professional Competencies

High-Tech Public Relations	Project Management
Strategic Communications	Detail Orientated
Executive Communications	Acquisition
PR Messaging & Media Relations	Positioning
Strong Writing Skills	Pitch Media
Media Training	Market Research
Multiple Projects	Build & Lead Teams
Story Placement	Mentor
Counsel Executives	Client Satisfaction
Tactics	Organizational Skills
Strong Editing Skills	Thought Leadership
Collateral Materials	PR
New Business	Social Media
Team Management	Leadership Branding
Budget Management	Story Telling
Account Management	Analyst Relations

And an example from a Hospitality Management CV:

Core Competencies

• Revenue Optimization	• Team Building
• Staff Development	• Time Management
• Spanish	• Productivity Growth
• Customer Service	• Client Relations
• Brand Integrity	• Turnover Reduction
• P&L	• 250 Covers Daily
• Payroll	• 300 Pre-Theater
• Food Cost Reduction	• Purchasing
• Training Manuals	• POS Systems
• Cost Containment	• Recruitment & Selection

- Operations Management
- Policy & Procedures
- Accounting/POS Support
- Inventory Control
- Problem Solving

- Liquor Inventory
- Cash Reconciliation
- Administration
- Marketing/Advertising

If you work in technology, or you have developed extensive technological competencies, you might choose to add a Technology Competencies section. It breaks up the page and it is easier to absorb when they are separated.

Here's an example of a separate Technology Competencies section:

Technology competencies

Operating Systems:	Unix, Windows
Languages:	C, C++, Java, Pascal, Assembly Languages (Z8000, 808x, DSP)
Methodologies:	TL9000, Digital Six Sigma
Software:	MS Office, Adobe FrameMaker, Matlab
RDBMS:	DOORS, Oracle 7.x
Protocols:	TCP/IP, SS7ISUP, A1, ANSI, TL1, SNMP
Tools:	Teamplay, ClearCase, ClearQuest, M-Gatekeeper, Exceed, Visio, DocExpress, Compass
Other:	CDMA Telecom Standards – 3GPP2 (Including TIA/EIA-2001, TIA-EIA-41, TIA/EIA-664), ITU-T, AMPS

Adding to professional competencies

Your CV is a living document, and its content may well change as your job search progresses. Whenever you come across keywords in job postings that reflect your capabilities, but which are not in your CV, it is time to add them. If nowhere else, at least put them in the Professional Competencies section.

Use keywords often

1 Give the most important of your professional competencies first in the Performance Profile section of your CV.

2 Include a complete list of your skills in the Professional Competencies section. It is the perfect spot to list the technical acronyms and professional jargon that demonstrate the range of your professional skills, especially if they won't fit into the Professional Experience section of your CV.

3 A Professional Competencies section should remind you to use as many of the keywords as you can in the Professional Experience part of your CV, where usage will show the context in which those skills were developed and applied.

This strategy will make your CV data dense for improved database performance, while also demonstrating that you have the relevant skills and putting them in context in a **visually accessible** manner. Yes, it will make your CV longer (we'll discuss this issue shortly); just know it has a much better chance of being picked from the databases, and because its content is completely relevant to the needs of the job and readily accessible to the employer, you will get an improved response rate.

Make room for supporting skills on your CV

If you want your CV read with serious attention, you know it needs to focus on the skills you bring to a single target job. However, employers still want to know about your supporting skills.

For example, a colleague in the IT world says, "I don't just want to see evidence that someone is a hotshot in, say, the .NET Framework; I also want to see that he/she can get on with other languages, so that I know (a) that the candidate understands programming as distinct from just .NET, and (b) that if my company introduces a new programming language/development environment in the future, I have someone who will be able to handle that."

You can still get this important information about *supporting skills* into your CV, without taking up too much room, by adding them to your Professional Competencies section.

You'll start the section with those skills most important to your target job, but you can then add all those skills that support your all-around professionalism.

The appearance of these *supporting skills* in the Professional Competencies section can help your cv's performance in database searches, and it helps put your primary skills in the larger context of your complete professional abilities. And because they are supporting skills, it doesn't matter that you don't include them in the context of the jobs you've held.

Skills prioritization

Your professional skills are most readily accessible when they appear in three or four columns. This section contains a list of your important professional skills and so needs to be near the top of your CV, for these reasons:

1 Coming after a Target Job Title and a Performance Summary that focuses on the skills you bring to the target job, you are helping both the discoverability of your CV in resume databases and its impact upon knowledgeable readers.

2 The programmes that employers use to search CV databases use algorithms that reward relevant words near the front of a document as a means of judging that document's relevance to the employer's search terms. So your professional skills need to be relevant to the target job and come near the top of your CV.

3 A recent study showed that once a CV has been picked from a CV database, employers spend an average of six seconds on a first-time scan of that CV. This means your skills have to jump out. You make them do so by using a Target Job Title, followed by a Performance Summary that reflects employer priorities as you determined in your TJD work, and followed in turn by a Professional Skills section that supports all the above claims of professional competency with a list of your relevant skills. This gives an employer plenty of time to see your abilities in that first six-second scan.

However there is another issue at play when it comes to the Professional Skills section. Ultimately it will be read by someone who really knows this job, who is aware of what's a "must-have" and what's a "nice to have."

The easiest way to explain this is with an example: A couple of years back we prepared a CV for a dental assistant, and she gave us a list of all the important *technical skills* of her job. We put these into three columns for visual accessibility, and something terrible jumped out at me: Her list started with "Teeth whitening" and ended with "Four-handed dentistry." What was so terrible about this? All the skills were there.

Yes they were, but common sense says that the most important skills for a job should come before the less important skills. We immediately switched these phrases so that "Four-handed dentistry" (a highly marketable skill) came first and "Teeth whitening" (a more routine skill) came last.

Bear this story in mind when you are creating your own Professional Skills section: By prioritizing the skills you are subtly telling the man or woman who will ultimately hire you that you have a firm grasp of the relative importance of all the necessary *professional skills* of your work. That point adds to the clear focus and power of the opening first half page of your CV. If you follow these directions, the opening sections of your CV will show that:

- You can do the job
- Your skills list backs up your statements of ability
- You understand the relative importance of the component parts of your job.

The result is that in the first half page of your CV, and well within the framework of a six-second scan, you have gone a long way toward making the short list of candidates who will be brought in for interview.

Performance/career highlights

Choose 2–4 of your achievements and contributions to your work, relevant to the Target Job you have chosen. Turn them into confident statements:

Performance Highlights
35% increase in on-time delivery + 20% reduction in client complaints

Effective Operations Management demands understanding every department's unique problems and timelines. Building these consider-ations into daily activities helped:

- Finance & Supply Chain, saved £55,000 in last three quarters
- Increased productivity, with a 35% increase in on-time delivery

These on-time delivery increases were achieved with improved com-munications, connecting Purchasing, Supply Chain, Customers, and Customer Service:

- Delivered 20% reduction in client complaints

Professional experience

Company names
Each job needs to be identified with an employer. There is no need to include specific contact information, although it can be useful to include the location. When working for a multidivision company, you may want to list the divisional employer.

Employment dates
A CV without employment dates considerably underperforms a CV that has dates, and those dates need to be accurate because they can be checked. With a steady work history and no employment gaps, you can be very specific:

January 2007–September 2011

If you had an employment gap of six months in, say, 2008, you can disguise this:

MBO Ltd.   2006–2008

XYZ Ltd.   2008–present

I am *not* suggesting that you should lie about your work history, and you must be prepared to answer honestly and without hesitation if you are asked.

If you abbreviate employment dates, be sure to do so consistently. It is quite acceptable to list annual dates, rather than month and year. Remember, when references get checked, the first things verified are dates of employment; untruths are grounds for dismissal, and that can dog your footsteps into the future.

Layout for dates and jobs

If you don't have problems with too many jobs in your work history, you want the dates to jump out because it makes information gathering easier for the reader. The best way to do this is to right justify dates like this:

Microsoft   **2009-Present**

If you have had promotions while with a company, you want to make this jump right off the page and this is the way you would do it. In our example the job hunter has held four progressively more responsible jobs in ten years, so the listing first captures the full scale of growth and then goes into the detail of each job as identified by title and dates.

Microsoft   **2009-Present**
Senior Business Analyst   2012–Present
Sales Operations Associate   2010–2012
Sales Compensation Analyst   2009–2010
DATES in the above must be vertically aligned, last entry is out of alignment

Senior Business Analyst   **2012-Present**
(Job detail would follow here)

Continuity of employment is clear, as is consistent professional growth, and we can see that each job is going to be handled in turn.

Achievements
Business has very limited interests. In fact, those interests can be reduced to a single phrase: making a profit. This is done in just three ways:

1 By *saving money* for the company

2 By *increasing productivity*, which in turn *saves money* and provides the opportunity to *make more money* in the time saved

3 By simply *earning money* for the company

That does not mean that you should address only these points in your CV and ignore valuable contributions that cannot be quantified. But it does mean that you should *try to quantify your achievements whenever you can*.

1. Did you increase sales/productivity/volume? Provide percentage or amount.

2. Did you generate new business or increase client base? How? What were the circumstances?

3. Did you forge affiliations, partnerships, or strategic alliances that increased company success? With whom, and what were the results?

4. Did you save your company money? If so, how and by how much?

5. Did you design and/or institute any new systems and procedures? If so, what were the results?

6. Did you meet an impossible deadline through extra effort? If so, what difference did this make to your company?

7. Did you bring a major project in under budget? If so, how did you make this happen? What was the budget? What were you responsible for saving in terms of time and/or money?

8. Did you conceive, design and/or help launch a new product or programme? If so, did you take the lead or provide support? How successful was the effort? What were the results?

9. Did you assume new responsibilities that weren't part of your job? Were they assigned or did you do so proactively? Why were you selected?

10. Did you improve communication in your firm? If so, with whom, and what was the outcome?

11. How did your company benefit from your performance?

12. Did you complete any special projects? What were they and what was the result?

Pick 2–4 accomplishments for each job title and edit them down to bite-sized chunks. Write as if you had to pay by the word—this approach can help you pack a lot of information into a short space. The resulting abbreviated style will help convey a sense of immediacy to the reader. I'll use an example we can all relate to:

Responsible for new and used car sales. Earned "Salesman of the Year" awards, 2014 and 2015. Record holder: Most Cars Sold in One Year.

Here's another example from a fundraiser's CV:

- Created an annual giving programme to raise operating funds. Raised £2,000,000.

- Targeted, cultivated, and solicited sources including individuals, corporations and foundations. Raised £1,650,000.

- Raised funds for development of the Performing Arts School facility, capital expense, and music and dance programmes. Raised £6,356,000.

Now, while you may tell the reader about these achievements, never explain how they were accomplished; the key phrase here is "specifically vague." The intention of your CV is to pique interest and to raise as many questions as you answer. Questions mean interest, interest means talking to you, and *getting conversations started is the primary goal of your CV*!

Prioritize your accomplishments, and quantify them whenever possible and appropriate.

You can cite achievements as part of a sentence/paragraph or as bullets, for example:

Collections:
Developed excellent rapport with customers while significantly shortening pay-out terms. Turned impending loss into profit. Personally salvaged and increased sales with two multimillion-pound accounts by providing remedial action for their sales/financial problems.

Individual jobs
Each section of the CV represents another opportunity to communicate your unique achievements and contributions. Replace time-worn descriptions in the Professional Experience section . . . :

- *Before:* Responsible for identifying and developing new accounts.

   . . . with strong action statements:

- *After:* Drove advances in market share and revitalized stalled business by persistently networking and pursuing forgotten market pockets—lost sales, smaller, untapped businesses/prospects overlooked by competition.

The area where you address your responsibilities and achievements in each job, *as they relate to the customer's needs you identified during TJD,* is the meat of your CV. When working on this part of your CV, constantly refer to your TJD to remind yourself of the details target employers are most likely to want to read about and the keywords and phrases that will help your CV perform in database searches.

The responsibilities and contributions you identify here are those functions that best relate to the needs of the target job. They do not necessarily correspond with how you spent the majority of your working day, nor are they related to how you might prefer to spend your working day. This can perhaps best be illustrated by showing you part of a CV that came to my desk recently. It is the work of a professional who listed her title and duties for one job like this:

"Motivated a sales staff of six, recruited, trained, managed. Hired to improve sales. Sales Manager increased sales."

The writer mistakenly listed everything in the reverse order of importance. She's not focused on the items' relative importance *to a future employer*, who, above all, will want to hire someone who can increase sales. She also wasted space stating the obvious about the reason she was hired as a sales manager: to improve sales. Let's look at what subsequent restructuring achieved:

Sales Manager: Hired to turn around stagnant sales force. Successfully recruited, trained, managed, and motivated sales staff of six. Result: 22 percent sales gain over first year. Notice how this is clearly focused on the essentials of any sales manager's job: to increase income for the company.

"Hired to turn around stagnant sales force": *Demonstrates her skills and responsibilities.*

"Successfully recruited, trained, managed, and motivated a sales staff of six. Result: 22 percent sales gain over first year": *Shows what she subsequently did with the sales staff, and exactly how well she did it.*

By making these changes, her responsibilities and achievements become more important in the light of the problems they solved. Be sure to match your narrative to employers' needs and to the priorities of that target job. Avoid exaggerating of your accomplishments. It isn't necessary.

Collections:

Developed excellent rapport with customers while significantly shortening pay-out terms:

- Evaluated sales performance; offered suggestions for financing/merchandising, turned impending loss into profit.
- Salvaged two multimillion-pound problem accounts by providing remedial action for their sales/financial problems. Subsequently increased sales.

Whenever you can, keep each paragraph to a maximum of four or five lines. This ensures that the finished product has plenty of white space so that it is easy on the reader's eyes. If necessary, split one paragraph into two.

When achievements are hard to define

Employers look to your past performance and what you achieved as an indication of your potential value to the team. If you are in Sales, for example, identifying achievements is a no-brainer, but for many jobs the case isn't so clear-cut.

There are two types of workers in every department: those who get things done and those who watch things being done; those who make a difference with their presence and those whose goal is to squeak by until the end of the working day. Recognizing how you try to make a difference with your presence everyday can help define your potential value.

Ask yourself how the department, company, or customer is better off because of your efforts, both in general and specific terms. Think about accomplishments of which you are proud, tough projects that turned out well, disasters that were averted. Think of days you left work feeling proud and why?

Use the following questions to jog your memory about accomplishments and achievements:

- Did you help or save a troubled customer?
- Did the quality of your work decrease typical problems or cause comment for other reasons?
- For what have you been praised on that job?
- Why do people like to work with you?
- Did you introduce any new or more effective systems, processes, or techniques for increasing productivity? What was the result?
- What budgets were you responsible for?

Education

Educational history is normally placed wherever it helps your case the most. The exact positioning will vary according to the length of your professional experience, and the importance of your academic achievements to the job and your profession.

If you are recently out of education with little practical experience, your educational credentials might constitute your primary asset and should appear near the beginning of the CV.

After two or three years in the professional world, your academic credentials become less important in most professions, and move to the end of your CV. The exceptions are in professions where academic qualifications dominate—medicine and law, for example. The highest level of academic attainment always comes first: a doctorate, then a master's, followed by a bachelor's degree. For degreed professionals, there is no need to go back further into educational history.

It is normal to abbreviate degrees (PhD, MA, BA, BSc, etc). In instances where educational attainment is paramount, it is acceptable to put that degree after your name. Traditionally, this has been the privilege of doctors and lawyers, but there is absolutely no reason that your name shouldn't be followed, for example, by MBA.

Recent graduates will usually give details of what was covered on their courses. How much depends on how relevant this is to the Target Job. Technical Skills gained on a technic course will, for example, be covered extensively when the Target Job is one that requires technical expertise.

Don't puff up your educational qualifications. Research has proven that three out of every ten CVs inflate educational qualifications. Consequently, verification of educational claims is quite common. If, after you have been hired, your employer discovers that you exaggerated your educational accomplishments, it could cost you your job.

Ongoing professional education

Identify all relevant professional training courses and seminars you've attended. It demonstrates your *commitment* to your profession. It also shows that an employer thought you worthy of the investment. Technology is rapidly changing the nature of all work, so if you aren't learning new skills every year, you are being paid for an increasingly obsolete skill set. Ongoing professional development is a smart career management strategy.

Accreditations, professional licences, and civil service grades

If licences, accreditations, or civil service grades are mandatory requirements in your profession, you must feature them clearly. If you are close to gaining a particular accreditation or licence you should identify it:

"Passed all parts of C.P.A. exam, September 2016 (expected certification March 2017)."

Civil service grades can be important if you are applying for jobs with government contractors, subcontractors, or any employers who do business with government agencies.

Professional associations

Membership in associations and societies related to your work demonstrates strong professional *commitment*, and offers great networking opportunities. If you are not currently a member of one of your industry's professional associations, give serious consideration to joining.

Note the emphasis on "professional" in the heading. An employer is almost exclusively interested in your professional associations and societies. Omit references to any religious, political, or otherwise potentially controversial affiliations unless your *certain* knowledge of that company assures that such affiliations will be positively received.

An exception to this rule is found in those jobs where a wide circle of acquaintance is regarded as an asset. Some examples might include jobs in public relations, sales, marketing, and insurance. In these cases, include your membership/involvement with community organizations and the like, as your involvement demonstrates a professional who is also involved in the community and shows an outgoing personality with a wide circle of contacts.

By the same token, a seat on the parish council, charitable cause involvement, or fundraising work are all activities that show a willingness to involve yourself and can demonstrate *organizational* abilities through positions held in those endeavours. Space permitting, these are all activities worthy of inclusion because they show you as a force for good in your community.

Companies that take their community responsibilities seriously often look for staff that feels and acts the same way. For instance, you could list yourself as:

West Somerset Youth Association: Area Fundraising Chair

If you are a recent entrant into the workplace, your meaningful extracurricular contributions are of even greater importance. List your position on the university newspaper or the student council, memberships in clubs, anything that demonstrates your potential as a productive employee. As your career progresses, however, prospective employers care less about your school life and more about your work life, so once you are two or three years into your career, the importance of these involvements should be replaced by similar activities in the adult world.

Publications, patents, and speaking

These three capabilities are rare and make powerful statements about *creativity*, organization, determination, and follow-through. They tell the reader that you invest considerable personal time and effort in your career and are therefore a cut above the competition.

Public speaking is respected in every profession because it is such a terrifying thing to do, and I say this as someone who has spoken all over the world for two decades! Publications are always respected but carry more weight in some professions (academia). You will notice in the CV examples in this book that the writers list dates and names of publications but do not often include copyright information or patent numbers, because it isn't necessary information for a CV. Here's an example of how to cite your publications:

"Radical Treatments for Chronic Pain." 2002. *Journal of American Medicine.*

"Pain: Is It Imagined or Real?" 2000. *Science & Health Magazine.*

Patents take years to achieve and cost a fortune in the process (I know; I have two optical patents). They demonstrate, *creativity*, attention to detail, and considerable tenacity. They are a definite plus in the technology and manufacturing fields.

As you are putting your CV together, it will almost certainly go beyond the one- and two-page mark. Do not worry about this. Traditional page-count considerations are out of date, and besides, you haven't go to the editing stage yet.

Languages

With the current state of communications technology, all companies can have an international presence. Consequently, you should always cite your cultural awareness and language abilities. If you speak a foreign language, say so:

Fluent in Spanish and French

Read German

Read and write Serbo-Croatian

Conversational Mandarin

If you are targeting companies that have an international presence, I suggest you cite your linguistic abilities in your performance profile and perhaps again at end of the resume.

Military

List any military experience. Military experience demonstrates, amongst other things, your determination, *teamwork*, goal orientation, and your understanding of *systems and procedures*.

Personal flexibility, relocation

If you are open to relocation for the right opportunity, make it clear. It will never, in and of itself, get you an interview, but it won't hurt. Place this information within the first half page so that it is within scanning distance of your address.

Judgment needed

Here are some things that do not normally go into your CV, but might. Whether you include them or not will depend on your personal circumstances.

Summer and part-time employment
This should only be included if you are just entering the workforce or re-entering it after a substantial absence. The entry-level person can feel comfortable listing dates and places and times. The returnee should include the skills gained but minimize the part-time aspect of the experience.

Reason for leaving
The topic is always covered during an interview, so why raise an issue that could have negative impact? You can usually use the space more productively, so your reason for leaving rarely belongs on a CV.

However, if you have frequently been caught in redundancies or mergers or recruited for more responsible positions, there can be a sound argument for listing these reasons to counteract the perception of your being a job hopper. You'll see examples in the CV section.

References
Employers assume that your references are available however, there is a case for putting "References Available Upon Request" at the end of your CV. It might not be absolutely necessary to say that references are there for the asking, but those four extra words certainly don't do any harm and may help you stand out from the crowd. Including the phrase sends a little message: "Hey, look, I have no skeletons in my closet." But only if space allows—if you have to cut a line anywhere, this should be one of the first to go.

Never list the names of references on a CV. Interviewers very rarely check them before meeting and developing a strong interest in you—it's too time-consuming.

Name changes and your references

If you have ever worked under a different surname, you must take this fact into account when giving your references.

A recently divorced woman I know wasted a strong interview performance because she was using her maiden name on her CV and at the interview. She forgot to tell the employer that her references would, of course, be under a different last name. The results of this oversight were catastrophic: Three prior employers denied ever having heard of anyone by the name supplied by the interviewer.

Personal interests

If space permits, always include personal interests that reflect well on you as a professional and as a human being. References to personal activities that demonstrate your ethics (you volunteer for hospice, for example) or are tied to the job in some way are the most effective.

A study once showed that executives with team sports on their CVs averaged £3,000 a year more than their more sedentary counterparts. Now, that makes giving a line to your personal interests worthwhile, if they fit into certain broad categories. If you participate in team sports, determination activities (running, climbing, bicycling), and "strategy activities" (bridge, chess, Dungeons & Dragons), consider including something about them. The rule of thumb, as always, is only to include activities that can, in some way, contribute to your chances of being hired.

What never goes in

Some information just doesn't belong in a CV. Make the mistake of including it, and at best, your CV loses a little power, while at worst, you fail to land the interview.

Personal flexibility and relocation issues

If you are open to relocation for the right opportunity, make it clear, but conversely, *never state that you* aren't *open to relocation*. Let nothing stand in the way of generating job offers!

Titles such as: CV, curriculum vitae, etc.

Their appearance on a properly structured CV is redundant. It makes it clear that your CV needs more work. Such titles take up a whole line, one that could be used more productively. Use the space you save for information with greater impact, or buy yourself an extra line of white space to help your reader's eyes.

Availability

All jobs exist because there are problems that need solutions. For that reason, interviewers rarely have time for candidates who aren't readily available. If you are not ready to start work, then why are you wasting everyone's time? As a rule of thumb, let the subject of availability come up at the face-to-face meeting. After meeting you, an employer is more likely to be prepared to wait until you are available, but will usually pass on an interview if you cannot start now or in the reasonably near future—say, two to three weeks.

The only justification for including this (and then only in your cover letter) is that you expect to be finishing a project and moving on at such-and-such a time, and not before.

Salary

Leave out all references to salary, past and present—it is far too risky. Too high or too low a salary can knock you out of the running even before you hear the starting gun. Even in responding to a job posting that specifically requests salary requirements, don't give the information in your CV. A good CV will still get you the interview, and in the course of the discussions with the company, you'll talk about salary anyway.

If you are obliged to give salary requirements, address them in your cover letter or use a separate Salary History page, you'll find an example in the samples chapter of this book.

Age, race, religion, sex, and national origin

Government legislation forbids employment discrimination in these areas under most instances, so it is wisest to avoid reference to them unless they are deemed relevant to the job.

Photographs

Careers in modeling, acting, and certain aspects of the media require headshots. In these professions, your appearance is an integral part of your product offering. Otherwise, no.

The place for your headshot is on your social networking profile on LinkedIn and other networking sites. We'll discuss your social networking profile as another version of your CV shortly.

Health/physical description

Unless your physical appearance (gym instructor, model, actor, media personality) is immediately relevant to the job, leave these issues out. If you need to demonstrate health, do it with your extracurricular interests.

5

HOW TO GIVE YOUR CV PUNCH

First impressions are important. Editing polishes your content and helps it deliver a greater punch.

The people who need to read and respond to your CV hate the mind-numbing grind of it all. It's an activity that makes the eyes tired and the mind wander, so your CV needs to be visually accessible, as we have already discussed. Next, you need to make sure the words you use make sense, read intelligently, and pack a punch by directly addressing your customers' needs.

You can assume that anyone who reads your CV has an open position to fill and is numb from reading CVs. Understanding exactly what this feels like will help you craft a finished CV that is most readily accessible to the tired eyes and distracted minds of employers.

Imagine you are an employer for a moment. Today, you have just completed a CV database search and have twenty CVs to read. Now, go and read six CVs from the sample section without a break. Really try to understand each one, but don't spend more than sixty seconds on each.

Three things will happen in sequence: first a ringing in the ears, followed by fuzzy vision and an inability to concentrate. After about fifteen minutes at this, you'll realize why your focus on relevant content, clear layout, and compelling language for your CV are critical for getting it read and understood . . . and why those headlines are so appreciated.

Customize the template

While the layouts and templates are based on common sense and market-response monitoring, you are still free to customize your layout. As a rule of thumb, the information most relevant to your application should always come first. For example, when you have no experience, your degree might be your strongest qualification, so put it front and centre. As experience increases with the passage of time, in most professions your education can become less important. This is why you will usually see education at the end of a CV, unless the job or the profession's particular demands require it up front. (There are some professions – medicine, education, and the law, for example – where essential academic and professional accreditations tend to be kept at the front of the CV. Bear this in mind if you work in one of these professions.)

However, the CV template isn't sacrosanct; you can customize the layout to suit your needs. For example, you might decide that moving languages, special training, or other information typically found at the end of the CV increases the strength of your argument when placed first. If that makes sense, go ahead and do it.

Filling in the template

Go through your template and transfer the information you developed earlier, and almost immediately, you have CV that begins to look like a finished product.

Tighten up sentences

Sentences gain power with action verbs. For example, a woman with ten years of law firm experience in a clerical position had written in her original CV:

I learned to use a new database.

After she thought about what was really involved, she gave this sentence more punch:

I analyzed and determined the need for a comprehensive upgrade of database, archival, and retrieval systems. I was responsible for selection and installation of cloud-based archival systems. Within one year, I had an integrated, company-wide archival system working.

Notice how verbs show that things happen when you are around the office; they bring action to a CV: they tell the reader what you did and how you did it.

Now, while the content is clearly more powerful, the sentences are clunky, too wordy, and need tightening.

Action verbs

In describing your work experience at each position you have held, it might be helpful to use the action verbs that best characterize your daily work, duties, responsibilities, and level of authority. Select from the following list or use other action verbs.

accepted	contained	extracted	moderated
accomplished	contracted	fabricated	monitored
achieved	contributed	facilitated	motivated
acted	controlled	familiarized	negotiated
adapted	coordinated	fashioned	operated
addressed	corresponded	focused	organized
administered	counselled	forecast	originated
advanced	created	formulated	overhauled
advised	critiqued	founded	oversaw
allocated	cut	generated	performed
analyzed	decreased	guided	persuaded
appraised	defined	headed	planned
approved	delegated	identified	prepared
arranged	demonstrated	illustrated	presented
assembled	designed	implemented	prioritized
assigned	developed	improved	processed
assisted	devised	increased	produced
attained	diagnosed	influenced	programmed
audited	directed	informed	projected
authored	dispatched	initiated	promoted
automated	distinguished	innovated	proposed
balanced	diversified	inspected	provided
budgeted	drafted	installed	publicized
built	edited	instigated	published
calculated	educated	instituted	purchased
catalogued	eliminated	instructed	recommended
chaired	emended	integrated	reconciled
clarified	enabled	interpreted	recorded
classified	encouraged	interviewed	recruited
coached	engineered	introduced	reduced
collected	enlisted	invented	referred
compiled	established	launched	regulated
completed	evaluated	lectured	rehabilitated
composed	examined	led	remodelled
computed	executed	maintained	repaired
conceptualized	expanded	managed	represented
conducted	expedited	marketed	researched
consolidated	explained	mediated	resolved

restored	screened	strengthened	translated
restructured	set	summarized	travelled
retrieved	shaped	supervised	trimmed
revamped	solidified	surveyed	upgraded
revitalized	solved	systemized	validated
saved	specified	tabulated	worked
scheduled	stimulated	taught	wrote
schooled	streamlined	trained	

Now, while the content is clearly more powerful, the sentences are clunky, too wordy, and need tightening.

Tight sentences have bigger impact

Space is at a premium, and reader impact is your goal, so keep your sentences under about twenty words. Always aim for simplicity and clarity:

- Shorten sentences by cutting unnecessary words.
- Make two short sentences out of one long one. At the same time, you don't want the writing to sound choppy, so vary the length of sentences when you can.

You can also start with a short phrase and follow with a colon:

- Followed by bullets of information
- Each one supporting the original phrase

See how these techniques tighten the writing and enliven the reading process from our law firm example:

Analyzed and determined need for comprehensive upgrade of database, archival, and retrieval systems:

- *Responsible for hardware and software selection.*
- *Responsible for selection and installation of cloud-based archival systems.*
- *Responsible for compatible hardware and software upgrades.*
- *Trained users from managing partner through administrators.*
- *Achieved full upgrade, integration, and compliance in six months.*

Notice in this example that by dropping personal pronouns and articles, the result is easier to read. It also demonstrates a professional who knows the importance of *getting to relevant information fast*.

Big words or little words?

Employers know every trick in the book; they've seen every eye-catching gimmick, and they're not impressed. Two of the biggest mistakes amateur (and professional) CV writers make is using:

1 Big words; in an effort to sound professional you end up sounding pompous and impenetrable.

2 Adjectives; when you use adjectives to describe yourself (excellent, superior, etc), the reader will often discount them, muttering, "I'll be the judge of that." You'll see examples in the CV section, but notice that the use of superlatives is kept under control and backed up with hard facts.

The goal of your CV is to communicate quickly and efficiently, using short sentences and familiar words; they are easy to understand and communicate clearly and efficiently. Remember: short words in short sentences in short paragraphs help tired eyes!

Voice and tense

The voice you use in your CV depends on a few important factors: getting a lot said in a small space, being factual, and presenting yourself in the best way possible.

Sentences can be truncated (up to a point) by omitting pronouns – *I, you, he, she, it, they* – and articles – *a* or *the*. Dropping pronouns is a technique that saves space and allows you to brag about yourself without seeming boastful, because it gives the impression that another party is writing about you.

"I automated the office" – becomes, "Automated office." At the same time, writing in the first person makes you sound, well, personable. Use whatever works best for you. If you use personal pronouns, don't use them in every sentence – they get monotonous and take up valuable space on the page. Use a third-person voice throughout the CV. Using the third person and dropping pronouns and articles throughout the body of the resume saves space and gives you an authoritative tone.

CV length

The rule used to be one page for every ten years of experience, and never more than two pages. However, as jobs have gotten more complex, they require more explanation. *The length of your CV is less important than its relevance to the target job*. The first half to two-thirds of the first page of your CV should be tightly focused on a specific target job and include a Target Job Title, Performance Profile, Professional Competencies, and perhaps Career Highlight sections. Do this and any reader can quickly see that you have the skills for the job.

If you are seen to be qualified, the reader will stay with you as you tell the story. Given the increasing complexity of jobs, the length and depth of your experience, and the need for data-dense CVs (which are overwhelmingly rewarded in database searches), it is idiotic to limit the length of your CV on the basis of outdated conventions from before the age of computers, let alone the Internet.

The worst – the most heinous crime of all – is to cram a seasoned professional's work history into tiny font sizes to get it onto one or two pages. Why? Here's a flash from reality: if you are a seasoned professional with a track record requiring a complex skillset and are climbing the ladder of success, it's likely your readers are also successful, seasoned professionals. Use tiny fonts and you annoy everyone whose eyesight has been weakened by prolonged computer use, and that means everyone. Busy senior managers simply won't read your CV because it suggests poor judgment and *communication skills*, both of which are mandatory for seasoned professionals.

Let form follow function with your CV. If it takes three tightly edited pages to tell a properly focused story and make it readable, just do it.

What's the alternative? Leaving stuff out means your CV is less likely to get picked from databases or convince the employer of your skills when it does get read.

Assuming your first page clearly demonstrates a thorough grasp of the target job, you can feel comfortable taking that second and third page, if necessary, to tell a concise story. In the CV samples, you'll see examples of justifiably longer executive CVs, requiring greater length to convey a concise message of ability in a complex job.

Worrying too much about length considerations while you write is counterproductive. If the first page makes the right argument, the rest of your CV will be read with serious attention. A longer CV also means that much more space for selling your skills with relevant keywords and more opportunities to establish your brand. However, you should make every effort to maintain focus and an "if in doubt, leave it out" editing approach.

If you have more than twenty years under your belt, many older skills from the first part of your career are now irrelevant. On the whole, the rule of one page for every ten years is still a sensible *guideline*. The bottom line is that your CV can be as long as it needs to be to tell a concise and compelling story. I have never,

ever heard of a qualified applicant being rejected because her CV exceeded some arbitrary page count; it just doesn't happen.

Does my CV tell the right story?

As you write, rewrite, edit, and polish your CV, concentrate on the story it needs to tell. You can keep this focus in mind by regularly referring to your TJD, and then layering fact and illustration until the story is told. When the story is complete, begin to polish by asking yourself the following questions:

- Are my statements relevant to the target job?
- Where have I repeated myself?
- Can I cut out any paragraphs?
- Can I cut out any sentences?
- Can I shorten two sentences into one? If not, perhaps I can break that one long sentence into two short ones?
- Can I cut out any words?
- Can I cut out any pronouns?

If in doubt, leave it out – leave nothing but the focused story and action words!

CVs evolve in layers

CVs are written in layers. They don't spring fully formed in one draft from anyone's keyboard. They are the result of numerous drafts, each of which inches the product forward. As I was writing this book, we worked with a public relations professional on her new CV. Before we were finished, we had completed eight different versions, each evolving until we had a great finished product. It took about two and a half weeks, but then generated eight interviews in a week, proof again that 50 percent of the success of any project is in the preparation.

Proofreading your final draft

Check your CV against the following points:

Contact information
- Are your name, address, phone numbers, and email address correct?

- Is your contact information on every page?
- Is the email address hyperlinked, so that a reader of your CV can read it on his computer and reach out to you instantly?

Target job title

- Do you have a target job title that echoes the words and intent of the job titles you collected when deconstructing the target job?
- Is this followed by a short, one-sentence statement that captures the essence of the *professional you*?

Performance profile

- Does it give a concise synopsis of the *professional you* as it relates to the target job?
- Does the language reflect that of typical job postings for this job?
- Is it prioritized in the same way employers are prioritizing their needs in this job?
- Is it no more than five lines long, so it can be read easily? If more, can you cut it into two paragraphs or use bullets?
- Does it include reference to the *transferable skills and professional values* that are critical to success? If they don't fit here, make sure they are at least in the core competencies section.

Professional competencies

- Is all spelling and capitalization correct?
- Are there any other keywords you should add?
- Do you have experience in each of the areas you've listed?
- Can you illustrate your experience in conversation?

Career highlights

- If you included a Career/Performance Highlights section, do the entries support the central arguments of your CV?

Professional experience

- Is your most relevant and qualifying work experience prioritized throughout the CV to correspond to the employers' needs as they have prioritized them?

- Have you avoided wasting space with unnecessarily detailed employer names and addresses?
- If employed, have you been discreet with the name of your current employer?
- Have you omitted any reference to reasons for leaving a particular job?
- Have you removed all references to past, current, or desired salaries?
- Have you removed references to your date of availability?

Education

- Is education placed in the appropriate position?
- Is your highest educational attainment shown first?
- Have you included professional courses that support your candidacy?

Chronology

- Is your work history in chronological order, with the most recent employment coming first?
- Does each company history start with details of your most senior position?
- Does your CV emphasize relevant experience, contributions, and achievements?
- Have you decided which combination of your *transferable skills* are most relevant, and come up with a statement of how this selection of *transferable skills* allows you to perform in the way you do.
- Have you kept punch and focus by eliminating extraneous information?
- Have you included any volunteer, community service, or extracurricular activities that can lend strength to your application?
- Have you left out lists of references and only mentioned the availability of references if there is nothing more valuable to fill up the space?
- Have you avoided treating your reader like a fool by heading your cv, "CV"?

Writing style

- Have you substituted short words for long words?
- Have you used one word where previously there were two?
- Is your *average* sentence no more than twenty words? Have you shortened any sentence of more than twenty-five words or broken it into two?

- Have you kept paragraphs under five lines?
- Do your sentences begin, wherever possible, with powerful action verbs and phrases?
- Have you omitted articles and personal pronouns?

Spelling and grammar

Incorrect spelling and poor grammar are guaranteed to annoy CV readers, besides drawing attention to your poor *written communication skills*. This is not a good opening statement in any job search. Spell checkers are *not* infallible. Check the spelling and grammar and then send your CV to the most literate person you know for input on grammar and spelling.

You need some distance from your creative efforts to gain detachment and objectivity. There is no hard-and-fast rule about how long it takes to come up with the finished product. Nevertheless, if you think you have finished, leave it alone at least overnight. The next day, read your TJD before reading your CV: Then you will be able to read it with the mindset of an employer and see the parts that need tweaking.

6

CV CUSTOMIZATION, ALTERNATIVE CVs AND FORMATS NEEDED FOR AN EFFECTIVE JOB SEARCH

With job searching the way it is today, you will almost certainly need more than one CV for your job search, and you may need to repackage your background into three of four different delivery vehicles.

You'll probably need:

- Customized CVs for specific openings
- One or more CV for other jobs you can do and want to pursue
- An ASCII CV
- A CV for your social networking site

And you might decide you need a *business card CV* and an HTML or *web-based CV*.

Customizing your CV for specific openings

Your CV is a living, breathing document, and the *primary* CV you so carefully developed is never really finished. It evolves throughout your job search as you learn more about the skills and experience your marketplace needs, and as you learn to express your possession of these skills and experiences in ways most accessible to your customer base.

Most important, it evolves every time you customize that CV in response to a particular job posting. Before sending your CV in response to any job opening, you should evaluate it against the job description, and tweak it *so that it reflects clearly and powerfully the stated needs of that job*.

You will notice that the *transferable skills* we talk about (*communication, critical thinking, multitasking, teamwork,* etc) crop up frequently in job postings:

"Work closely with" means you are a *team player* and work for the good of the team and the results to which you are collectively committed.

"Communication skills" means you listen to understand and that you can take direction in all circumstances. It also refers to verbal and written skills, dress, body language, your social skills, and emotional maturity.

"Multitasking" does not mean you rush heedlessly from one emergency to the next; it means that you carefully order your activities based on sound time management and *organizational skills*.

"Problem-solving skills" means you think through the likely effects of your actions before taking them, and that you know your area of expertise well enough to identify, prevent, and solve the problems it generates on a daily basis.

Tweak your CV for keyword *resonance*

Match the job posting against your CV to see that the words you use to describe certain skills match the words the employer is using.

Then think through how the job posting requirement of, say, "work closely with others," applies to each of the employer's specific skill requirements that require you interact with other people and other departments to get your work done. For example, an accountant working with accounts receivable might, on hearing "work closely with others," think about problem accounts and working with sales and the nonpaying customer, as well as working laterally and upward within the accounting department.

When you think through your work experience and discover achievements that reflect the stated needs of an employer, you can draw attention to your close match in either your CV or a cover letter.

Keywords in a cover letter

In a cover letter, these might appear as the company statement in quotation marks followed by an achievement in that area:

"Analytical/Critical thinking/Problem-solving skills"

- Thorough knowledge of the issues that impact productivity in Operations has resulted in a 35% increase in on-time delivery.

"Work closely with" and "Communication skills"

- Improvements in on-time delivery also made possible by improved communications with stakeholders: Purchasing, Supply Chain, Customer, and Customer Service, which also delivered a 20% reduction in client complaints.

"Multitasking"

- Effective Operations Management demands understanding every department's critical functions and timelines. Building these considerations into daily activities helped Finance & Supply Chain save £55,000 in last three quarters.

Keywords in a CV

In a CV, you might decide to highlight relevant achievements with a *Performance Highlights* or a *Career Highlights* section, coming right after the *Professional Competencies* section.

This section will comprise a short sequence of bulleted statements, each addressing one of the company's stated requirements, and so emphasizing the fit between the employer's needs and your capabilities. Use an example to illustrate if you can do so succinctly.

However, in your CV, space might be at more of a premium than in your cover letter, and so you would use the achievements without the quotes:

Performance Highlights
35% increase in on-time delivery + 20% reduction in client complaints

Effective Operations Management demands understanding every department's unique problems and timelines. Building these considerations into daily activities helped:

- Finance & Supply Chain, saved £55,000 in last three quarters
- Increased productivity, with a 35% increase in on-time delivery

These on-time delivery increases were achieved with improved communications, connecting Purchasing, Supply Chain, Customers, and Customer Service:

- Delivered 20% reduction in client complaints

A job-targeted CV for that other job

With just a few years' experience in the professional world, most people reach a point where they have experience that qualifies them for more than one job. You built your *primary CV* around the job for which the odds are shortest. But that doesn't mean there aren't other jobs you can do and want to pursue.

After your primary CV is completed, it is fairly easy to create a CV for any additional job you want to pursue. Given your completed primary CV, you already have a template to start with; plus the dates, layout, chronology, contact information, and possibly the employers are all going to remain the same. There's a methodology that quickly helps you refocus and edit your primary CV into a CV for that second or third target job:

1 Save a duplicate copy of your primary CV, and save it under the new target job title, because although the job is different, a great deal of the information and CV layout will remain the same.

2 Complete Target Job Deconstruction exercise on the next target job.

3 On the duplicate copy of your CV, saved under the name of the second target job, use the new TJD to edit out less relevant details and replace them with the higher-impact information that is more relevant to the new target job.

4 Edit and polish, and you have a customized CV for that second or third target job.

The major CV formats and why you need them

An online job search means that you will be able to customize your CV for specific openings, upload it to CV databases, and send it directly to an employer or networking contact. Each of these major needs is served by having your CV prepared in three different formats:

1 MSWord

2 PDF

3 ATS Friendly

Your CV in MSWord

You will be saving and using your CV in MSWord, PDF, and ATS-Friendly formats, but always develop your original document in MSWord because it gives you the greatest flexibility for design, layout, colour, and text enhancements.

I recommend you create your primary CV document in MSWord because if a job is worth applying to, then it is worth customizing your CV for that opportunity, and the aforementioned design flexibility gives you the greatest range of options for doing so.

However, MSWord has certain problems, which means the CV versions you use most in your search are likely to be PDF-and ATS-Friendly. Microsoft Word can have problems:

- crossing from a PC platform to a Mac platform
- moving from one version of MSWord to another
- printing on one of the many thousands of printers available

An example of the problems you will encounter in sending out MSWord versions of your CV is a line at the bottom of one page jumping onto the top of the next page; sometimes Word even leaves the balance of that page blank. This does not support the professional image that will advance your career. This only happens occasionally, but it does happen, and Murphy's Law tells us that it will happen at the most damaging of times.

Create your CV in MS Word (use .docx when available) because this gives you the greatest flexibility for delivering your message in a clear and visually attractive way. However, once created you should keep this as a clean source document from which you will make copies to customize for specific openings, and to save the revised CV document in other formats – as we'll discuss. But you are not advised to send an MSWord CV in response to job posting openings, headhunters, or potential employers, unless specifically requested to do so.

MSWord conversion problems

Word can create problems when a transmitted document crosses from a PC to a Mac, or when the sender and the viewer are using different versions of MSWord – or any combination of these factors. Consequently, if you are specifically requested to send an MSWord version of your CV, you should be aware of the conversion problems over which you can exhibit some control.

Page jumps

If you discover, while testing your CV by sending to and receiving from a variety of friends and colleagues, that the bottom line of a page is throwing off the whole layout of your document by jumping to the top of the next page, you have a couple of options, depending on your machine and version of MSWord:

- With your MSWord document open, you can insert a hard page break by going to the "Insert" menu along the top of your page and inserting a page break from the options offered in the drop-down menu under "Break."

- You can also key CTRL ENTER to insert a hard page break at the end of the page.
- If you like to use paragraph marks when writing you must remove these once the CV is finished. A stray paragraph mark at the end of a page could cause your CV to jump to an additional blank page,

Using symbols

CVs can be enlivened by using symbols, but you must be careful:

- To use symbols that increase comprehension rather than just serve as an attempt to prettify the document.
- To use symbols that are recognizable across computer platforms and CV-tracking systems.

Symbols that can enhance comprehension and be intelligible regardless of computer platform or software opening the document are called Unicode symbols. You can find all you need by searching for "Unicode symbols" on Google.

You can find a complete list of Unicode symbols and typography at *http://unicode-table.com/en/miscellaneous-symbols*, although this might be overkill for some people.

Margins and printing your CV

Today's printers can handle margins of as little as 0.35 inches at the top and bottom of your CV and 0.5 inches on the left and right sides; this gives you more space to tell your story on a page and still have plenty of white space to make your message easily accessible to the eye. Sticking to these conventions, your CV should print on any standard printer.

If you have an older printer it might not be able to handle such tight margins – they sometimes require margins of 0.75 inches on all sides. If this applies to you, make sure you test print your CV out on a printer that can handle the tighter margins; all company printers are likely to be able to handle these tighter margins.

PDF CVs

Save a version of your CV in PDF – its an acronym for Portable Downloadable File; you'll find this option within the "Save As" dialog box within MSWord that pops up when you give your document a title. Click on format choices and choose PDF. The PDF format is a permanent, locked, and incorruptible format that cannot change no matter what device it is viewed or printed on; it will appear exactly as you send it. You should:

- Use a PDF to send as an email attachment to networking contacts, employers, headhunters, and managers.
- *Never* use a PDF for uploading your CV to databases, because ATS (Applicant Tracking Systems) have difficulty accessing the locked information.

When sending an attached PDF CV by email, mention the attachment in the body of your email: "My CV is attached in a PDF document."

ATS-friendly CVs

CV databases are a fact of life, and during a job search you are likely to upload a version of your CV into these databases a number of times. Recruiters access these databases using applicant tracking system (ATS) software.

What is an ATS-Friendly format? Basically it is a version of your CV saved in MSWord 97-2003, and stripped of most of its formatting (you'll find this option within the "Save As" dialog box within MSWord that pops up when you give your document a title).

Most ATS software can read a properly formatted CV in MSWord but in case you apply to a company that has an older system we continue to recommend the SATS-Friendly format, in the older version of MSWord. In the example here you will see a CV in a single font size, left justified, stripped of columns, colour, and many of the other niceties of formatting.

Use your ATS CV version to cut and paste information into employer or commercial CV database dialog boxes. If you want to cover all the bases, you can upload an MSWord 2013 /.docx version as well.

TXT versus ATS friendly

We used to use .txt versions of a CV for uploading to CV databases, but ATS-Friendly formats have made the less attractive .txt format obsolete for these purposes.

In the unlikely event that a database or employer, asks for a .txt or .rtf (Rich text format) version of your CV, you can create one in sixty seconds: Make a copy of your ATS CV and save it; this will open the "Save As" dialog box. Click

Jen Ellis

11 Any Avenue, Anytown AA0 0AA   01234 567890   j.ellis@gmail.com

---

Underwriter – Senior Credit Analyst – Loan Closer / Banking & Mortgage Lending Industry

Professional Profile
Branch Manager & Loan Officer with 12 years of experience managing branch banking and lending activities, improving business processes, and leading a team of financial services professionals who generate approximately £9 million in loanseach year.

Professional Skills

Banking Products & Financial Services	Strategic Business Planning	New Business Development
Mortgage Lending & Underwriting	Economics, Accounting, & Finance	Staff Training & Supervision
Asset Management / Portfolio Valuation	Statistical Analysis & Market Trends	Teamwork & Collaboration
Asset Preservation & Loss Prevention	Regulatory Compliance	Verbal & Written Communications
Loan Applications & Processing	Requirements Elicitation	Lead Generation / Prospecting
Credit Administration / Credit Analysis	Financial Statements & Financial Audits	Customer Accounts Setup
Credit Quality / FICO Credit Scores	Data Entry & Database Management	Customer Relationship Management
Loan Reviews, Approvals, & Closings	Spreadsheets, Flat Files, & Databases	Exceptional Customer Service
Documentation for Funding	General Ledger Accounting	Cross-Selling Opportunities
Collateral Analysis for Secured Loans	AR/AP, Billing/Collections, & Payroll	Critical Thinking & Sound Judgment
Data Verification / Fraud Analysis	Investigative Research	Organization & Time Management
Data Integrity, Security, & Confidentiality	Loss Prevention & Claims Mitigation	Ability to Manage Multiple Priorities

Computer Skills
Microsoft Office Suite: Word, Excel, PowerPoint, Access, Outlook, SharePoint

Performance Highlights
- Strategic Business Leader who uses financial data and market trends analysis to drive business decisions.
- Credit Administrator proficient in interviewing clients, gathering financial information, processing loan applications, analyzing and interpreting credit quality for loan approval or denial, and closing asset-based loans. Train, coach, and mentor branch banking employees in best practices for selling bank products and providing exceptional customer service.
- Compliance Resource for fair lending and responsible banking laws.
- Loan Manager with knowledge and experience in asset management/valuation. Capable of managing multimillion-pound portfolios. Experience working with distressed properties and reviewing collateral reporting packages comprised of accounts receivable aging, inventory reports, sales journals, cash receipts registers, accounts payable listings, and other financial reports. Meticulous in analyzing field examination findings, reconciling all pertinent information to the bank's loan system, administering loan status reports, and overseeing billing and collections.

Professional Experience

Branch Manager / Assistant Branch Manager   May 2003 to Present
XYZ Bank   Anytown

Promoted from Assistant Branch Manager to Branch Manager in July 2004. Serve in a business development and sales role. Offer personal and real loans as well as credit insurance. Generate £9 million in loans each year, provide exceptional customer service, and build strong customer relationships.

- Recruit, hire, train, supervise, and evaluate performance of branch employees working in lending and loan collection.
- Monitor and direct loan activities. Analyze and deter risks associated with personal and property loans. Perform due diligence and conduct thorough credit risk assessments to provide an accurate risk profile and portfolio analysis pertinent to sustaining portfolio value and branch growth.
- Meet clients to determine loan needs and discuss rates, terms, and underwriting requirements. Assist clients in loan application process. Analyze loan applicants' financial data to determine credit worthiness, including income, property valuations, credit report, credit history, etc.

TXT versus ATS friendly

We used to use .txt versions of a CV for uploading to CV databasees, but ATS-Friendly formats have made the less attractive .txt format obsolete for these pirposes.

In the unlikely event that a database or employer, aska for a .txt or (Rich text format) version of your CV, you can create one in sixty seconds: Make a copy of your ATS CV and save it; this will open the "Save As" dialog box. Click on format choices and you'll find both .txt and .rtf as options; click on the one you need and you are finished.

Employer-preferred formats

We have discussed the logical and generally preferred ways to format and deliver your CV, but there are two instances that trump everything I have said: the stated submission requirements of a database or an employer.

Always check to see how that database or employer wants your CV delivered. They will invariably define a specific format. Whatever is requested, or suggested, is the format you use in that instance.

Web-based or HTML CV

A web-based/HTML CV is a "nice to have," not a "must-have." Don't even think about it until you have a properly constructed CV that portrays you exactly as you wish to be seen and have created formats in .docx, PDF, and ATS Friendly.

An HTML, web-based, or e-portfolio CV is essentially a website dedicated to extolling your professional credentials. Apart from a simple CV, it can have additional features such as video and sound.

It is one of those approaches touted as the next big thing, but your LinkedIn profile can achieve everything your own website can. There are a handful of instances when this option might be viable: if you work in the arts, education, certain areas of communications, or technology, the ability to include audio and video clips, music, and pictures can be a plus. It also works in areas of technology where you need to control the bandwidth to ensure the quality of the viewer experience that presents your skills and credentials. Your time is better spent building a LinkedIn Profile which achieves the same thing.

Your CV and databases

Your CV will go into databases, and to be found once uploaded it must contain the right balance of relevant information. We started the CV-building process with understanding employer priorities and the words they use to explain those priorities, through a process we call TJD or Target Job Deconstruction.

You used this information as a general guideline for the story your CV needs to tell, then you made a special effort to see that these TJD-identified priorities and the keywords that express them appear in a number of places throughout your CV:

- Target Job Title
- Performance Profile or Summary
- Professional Skills section
- Within the context of the jobs in which those skills have been developed and applied

ATS software is now able to recognize keywords in context and rewards CVs that use keywords within the context of their application at work so make every effort to do this.

Updating Your CV

Once you have landed in the new job and are starting the next steps of your career, you need to keep your work and achievements tracked on a weekly or monthly basis in your CV folder. If you keep a record of your work on a regular basis, it will make updating your CV for the next step that much easier.

When do you need to update your CV for a job search? Most people leave it until the last minute, but this is too important a document to rush. My best advice is that you need to update the CV about ninety days before you start a job search.

Your social networking profile

There are many options for social media sites, but for professional networking there is one dominant site on which you must have a presence: LinkedIn.

With well over half a billion professionals around the world using LinkedIn for networking, you would be crazy to ignore it. There are two reasons for a social networking site: to find people and to be found. As a professional working in a world without any reliable job security, having a presence on a social media site like LinkedIn keeps you visible not just when you are job hunting but on an ongoing basis. This means you will have the opportunity to build ever-growing networks of similar professionals, employers, and headhunters. Even if you aren't interested in the job, knowing of a company that hires people like you is useful intelligence. Always be polite, professional, and helpful whenever you can; you might not need them now, but six months or a year from now?

When employers are looking for someone like you, they use keywords and phrases from the job posting that they are working from; the relevance of your profile determines:

- Whether you will be found amongst those 400 million-plus other LI users
- Whether the recruiter follows his review with a contact

First things first

As you look at the headlines and categories of a LinkedIn profile, does the flow of information requested remind you of anything? Perhaps the exact flow that your CV follows? I want to make two points:

1 The similarities should give you considerable confidence in what you are doing.
2 You can get a fast start on creating, or upgrading your profile, by cutting and pasting sections of your ATS-Friendly CV into the appropriate section of the LI profile.

However I want you to do something else first: Upload your CV to your profile so that it can be seen and downloaded by others. To upload your CV, follow these steps:

1 Click **Profile** at the top of your homepage.
2 Move your cursor over the Down arrow next to the **View Profile As** button and select **Import CV**.
3 Click **Choose file** or **Browse** to locate your CV on your computer.
4 Click **Upload CV**. You'll be taken to a page where you can review the infor-mation extracted from your CV.
5 Double-check all fields to be sure the information is completed and correct.

Click **Save**.

How to create a brilliant LinkedIn Profile

The profile you create will give you visibility with search engines and enable others to find you. It's like having an advertising hoarding on the side of a road travelled by the people you want to be visible to. Additionally, employers, head-hunters, and managers who have already seen your CV often like to check your social profile(s) to find out more about you. This is why – once you are satisfied that your CV and profile echo the same messaging – I suggest adding a link on your CV to your LI profile.

Your LinkedIn profile, and any other social networking profiles you subse-quently develop, are your public face and your most important passive market-ing tool, keeping you constantly visible to the very people who quite possibly hold the keys to the next step in your career.

It all starts with your headshot

Your headshot appears at the top left of your LinkedIn profile, and it's the first thing anyone who visits your profile sees. An increasing number of Human Resources people say they check out social media profiles, especially LinkedIn and Facebook, before inviting a candidate in for an interview. As the face you show to the world, your headshot is your professional image.

Every picture tells a story

Headshots have become an important part of establishing a credible profes-sional image for all of us. Like it or not, your headshot tells a story, so make sure yours is telling the right story.

We all make judgments based on visual first impressions; with search results, a profile with a headshot will get many more clicks than a profile without one, and the people who come to your profile will form an opinion based on your headshot before they read anything you have written. How professional and accessible your headshot makes you look will also colour the impressions of anyone who then reads your profile. It's safe to say that getting your headshot right is extremely important. Make sure yours presents a confident professional.

Can you get away with a DIY headshot?

The headshot doesn't have to be done by a professional, but you should dress as you would for a job interview.

You can probably get a friend to photograph you against a plain background and it will come out as an acceptable candid shot.

The beauty of a digital camera is that you can take as many shots as you want, pick the best one, and maybe even do some basic cleanups. Shoot straight on and then experiment with distance. Once you've settled on a distance (between four and eight feet for many cameras), experiment with angles to see which is most flattering; adjust the lighting to get the most complimentary result.

You need the best headshot you can generate for immediate use, but bear in mind that summer is the best time to upgrade your social media headshots: you look happier and more relaxed because it's summer, and for paler skins any kind of tan makes you look healthier.

Your headline

After your headshot, the next thing people notice is your headline. This headline should say who you are and what you do; it is important to give a focus, and this is one of the areas the search engine rates as important in establishing your ranking in searches. (called search engine optimization or SEO.) This headline is limited to a 120-character thumbnail description about you and works as a brief biography of the person behind the headshot. You have just these 120 characters to say who you are, so your headline should include your Target Job Title and the keywords that most succinctly capture what you do. You increase the odds of these working well by doing searches on LinkedIn for your own target job title and looking at how the people who show up on the first few pages of results build a winning headline. Use this insight to adapt what you have to offer to synchronize with your findings.

Summary

This should include information that will maximize your *discoverability* when an employer searches for someone like you. Information in your Summary section should be geared to drawing a concise picture of your professional capabilities – not your hopes and dreams but your *capabilities*, because you get hired based on your credentials, not your potential.

The summary on your LinkedIn profile (as on other social networking sites) provides more space than you would usually use in the Summary or Performance Profile section of a job-targeted CV. However, if you have already built a CV, you will have a Performance Profile that reflects the skills, experience, priorities, and word choices employers use to define the job they need to fill. If so, just upload the CV and change it to a first-person voice. Alternatively, you could write six sentences that succinctly capture your capabilities in each of the employer priority areas identified in your TJD.

The summary and work experience sections of your LinkedIn profile accommodate a considerable word count. However, anything you write needs to be accessible to the human eye, and long blocks of text become visually inaccessible very quickly, especially to anyone scanning briefly rather than reading. Consequently, you need to make sure that no paragraph is more than six lines of unbroken text. You can also use bullet points to share important information and deliver visual variety.

Some career "experts" suggest writing about your hobbies here. However, no employer cares about your personal interests until they know you can do the job, so such information is irrelevant, a waste of this valuable selling space, and will cost you readers. Besides, LinkedIn has provided a space for this, where it belongs: at the *end* of your profile.

Instead, use any remaining available space to list critically important skill sets for your work. There is a place for peer-reviewed professional skills later, but listing them here is very helpful to employers, and you certainly won't diminish the impact of your profile by mentioning these skills more than once.

A first- or third-person voice?

While your CV invariably uses a third-person voice, a social media profile has evolved as a longer, more revealing, and personal document, and many people think you should use a first person voice, "I did this, I did that, etc."

I disagree with this thinking, because talking about your responsibilities and accomplishments in first person can make you sound boastful. There is a saying from the world of architectural design that "form follows function"; it applies here. You want a presence on LinkedIn to build networks of professional contacts and to be discovered by employers and headhunters; to me this says that the universally adopted rule for professional CVs should apply here.

We always give our clients the option and recently we were doing a profile for a man who owns a couple of investment companies but whose main focus was sitting on company boards as a board member and external advisor; in response to the question he replied,

"Third person please, if we used first person with my background I'd sound like a narcissistic buffoon. No one wants to work with someone like that."

Contact information

The whole point of having a social media profile is to be in closer contact and better *communication* with your professional world. To this end LI offers multiple ways for others to connect with you; most importantly is the In mail function. As well, you need to have adequate connection information on your profile.

There are two places for this – the most important comes right after your name and headline and before your Summary. The section is referred to as "Contact Info." If you are smart, you will put your personal email address in here. I'm sorry to say that about a quarter of the connection requests I receive everyday lack an email address.

There is also the opportunity to add contact info at the end of your profile, and you should replicate all appropriate contact info here. With email addresses at start and finish of your profile you make contact that much easier for people who want to communicate with you, perhaps by opening doors of opportunity – help them as much as you can.

Work experience

The experience section of your profile begins with your current job and work experience. Again, you can cut and paste the entry from your CV first, then add to this with additional information that you feel is relevant.

Review your entries to see if there is additional experience you would like to add. You have plenty of space here, so as long as your headline and entries for each job start with the most important information as determined by your TJD – you can continue to add additional supporting information until you run out of space.

Whatever you do, don't be lazy and just list your current job: That gives the impression that you have only had the one. LinkedIn will tell you that you're twelve times more likely to be found by employers when you have more than one job listed – perhaps because those other jobs allow you to weight your profile with enough relevant keywords in each job's headline to increase your profile in database searches.

The inclusion of keywords in each job's headline and in the details of that work experience helps make you more visible. This helps employers see your claims of professional competency in context and will dramatically increase the frequency of keyword usage. Do this with each job and your visibility will steadily rise.

Special projects

If you want to add greater detail about your work, perhaps the story that goes behind special achievements or description of an important project, then you can add these experiences (as many as you like) to each job as Special Projects. Now this is a nice option, but don't get carried away and detail the minutiae of your every working moment. Keep in mind that your goal in a job search is to get into *communication* with the people who can hire you as quickly and frequently as you can, so your LI profile is a marketing device to attract people and start a conversation. This means that too much information can help rule you out of consideration before a conversation even occurs. As a rule of thumb think *moderation*, and in this context it means telling potential employers what you can do but never how you did it – that's for conversation.

Professional and technology competencies

LinkedIn has a Skills area that allows you to identify up to fifty different skills. Using your Target Job Deconstruction to determine the skills your customers seek in someone with your professional title, you should add a list of *professional skills* to your LinkedIn profile.

Getting and controlling skill endorsements

Once your profile is visible to the public, people can endorse you for each of these skills (a favour you can initiate and return). The more endorsements you have of your skills, the more visible you become to employers. Adding skills to your LinkedIn profile has the same benefits as adding it to your CV: it makes your profile more visible in database searches and your skills more readily accessible to readers.

You can post up to fifty skills in the dialogue box; however, you will also want your contacts to endorse you for these skills, so listing fewer skills can mean more endorsements for each, and more endorsements help your visibility. As your networks grow, they'll certainly include others who are job hunting, and mutual skill endorsements can help you both.

Your visibility in LI database searches does not depend on how many skills you have listed, but rather the volume of endorsements you have for those skills: Ten skills with 100 endorsements each is much better than fifty skills with ten endorsements each, not only for the database algorithms but for the message it sends to the reader.

On the personal settings page you can also decide if you want to permit others to add skills to your list or not. It is best to keep control of what appears on your profile so do not allow this option.

Education

Start with your highest educational level and work backward. While your educational attainments will usually stop with postsecondary education in your CV, with a LinkedIn profile you might want to consider listing secondary school as well: This increases your networking opportunities. Just a week before the time of writing, I received a connect request from a school friend living half a world away, whom I'd lost touch with many years ago.

Certifications

Add all your professional certifications; they demonstrate that either your employers, or you personally, have seen fit to invest in your ongoing professional education. Additionally, they can be used by headhunters as search terms, making you more discoverable.

Interests

Finally, the place where it is appropriate to add something about your outside interests! If someone has read this far, learning that I enjoy history, historical fiction, kayaking, swing, rhumba, and country dancing, am an obsessed collector of phonographs, and am the world's worst bass player might be of interest, because it allows the reader to see a three-dimensional person; but coming earlier in my profile it would only be a distraction.

Associations and awards

Include membership in any associations or societies. List profession-related organizations and professional awards first, then follow with groups and awards related to your personal interests.

Reading List

You should include professionally relevant materials here.

Spelling, punctuation, and grammar

The same considerations you applied to spelling, punctuation, and grammar in your CV also apply here.

Recommendations

LinkedIn likes your profile to have at least three recommendations and doesn't recognize it as complete until you do. This is in your best interests too, as recommendations from colleagues, co-workers, and past managers give your profile depth and increase your appeal. The easiest way to get recommendations is to do them for your colleagues and then ask them to reciprocate. LinkedIn will send a recommendation to the recipient and ask him (a) if he would like to upload it, and (b) if he would like to reciprocate. If he doesn't reciprocate within a couple of days, send a personal request. You don't need to tell someone he *owes* you a reference in return for yours, just that you'd appreciate it.

If you are returning to the workforce after an absence, you can use recommendations from volunteer work. Also, you can reach out to people who gave you written recommendations and ask them to be duplicated on LinkedIn. You can make things easier by sending such people an email with a copy of the recommendation.

Link your CV to your social media profile

Once your profile is complete and supports the story told in your CV, upload the CV as directed. Linking to your CV is useful because a CV is still the most succinct vehicle for sharing your professional skills, and employers will use it for their records.

Your CV should also have a mutual link to your LinkedIn profile (beneath your hyperlinked email address), so that HR or the manager can click through and gather more insight into your potential suitability.

Privacy and saving your work

Building your profile may take a week before you have it exactly right, so you should know that every time you change a sentence on your LinkedIn profile and log out, LinkedIn can automatically send a change of status to your network. As you may make many changes to get it right, you don't want your contacts notified every few minutes. To avoid this, do three things:

1 Write your early drafts on a Word document with headings that match the site's profile subject headers. Then make changes to your heart's content without any danger of unwittingly sharing your edits with the world. When you do upload, you'll invariably still want to tweak your copy and so still want to maintain privacy.

2 Go to *Settings* from the drop-down menu under your name on the top right of your homepage and look for *Privacy Controls*. Choose *Private* while you are making profile changes. This will keep your changes private until your profile is complete and you release it for public display.

3 Save everything in the final published draft in a Microsoft Word document. This will give you a complete social media profile ready for fast adaptation when you join other social networking sites. Back up your work, because if you don't, somewhere along the line you are going to lose it.

You can also use the *Public Profile Settings* to customize your existing LinkedIn URL to make it more attention grabbing and informative – perhaps reflecting your job title.

LI personalized URL address

LinkedIn automatically gives your profile an address along the lines of *https://www.linkedin.com/in/Jim-Dowe-715594236*; this allows others to find you and you to refer people to your profile but you can do better. LI allows you to create a personalized URL for your profile to shorten it up and remove the numbers after your name.

Your name is okay, but something that mentions your job like "TopAccountant" or "HClexpert" is much better, because LI profile addresses and email addresses are often the very first thing an employer sees, so an address that helps identify your professional persona is a distinct benefit.

HTML/multimedia CV considerations

An HTML or multimedia CV can be a sensible option if you work in a field where visuals and sound and/or graphics represent critical skills. A good percentage of CV banks and social networking sites accept HTML CVs; plus a simple HTML CV can be created by using the "Save as HTML" command, which you can access in Microsoft Word when you save and name your documents.

If you want to create a small website, you can create a much richer experience for the viewer, adding audio and video and other bells and whistles if they will help. You can add a hyperlink in your standard CV, or in your cover letter/email, that takes the reader to your web-hosted CV. This has the advantage of allowing the viewer to see your background exactly as you wish it to be, with the enrichment of additional media.

HTML and multimedia design considerations

- Don't be seduced by design capabilities for the sake of their flashiness; remember the needs of your customer and your communication goals. Use technology to make life easier for the visitor. For example, your email address can be a hyperlink, so that clicking on it immediately launches the user's email to contact you.

- If the HTML CV ends up being a complex document with graphics, sound, and video, layout is going to be a major consideration. You don't want the mission-critical topics – performance profile, core and technical competencies, education, work samples, etc. – to get lost in the glitz. It is all too easy to get caught up in building a website, because it's a convenient and fun way to put off the real work of building your CV.

- Provide a hyperlink that allows the user to print out that beautifully formatted PDF version of your CV.
- Don't start from ground zero; find an example you like and copy it.

Is an interactive portfolio/web-based CV a waste of time?

Much depends on your situation. It's a nice thing for anyone to have, but not mandatory unless:

- Your profession is web based
- Your work involves visual and auditory components
- Your work is technology based with a communications component
- Demonstrating technological expertise is a plus for your job

Since an online portfolio is the most complex CV document you can create, you want the core content of the site to be finished before you start creating this version with all its bells and whistles. The most practical approach is to get your Microsoft Word CV completed, along with the necessary ASCII text versions. Once you've developed the other versions, and have your job search up to speed, you can decide if you need to develop this third variation.

Some disadvantages include:

- Adding graphics, visuals, video, and audio is a time-consuming process, and can be expensive if you hire someone to do it for you; most professionals don't need to present themselves in this way.
- If you want an HTML or web-based CV, you'll need to build a website or have one built. This website will then have to be hosted somewhere and you'll have registration fees, hosting fees, and announcement fees (elementary optimization); if this is a foreign language to you, as a website owner you'll have to learn it, because all these things cost money. Apart from paying to have such a site built, these costs are usually small, but they are ongoing and add up over time.
- If you want to build it yourself without any experience, there is a learning curve involved.
- Because the content is more complex, these documents take longer to open and work through, so the content needs to be compelling if you are going to hold anyone's attention.

- You will build a web-based CV because you hope to *send* people to see it. You can't expect employers to flock to it, since there is fierce competition to achieve a reasonable search ranking in the world of CVs. So unless you spend a small fortune on optimization, you can't realistically expect much passing traffic;

For most people, having a LinkedIn Profile will be a perfectly adequate substitute for a personal website. On top of this, I know a lot of headhunters, and they almost all express a bias against these websites – people who use them are seen as desperate; they'll try anything to get a job. The exceptions are the circumstances mentioned above where the profession makes such a initiative relevant and useful.

The business card CV

The first time you hear about a business card CV, it can sound like a gimmick, and you should know better than to waste valuable job search time pursuing gimmicks. That said, business cards are an accepted sales tool the world over, and for a job hunter they're so much less intrusive than carrying around a wad of CVs under your arm.

If you want to try a business card CV, you must consider the severely limited space available to you and use that space wisely:

Front of the card

- List critical information: Your name, Target Job Title, telephone number, and email address.
- Use legible, businesslike (Times Roman, Arial) fonts.
- Make it readable. Limit the word count so that you can maximize font size to increase readability; better to have one legible email address than add a social network address and have them both be illegible.
- No one in a position to hire you can read an 8-point font, and reminding someone that he/she is old and has failing eyesight is not a good sales pitch.

Back of the card

Space is minimal, so less is more and readability is everything; the words you choose must communicate *both* your understanding of the job and your ability to deliver when you are doing that job:

1 Repeat your Target Job Title.

2 This is followed by a two-word headline on the next line: Performance Profile.

3 Follow this with a single short sentence that addresses the most important part of your target job. The most important part of your job (and all jobs) is – say it with me now – the identification, prevention, and solution of problems within a specific area of professional expertise. It is ultimately what we all get hired to do.

4 Finish with a social network address that delivers a comprehensive professional profile to any interested reader, such as your LinkedIn profile, your web-based CV, or any other URL that delivers the full story on your professional capabilities.

As an example, an accounting professional who worked in accounts receivable, might have the rear side of a business card CV that looks something like this:

Martin Yate   01234 567890

Accounts Receivable

Performance Profile/Performance Summary
Focused on the ID, prevention, and solution of all
recurrent A/R problems.

http://www.linkedin.com/martiny

Notice that by starting this mini-CV with a verb, you not only show understanding of what is at the heart of this job, you also deliver a powerful personal statement by telling the reader what to expect.

CV for promotions

We tend to think of our CV as a tool to get a new job at another company, and forget that we can use it to get a promotion where we already are.

You need a job-targeted CV for pursuing internal promotions because:

- No one is paying as much attention to you as you would like.
- It shows an employer you are serious about growth.

- It's a powerful way to get yourself viewed in a different light.
- It puts you on a par with external applicants who will have job-targeted CVs.
- It puts you ahead of these applicants, because you are a known quantity.
- When you have the required skills, it's much easier to get promoted from within.

Promotions come to those who earn them, not as a reward for watching the clock for three years. Thinking through what's really needed for your next step up the ladder, building the skills to earn that promotion, and then creating a CV that positions you for the job, is smart strategic thinking.

Your promotion campaign starts with determining a specific target job for the next logical step up the ladder, and then understanding the requirements for someone holding that job title.

Collect job postings for that next step and deconstruct the target job's specific responsibilities.

Once you have a crystal-clear idea of what is needed to succeed in the target job:

- Identify areas for skill development.
- Determine how you will develop these skills.
- Volunteer for assignments that build these skills and give you practical experience that can become part of your CV.

Once your skills have reached 70 percent of those required for the new job, you can start building a CV targeted to that promotion.

Proofread and test-email all versions of your CV

Before you send any version of your CV, proofread it carefully. Send your email cover letters and CV attachments to yourself and to a friend or family member. Ask them for printouts of your practice email messages and CVs to ensure that what you intended to send is actually what was received, and can be printed out. Often, this exercise will help you find mistakes or larger problems incurred during the conversion process. The most common and annoying problem is that the contact information you carefully put at the top of the second page now appears halfway down it; these are the important mistakes you can easily catch with this exercise.

7

READY TO LAUNCH

Why everyone hates reading CVs and what you can do about it. Here are some powerful construction strategies to simultaneously make your CV information dense and visually accessible.

You are in the home stretch, giving your CV the final polish before releasing it to a very discriminating public. It has to be:

- Job focused and data dense to beat out the competition in the CV database wars.
- Typographically clean, and visually accessible to accommodate the recruiters' initial scan.
- Headline rich and textually concise to deliver a compelling message.

Make this happen and your CV will get picked for review from the databases. It will then get serious attention from employers.

The importance of immediate impact

Your CV will get between five and forty seconds of initial attention, and the more accessible it is to the tired and distracted eyes of managers, the closer the attention it will receive. You'll improve the chances that your CV will receive attention if you:

1 *Make it readable.* Stop worrying about page count. In CVs, as in everything, *form follows function*; use the space you need to tell the story you need to tell. Use 11- and 12-point fonts that are easier on adult eyes.

2 *Check your headlines.* They help a reader achieve and maintain focus. The first page of your CV always needs to start off strong, and there is

no better way of doing this than with headlines that help accessibility and comprehension.

Target Job Title
(What the CV is about)

Performance Profile
(A snapshot of what I can do)

Professional Competencies
(The key professional skills that help me do my job well)

Technology Competencies
(Optional: the technical skills that help me do my job well)

Performance Highlights
(Optional: my outstanding achievements as they relate to the job)

Professional Experience ....
(Where and when everything happened)

3 *Check Professional Competencies and Technology Competencies.* These are the hard skills that enable you to do what you do. Each word or phrase should act as a headline of capability and topic for discussion.

4 *Performance/Career Highlights.* This is an optional section, provided that your experience has the achievements to support it.

A first page with these headlines and job-focused content in readable fonts will draw in the reader.

Fonts and font sizes

You can use one font throughout your CV, but never use more than two fonts: one for headlines and the other for the body copy. The most popular fonts for business *communication* are Arial and Times or Times New Roman. They probably look boring because you are so used to seeing them, but you see them so much because they are clear and very readable. Bottom line: they work. The biggest criticism of these fonts is their lack of flair and design value. Below are some other fonts that are good for headlines and body copy, since they are readable and almost universally recognized by printers (obviously a plus if you plan on having someone actually read your CV). The nature of each font is unique and the actual size of each is going to vary. Don't be a slave to 12-point:

Sometimes 11-point might work with a particular font. Just don't use a smaller font size to keep your CV to one or two pages. Your CV must be easily readable by those tired and distracted eyes.

Avoid or minimize capitalized text, as it's tough on the eyes. Many people think it makes a powerful statement when used in headlines, but all it does is cause eyestrain and give the reader the impression that you are shouting.

Good for headlines:

Arial	Verdana
Times/Times New Roman	Gill Sans
Century Gothic	Lucida Sans

Good for body copy:

Arial	Georgia
Times/Times New Roman	Goudy Old Style
Garamond	

Each of the above is in 12-point font, but you can see that the nature of each font is unique and the actual size of each is going to vary.

Avoid "script" fonts that look similar to handwriting. While they look attractive to the occasional reader, they are harder on the eyes. That said, in the CVs later in this book you will see examples of just this sort of font. For example, the arts, education, and (sometimes) healthcare are areas where the warmer and more personal look of a script font can work and still present a professional-looking CV. Use with discretion.

Once you decide on font(s), stick with them. More than two fonts will be disquieting to the reader. You can do plenty to liven up the visual impact of the page and create emphasis with **bold**, *italic*, ***bold italic***, underlining, sizing of words, and highlighting, used judiciously.

Avoid typos like the plague!

CVs that are riddled with misspeltings rejected. You have a spellchecker; use it.

A couple of years back, I counselled an executive director in the £100-per-year range. He was having problems getting in front of the right people. The first paragraph of his CV stated that he was an executive with "superior communication skills." Unfortunately, the other twelve words of the sentence contained a spelling error! Fortunately, we caught it. In an age of spellcheckers, this sloppiness isn't acceptable at any level.

A word of caution: the spellchecker can't catch everything, so you'll have to do some editing work yourself. For example, spellcheck won't catch the common mistyping of "form" for "from" because "form" is a word. Similarly, your spellchecker can't help you distinguish *too* from *to* and *two*, *your* from *you're*, or *it's* from *its*, so get someone you trust to check it over as well.

Proofing the print resume

Even in the age of email and databases, you will need print versions of your CV. For example, you should always take printed copies to your interviews: This guarantees each interviewer will have your background laid out in the way you want it. Print it out now to ensure that the onscreen layout matches that of the printed document. Make sure the pagination of the printed copy works the way you intend. Double-check the printed copy for:

- Layout and balance
- Typos and grammatical errors
- Punctuation and capitalization
- Page alignment errors
- That everything has been underlined, capitalized, in bold, italicized, and indented exactly as you intended

Print it out on as many different printers as you reasonably can. Why? Depending on the printer, you can find fonts performing differently. That's one of the reasons for using *Times* and *Arial*: they print without problems on every printer.

Appearance checklist

Let the CV rest overnight or longer, then pick it up and review it with fresh eyes, immediately after you have reread your TJD.

- What's your immediate reaction to it? Is it clear who and what this document is about? Does it clearly address the needs of your TJD? Are the lines clean?
- Does the copy under each of your headlines tell a convincing story?
- Does the first page of the CV identify you as someone clearly capable of delivering the job's requirements?
- Have you used only one side of the page?
- Are your fonts readable, in the 11- to 12-point range?
- Does the layout accommodate the reader's needs, rather than outmoded concerns on CV length?

- Are your paragraphs no more than five lines long? Are your sentences fewer than twenty words long?

- Are your sentences short on personal pronouns and long on action verbs?

- Is there plenty of white space around important areas, such as Target Job Title and your Opening Statement? Managers may be reviewing CVs on handheld devices, and plenty of space helps readability.

The final product

The paper version of your CV should be printed on standard, A4 paper. Paper comes in different weights and textures; good CV-quality paper has a weight designation of around 80gsm. Lighter paper feels flimsy and curls; heavier paper is unwieldy. Most office supply stores have paper and envelopes suitable for CVs and cover letters.

As for paper colour, white, pale gray, and cream are the prime choices. They are straightforward, no-nonsense colours that look professional.

Cover letter stationery should have the same contact information as your CV and should *always* match the colour and weight of the paper used. Again, it's part of the professional image that underlies all the little things you pay attention to in a job search.

Set up letterhead for your cover letter stationery, using the same fonts you used on the CV. The coordinated paper size, colour, weight, and fonts will give your CV and cover letter a cohesive look.

8

THE CVs

I have included CVs from a wide range of jobs so that you will be able to find a CV telling a story similar to yours. However, *CV layouts are tailored not to the job but to the person and his or her story*. So when you see a CV layout that works for you, use it Don't be put off because the example is of someone in another profession.

Zoe Blake

Linked**in** profile

11 Any Avenue
Anytown AA0 0AA

01234 567890
zoe.blake@gmail.com

Accounting / Finance

PERFORMANCE PROFILE

A highly astute, energetic, and team-spirited accounting graduate seeking opportunity to contribute to an organization's goals and objectives. Accurate, precise, and ethically responsible in all work-related assignments. Quick learner with an eagerness for learning and expanding accounting capabilities. Proven ability in identifying problems and implementing innovative solutions.

- Recent graduate with proven analytical and critical thinking skills.
- Disciplined with a desire to succeed as evidenced by working 20 hours per week while attending college full-time.
- Exceptional skills in written documentation and verbal communication.
- Effective interpersonal and leadership skills supported by an enthusiastic, team player attitude.
- Foreign Language—proficient in Chinese.
- Technology: MS Word, Excel, PowerPoint, Access, Database, and Adobe Photoshop; Internet savvy.

PROFESSIONAL SKILLS

- Customer Service Skills
- Accounts Payable
- Accounts Receivable
- Budget Forecasting

- GAAP
- Inventory Analysis
- Bookkeeping
- Journal Entries

- Financial Presentations
- Management Skills
- Cost Control
- Market Research

EDUCATION

BSc in Accounting/Finance, Southern University   2016
Relevant Course Work: Intermediate Accounting I, Intermediate Accounting II, Accounting Theory, Accounting Principles, Government Accounting, Income Tax, and Auditing.

ACTIVITIES

Volunteer Income Tax Assistance
Prepared income tax returns for non-profit and small businesses

EXPERIENCE

Southern University,   January 2014–Current
Student Manager, Dining Services
- Calculate weekly payroll for all employees.
- Conduct store management as well as accounting and financial presentations for daily business performance to enhance utilization of funds.
- Supervise daily sales operations and training for new employees to maintain quality and efficiency.

Student Employee   January 2012–December 2014
- Provided high-quality customer services and efficiently carried out monetary transactions.
- Assisted with opening and closing accounting procedures for Coffee shop and campus deli store.

Student Worker, Rivers Centre   January 2010–December 2012
- Arranged services to meet a large portion of the leisure, recreational, conference, and meeting needs on campus.
- Managed procedures of business conferences and banquets for campus needs.
- Successfully promoted student-faculty interaction and learning outside of the classroom environment.

HOLLY BOYETTE

11 Any Ave., Anytown AA0 0AA • 01234 567890 • auditeagle@gmail.com

Auditor

Performance Profile

Top-performing ACCA with five years of comprehensive accounting and auditing experience in domestic and international settings. Progressively responsible positioning with a top-ranked accounting firm serving a wide range of clients. Broad knowledge of IFRS and GAAP UK with the ability to work productively and deliver results in pressure-intensive situations.

♦ Strong analytical and critical thinking skills with a consistent record of anticipating problems and finding solutions, while exhibiting superior judgment and a balanced, realistic understanding of issues.
♦ A willing and eager learner who is constantly updating knowledge and skills. Completed all four parts of the CPA exam within four months while working full-time. Passed all exams on the first try.
♦ A lead-by-example, self-motivated mindset; able to set effective priorities and implement decisions to achieve immediate and long-term goals and meet operational deadlines.
♦ Builds and maintains excellent client relationships to ensure customer satisfaction.
♦ Fluent in English, French, and Afrikaans.

Professional Competencies

- Certified Chartered Accountant
- General Accounting Operations
- Analytical
- Organizational
- Troubleshooting

- UK GAAP
- IFRS
- Sarbanes-Oxley Compliance
- Resource Management
- Project Management
- Staff Training & Development

- Audit Methodology
- Financial Audits
- Business Development
- Communication
- Presentation
- Report Writing

Professional Experience

XYZ Associates, Anytown   2009–Present
International assurance, tax advisory services firm. 35,000 employees and £4B in global revenue.

AUDITOR   2014–Present

♦ Working collaboratively and independently, conduct client engagements from start to finish, including planning, executing, directing, and completing financial audits and managing to budget. Supervise three to five interns and audit associates.
♦ Charged with assurance services, including assisting Senior Audit Associates, Audit Managers, and Audit Partners in performing external audits of public and private companies.
♦ Maintain excellent client relationships to ensure customer satisfaction; partner with all levels of client management and staff to effectively perform audit services.
♦ Proactively work with key client management to gather information, resolve audit-related issues, and offer recommendations for business and process improvements.
♦ Perform tests of controls including Sarbanes-Oxley Compliance and substantive procedures of audit. Compose project performance and budget reports for managers, partners, and clients.
♦ Prepare and review journal entries in accordance with GAAP; research errors and perform balance sheet reconciliations.
♦ Provide strategic support to Junior Audit Associates, advising, reviewing, and assisting with work.

| HOLLY BOYETTE | 01234 567890 | auditeagle@gmail.com | Page Two |

BUSINESS ADVISORY SERVICES ASSOCIATE 2011–2014

Selected to work on confidential investigative project with one of the largest banks in the UK.
♦ Accountable for review and test of controls of bank's credit agreements in terms of their own and government credit guidelines.
♦ Involved in team and client discussion for review comments and recommendations.
♦ Performed review and quality control assessment of colleagues' and junior team members' work.
♦ Provided strategic support to Junior BAS Associates, advising, reviewing, and assisting with work.

AUDIT ASSOCIATE 2010–2011

Offered full-time permanent position with Hepburn & Associates in FL as result of performance excellence.
♦ Tasked with assurance services, including assisting Senior Audit Associates, Audit Managers, and Audit Partners in performing external audits of public and private companies.

SENIOR TRAINEE ACCOUNTANT
JUNIOR TRAINEE ACCOUNTANT 2009

Assisted with audits while acquiring experience for Chartered Accounting programme.

Education
~Chartered Certified Accountant 2012
~Proposal Writing, University of London 2012

Professional Organizations / Affiliations
Certified Public Accountants Association (CPAA)
British Institute of Chartered Accountants (SAICA)

Computer Skills
Software: Microsoft Access, Word, Excel; SharePoint; J.D. Edwards; AS400 (eServer iSeries/400)
Operating Systems: Microsoft XP, Windows7

Languages
Fluent in English, French, and Afrikaans, verbal and written

Kanji Mosoui

Anytown AA0 0AA   01234 567890   finance_focused@gmail.com

QUALIFICATIONS FOR FINANCIAL SERVICES INTERNSHIP

- ➤ Committed to a career combining formal education in economics with practical work. Experienced with analyses for project management, including budgets, labour resources, and timelines.
- ➤ Prepared and delivered numerous presentations on project status. Reserched and presented options to property owners and investors for construction materials.
- ➤ History of taking on responsibility and successfully managing personnel for multimillion-pound projects. Excellent communication with individuals, businesses, and professional firms.
- ➤ Conversational Spanish.

Education

MIDLANDS UNIVERSITY,

MA, Economics   Anticipated Dec 2017

BSc, Economics   Graduated 2016

Leadership Experience

MU Student Wellfare Association   2014 – 2016

Consecutively **Treasurer, Vice Chair, Chair**

Professional Experience

XYZ   2010 – 2014

Installer of wet and dry underground utilities for new developers

Project Manager

- Managed £3.6M project to install new underground dry utilities and new street lights. Worked with telephone and cable companies. Project took approximately 1 1/2 year for planning, execution, and completion. Averaged approximately 15 full-time crew.

DAVÉ CONSTRUCTION, San Jose, CA   2009

Residential and investment property new construction and renovation

Construction Manager / Project Manager

- Functioned as general contractor for construction of new £2M, 4,700-square-foot residential property. Hired and managed approximately 300 subcontractors and suppliers over the course of the project.
- Worked with general contractors and clients on architectural plans. Oversaw daily construction, and handled accounting, including paying all subcontractors.
- Worked with owner to convert 1,000-square-foot home to 3,200 square feet. Same duties noted as above. Sale of home resulted in net profit of almost £400K for property owner.

Excellent references available

JAMES MARTIN

11 Any Ave., Anytown AA0 0AA
01234 567890 | james.martin@comcast.net
Linked **in** profile

REGULATORY COMPLIANCE SPECIALIST

Protecting companies from financial and legal risk through the development of compliance policy.

Compliance expert offering 15+ years of related experience in banking capital markets, brokerage and investment firms, and insurance sector, ensuring strict adherence to legal and financial regulations to alleviate risk exposure, facilitate smooth audits, and enable company profitability. Adept at maintaining focus on company operations to monitor, investigate, and ensure fulfillment of regulatory obligations and alignment of compliance policies. Advise key decision makers on regulatory and compliance requirements to aid in development of strategic solutions that support new programs.

Registered financial advisor whose wide-ranging expertise spans implementing and managing compliance monitoring programme; following compliance policies and procedures; ensuring appropriate compliance training; monitoring FCA regulations and their application; preparing and submitting FCA regulatory returns. Thrives in high pressure environments where swift, effective resolution of identified risk is paramount.

PROFESSIONAL SKILLS

Regulatory Compliance	Due Diligence	Performance Management
Legal Analysis	Staff Development	Fiduciary Responsibility
Risk Assessments	Team Leadership	Anti-money Laundering (AML)
Controls	Account Surveillance	Know-Your-Customer (KYC)
Negotiations	Mediations/Arbitrations	Training & Development

PERFORMANCE HIGHLIGHTS

- Played pivotal role in alleviating AML concerns through automation of new international account forms.
- Thwarted reputational and financial damage of firm by uncovering and remediating adverse practices among select financial advisors via conducting surveillance on personal trading and researching patterns.
- Increased volume of licensed support staff through implementation of Series 7 training programme as well as raised number of certifications held by financial advisors by offering incentives and training programme for office staff.

PROFESSIONAL EXPERIENCE

ABC Bank | Anytown   1998 – 2015

Administrative Manager – Global Wealth Management (1999 – 2015)
Appointed to ensure branch adherence to internal and regulatory agency requirements as well as to provide guidance on trading strategy policies, including options, commodities, derivatives, and structured investments.

Monitored office activities, from trading to complaint resolution, and facilitated biweekly performance management meetings, liaising with senior compliance executives.

Guided branch to earn satisfactory FCA and branch audit ratings. Supervised 250 employees and negotiated employee disciplinary actions and client complaints via mediation or arbitration.

- Spearheaded smooth transition of million-pound wealth management teams.
- Bolstered office productivity by analyzing product profitability, helping financial advisors better understand products to increase their payout.
- Championed 1st successful internal audit with no significant findings, examining recordkeeping, trade tickets, correspondence, structured investments, trading activity, and client activity to ensure compliance.
- Fostered numerous strategic business relationships, forging alliance between XYZ College and branch office for summer intern programme as well as proposing partnership between ABC Bank and central African Financial Advisers.
- Implemented and led annual project, fostering team building and boosting morale among staff members.

Financial Adviser   1998 – 1999

Managed portfolios for more than 100 clients, facilitating financial seminars and providing financial planning expertise for individual, corporate, institutional, and nonprofit clients.

EARLIER CAREER

Bank South | **Compliance/Quality Control Associate**	1997 – 1998
A & B | **Compliance Associate**	1996 – 1997
Securities International | **Compliance Associate**	1994 – 1996
Securities International | **Sales Associate**	1990 – 1994

EDUCATION

- **BBA Business Administration:** Southern University
- ICA Professional Postgraduate Diploma in Governance, Risk & Compliance
- ICA Professional Postgraduate Diploma in Financial Crime Compliance

Sylvana Cecchini

Anytown AA0 0AA   01234 567890   syl.cecchini@anyisp.com

Senior Credit Analyst with MBA and 10 years of investment banking experience.
With Expertise in Credit Evaluation, Risk Analysis, & Risk Mitigation

Credit Review, Analysis, & Structuring	Underwriting & Portfolio Management	Bonds/Securities Market
Corporate & Industry Research	Risk Infrastructure Advisement	C-Level Communications
Financial Analysis & Reporting	Risk Assessment/Risk Assignment Plans	Global Business Relationships
Presentations & Negotiations	Investment Banking/Corporate Lending	Tax Laws & Regulations

Performance Highlights

- **Chartered Accountant** with substantial experience managing all aspects of credit analysis, credit risk, credit approval processes, including corporate/industry research, financial statement review, credit evaluation, and risk mitigation for multibillion-pound portfolios.
- **Communicator** with the ability to condense complex financial data into a readable format and present evidence-based opinions regarding financial health and credit worthiness of new and existing bank clients.
- **Integral part of investment banking teams** that:
  - **Financed the first geothermal power plant in Indonesia** out of a bank in Japan.
  - **Built banking relationships** with some of the largest oil and gas corporations in Southeast Asia.
  - **Loaned funds to diverse corporations and structured finance transactions in Oceania and Asia** including key markets of Australia, Singapore, Indonesia, Thailand, Malaysia, Philippines, Vietnam, Hong Kong, India, and New Zealand.
- **Worked for the Malaysian Ministry of Finance** as a part of the startup team that implemented the framework for operations of the first Malaysian financial guarantor of Malaysian bonds and Islamic securities market (sukuk) valued at £ billion annually.

Professional Experience

ABC BANK, Anytown **Senior Analyst, Credit Division**	September 2011–Present
XYZ BANK, Anytown **Head, Portfolio Risk**	September 2009–August 2011
A & B BANK, Othertown **Credit Research**	January 2008–July 2009
X & Y Building Society, Othertown **Credit Analyst, Department of Industrial and Consumer Products**	November 2004–December 2007
TAX PREPARATION SERVICES, Othertown **Tax Accountant**	April 2003–October 2004

Education

Master of Business Administration, MBA–London University
BSc Accounting–Othertown University

Personal Data	**Professional Affiliations**
Languages: Fluent in English, Italian, and Portuguese	Institute of Chartered Accountants in England and Wales (ICAEW)

Caroline Olivero, CFA

11 Any Avenue
Anytown AA0 0AA

01234 567890
cpa66103@gmail.com

Financial Analyst

Performance Summary

Senior-level Accountant, Financial Analyst, and Internal Auditor with more than 15 years of experience in accounting and finance. Skilled in gathering and analyzing data, confirming accuracy, and performing monthly review of financial information. Quick, decisive, and highly effective financial strategist with proven success ensuring compliance with FCA regulations, internal regulations and policies. Maintains the overall integrity of accounting and financial systems. Skilled in coordinating with regional finance teams on statement preparation. Able to prepare financial statements and summarize results for management and key stakeholders. Impeccable integrity and work ethic.

Professional Skills

Financial Analysis	Variance Analysis	GAAP UK	SAP & PeopleSoft
Financial Close	Sarbanes-Oxley	Bribery Act	Staff Leadership
SOX/non-SOX Controls	Communication	Relationship Development	Report Development
Account Reconciliations	Financial Statements	Internal Controls	Documentation
Microsoft Office Suite	Issue Resolution	Financial Reports	Compliance

——Professional Experience——

International Paper Company, Anytown   2013 – 2017
World's largest pulp and paper producer with £26B in annual revenue and 61,500 employees worldwide.

Senior Financial Analyst

Assisted in performing internal control reviews of Beverage Packaging Division manufacturing facilities in Europe, Asia, and Latin America. Provided assistance with development and implementation of audit control activities for the division. Ensured audit programmes were compliant with International Paper's SOX compliance programme by coordinating with the compliance group. Developed new process narratives and Visio flowcharts for identification of control deficiencies and improvement of audit efficiency for Latin American locations. Prepared 2005 and 2006 GAAP financial statements and footnotes for division audits in preparation for divestiture, including coordination with external auditors and management.

- Coordinated with International Paper Accounting Staff in preparation of GAAP consolidated financial statements for Liquid Packaging Division.
- Coordinated with the International Paper's SOX compliance group to ensure compliance with SOX compliance programme.
- Developed and implemented audit procedures used by the Liquid Packaging Division subsequent to acquisition by coordinating with International Paper's Internal Audit Group.

XYZ Express, Othertown   2008 – 2013
The largest business unit within XYZ which has £43B in annual revenue and 300,000 employees worldwide.

Senior Accounting Research Analyst

Provided maintenance of the accounting data for long-term aircraft leases, including ensuring all leases were accrued on straight-line basis and amortizing gain on sale-lease aircraft. Reviewed expense line items for leased property and equipment expense, as well as long-term aircraft lease expense, including analyzing account variations, obtaining explanations for business reason for variation, and reporting findings to management. Provided quarterly summary of accounting information for management review. Prepared monthly summary of underutilized leased property.

- Selected to research accounting matters for the Corporate Accounting Group through preparation of a quarterly summary of accounting-related information for management review.

ABC Enterprises, Anytown   1997 – 2008
One of Europe's leading beverage companies with £8B in annual revenue and 13,250 employees.

Senior Financial Analyst   1999 – 2008

Charged with providing management and support for the operating budget within the Midlands Division. Traveled to various locations and coordinated with Branch Managers, Division, and Senior Management to ensure budget reflected expenditures.

- Spearheaded new method of analyzing contract profitability with local and primary schools, as well as colleges and universities. Project included downloading sales reports and incorporating into NPV analysis.

Senior Accountant   1997 – 1999

Prepared entries for month-end close, performed analysis, and provided explanations for various operating expense variances for management. Designed and delivered ad hoc reports. Provided management and training for senior accountant and staff accountant. Reconciled balance sheet accounts, including third-party marketing accounts, bank accounts, and division payroll account.

- Assisted in the implementation of a systematic method of accruing invoices by developing a database application utilized to track invoices and follow up on outstanding items.

―――― **Education and Complementary Experience**――――

BSc Accounting and Finance, Midlands University

Chartered Financial Analyst (CFA)

Meredith Sommers

Linked **in** profile

11 Any Avenue
Anytown AA0 0AA

01234 567890
meredith.sommers@gmail.com

Healthcare Sales Management

Performance Profile

Eighteen years of Medical/Healthcare sales and a proven track record of consistently outperforming sales quotas, developing new business, building strong customer relationships, and effectively managing time and territory. Proficient and persistent in all stages of the sales cycle. Uncompromising commitment to management and customer service excellence balanced by the highest degree of integrity in all relationships and transactions.

Proven abilities include:

- Excel in prospecting, qualifying, developing, and closing sales opportunities.
- Experienced sales trainer in classroom settings in addition to field training.
- Expert in consultative and solution selling with proven ability to capitalize on sales opportunities.
- Ability to gain cooperation and buy-in of multiple decision-makers in complex business environments.
- Strong healthcare IT industry knowledge and experience.
- Visionary strategist with the ability to articulate solutions to customer problems and maximize revenues.
- Strong ability to work effectively, independently, and collaboratively with internal and external sales teams.
- Change agent with expertise in indentifying business needs and delivering innovative solutions.
- Exceptional customer relationship management skills.
- Notable efficiency, organizational skills, and ability to multitask projects and set priorities.
- Strong communication and presentation skills.

Core Skills

Contract Negotiations	Margin Enhancement	Lead Generation	Presentations
Consultative Selling	Business Development	Change Agent	Prospecting & Closing
Revenue Growth	Cost Containment	Customer Retention	Team Building
Solution Selling	Key Account Management	Training & Educating	OEM/E-commerce

Professional Experience

XYZ Ltd, Anytown
Manager of Business Development - Integrated Healthcare Solutions

2011 – Present

(continued)

Selected to build XYZ's Integrated Healthcare Solutions market share. Established strategic vision and developed team of Business Development Healthcare representatives. Managed new product integrations, new partnerships, and new product solutions.

- Instrumental in building new and existing national distribution channels and vertical business partners.
- Completed certification and validation of 87+ EMR/EHR/Practice Management Software integrations with company's products leading to peripheral bundles, assessment add-in, and multiple purchasing channels, creating 33% new organic growth revenue in EMR category sales in 2011.
- Initiated, negotiated, and created ABC partnership resulting in £329K of new sales in 2014.
- Essential role in hiring team of new Healthcare Business Development managers. Designed strategy, trained new employees, set direction, directed team, and managed multiple projects simultaneously.
- Negotiated, procured, and managed new distributor partner, SYNNEX. Drove sales of SYNNEX products from zero to over £5 million in sales from 2012 to 2016.
- Received National Sales Award 2013; £1.4 million in growth for a territory total of £4,895,854.

ABC Ltd., Anytown   2005 – 2011
Surgical Sales Specialist
Quickly re-established market presence in a territory that had been vacant for over two years. Managed and led all sales activities in hospitals, and surgery centres. Collaborated with local architects, hospital administrators, and department leaders to develop an in-depth understanding of customer needs and align focus and scope of territory management.

- Successfully developed new revenue-generating customer base with no prior information or CRM content data; generated £540K in new sales.
- Closed sale on first Bariatric Surgery Centre in country with all ABC equipment.
- Earned prestigious "Summit Award" for No. 1 Region 2006.
- Increased sales 83% from £157K to £1.3M.

Technology

Operating Systems: Mac OSX, Windows; Software: SalesForce.com, Microsoft Office Suites and Windows, MS Word, Excel, PowerPoint, Office Communicator, Adobe Acrobat 8 Pro, SAP, Sales Perspectives, ACT, Gold Mine

Education

BSc, Business Administration, London University   1986

Professional Development

Growth Partnering Sales: Value-Added Strategies for the 21st Century   2005
XYZ Sponsored

Gemba Kaizen Training, London   2003
Kaizen Certificate of Completion
Esselte – ABC Sponsored

11 Any Avenue
Anytown AA0 0AA

Rex Moore

01234 567890
rex_moore@anyisp.com

Healthcare Coordinator

Performance Summary

Unique blend of academic achievement with strong knowledge and practical experience within the healthcare sector. Selected for internship at University School of Medicine within the Division of Dermatology for management of multiple projects while gaining understanding of Academic Medical Centres. Experienced in providing customer support. Outstanding customer service, analytical skills, strategic planning, and communication skills.

——Professional Skills——

Healthcare Knowledge	Analytical Skills	Communication	Technology
* Defining care needs	* Data Analysis	* Team Collaboration	* Microsoft Office/PowerPoint
* Assessment of service users	* Strategic Planning	* Customer Service	* Data Entry
* Clinical monitoring	* Report Development	* SPSS	* OSX Mountain Lion
* Academic Medical Centre	* Issue Resolution	* Patient Support	* Mentoring & Leadership

——Education——

MSc Health Administration, School of Medicine University   **2015**

BSc Psychology •   **2013**
Diploma Business Administration, University of the North

——Professional Experience——

XYZ Healthcare, Anytown   2013 to Present
Healthcare Report Coordinator

Provide support to service users and staff by answering a variety of questions on special care needs and identification of specific service user issues, monitoring and reviewing as appropriate. Complete research on physicians, hospitals, and medical equipment companies to locate providers, review outcomes, plan care packages, and provide general information.

* Achieved a quality score of 92% by following approval processes and researching information prior to reports.
* Expanded personal knowledge of regulations and guidelines.

University School of Medicine, Anytown   Summer 2012
Intern
Managed multiple projects within Dermatology and Medical Oncology.

Institute of Addiction Recovery, Anytown   Summer 2011
Intern
Gained strong knowledge of addictions and recovery, including the 12-step process. Attended group and individual meetings. Communicated with staff, physicians, and patients.

Hillary Sanders

 View my profile

11 Any Avenue
Anytown AA0 0AA

01234 567890
OrthoSales@outlook.com

Orthopaedics Account Manager

PERFORMANCE PROFILE

Top-producing medical device sales professional with 12+ years' experience and proven track record of surpassing sales quotas, developing new business, via effective time and territory management. Extensive orthopaedic knowledge of reconstructive, trauma, orthobiologics, hand, foot, and ankle technologies. Strong business acumen with the ability to execute the sales cycle, leading customer to action. Ability to build relationships with physicians, surgeons, and other healthcare professionals. Excellent interpersonal, cross-functional teams, networking, presentation, negotiation, and closing skills.

- Ability to handle customer questions and objections in a way that is consistent with product indications and sales training methodology.
- Increases territory growth by building and maintaining strong business relationships with key accounts and key opinion leaders.
- Adheres to all policies and SOPs regarding interactions with healthcare professionals, including product handling and complaints, expense reporting, sales activities, and training.
- Strong organizational and time management skills with the ability to think strategically and analytically.
- Maintains training in sales skills, product features, benefits, competitive data, and industry trends.

PROFESSIONAL SKILLS

*Strategic Sales Development
*Surgical Case Coverage
*Customer Solution Skills
*Product Demonstration
*Orthopaedic Device Sales
*Exceeds Sales Quotas
*Inventory Management

*Consultative Selling Techniques
*Customer Acquisition
*Maintains Sales and Product Training
*New Production Introductions
*Customer Relationship Management
*Clinical Knowledge
*Industry Trends & Territory Analysis

*Post-Sale Follow-Up
*Presentation Skills
*In-Service Training
*Policies & Procedures
*Full Sales Cycle Skills
*Professional Work Ethics
*Product Portfolio

PROFESSIONAL EXPERIENCE

XYZ Orthopaedics, Anytown
Sales Representative

2009–Present

Manages sales territory by planning and implementing sales strategies to retain current business and converting new business in the orthopaedic sales climate. Promotes and presents company's medical-device products at hospitals, doctors' offices, surgical centres, and other healthcare facilities to raise awareness of latest medical devices offered. Provides customer base with excellent post-sale follow-up.

- Attained sales quota of £1.3M+, subsequently receiving 2009 National Sales award.
- Converted new customers, resulting in increased sales of £400K.
- Increases sales growth within sensitive pricing accounts by conducting customer needs analysis to aid customer in identification of product benefits.
- Develops and maintains key customer relationships within territory.
- Manages inventory turns by implementing best strategy for utilizing inventory.

ABC Osteologic, Anytown   2007–2012
Sales Representative

ABC Orthopedics Dublin and Belfast branches become part of ABC Osteologic, one of the largest
agencies within ABC with a total of £60M in sales.
- Total sales £1M+ resulting in a 47% growth.
- Managed £10M territory; worked independently and as team of three sales representatives to achieve
  quotas and meet agency target sales goals.
- Demonstrated ability to identify and close new customers while managing existing accounts.
- Created sales strategies for territory, resulting in increased sales.

ABC Osteonics, Belfast   2005–2007
Sales Representative

Producer of orthopaedic implants for reconstructive, trauma, and spine surgery. Hired to manage sales territory
generating £6M in sales. Responsible for hospital services, including assisting current sales representatives in
increasing sales by helping with customer relationship management, building relationships with new surgeons,
contributing to day-to-day operations of covering cases, and setting up instruments and implants for surgeries.

- Increased sales by £26K+ for a total of £558K+ in total sales; first year 100.12% to quota.
- Established relationships with current and potential customers by establishing a reputation for strong
  product knowledge.
- Converted competitive business by identifying needs not met by competitors, resulting in increased
  sales.
- Assisted company sales representatives in achieving quotas and meeting organizational goals.

AWARDS / RECOGNITION

Quota Achiever: 102% to Quota (2015)   Quota Achiever: 108.9% to Quota (2012)
Quota Achiever: 101.5% to Quota (2014)   Quota Achiever: 100.12% to Quota (2011)

EDUCATION
East of England University   2005
BA, Business Administration

PROFESSIONAL DEVELOPMENT
Sponsored by ABC Orthopaedics

Customer-Centric Selling   Gallup Strength Finder
ABC Revision Training   ABC Reconstructive Product Training
ABC Product Trauma Training   ABC Orthobiologic Training

Superior references available

Gayle Ramirez-Chung

Trenton, NJ 08601   609.567.1569   opthalmictech@sbcglobal.net

OPHTHALMIC TECHNICIAN
Building organizational value by assisting with diagnostic and treatment-oriented procedures

Performance Summary

Technical Skills:

Precise Refracting/Workup
Scribing
Goniometry
Sterile Techniques

Personable and capable professional experienced in conducting diagnostic tests; measuring and recording vision; testing eye muscle function; inserting, removing, and caring for contact lenses; and applying eye dressings. Competently assist physicians during surgery, maintain optical and surgical instruments, and administer eye medications. Extensive knowledge in ophthalmic medications dealing with glaucoma, cataract surgery, and a wide variety of other diagnoses.

Professional Experience

Procedures & Treatments:

Chalazion Surgery
Glaucoma Treatments
Conjunctivitis
Diabetes Monitoring
Retinopathy of Prematurity
Macular Degeneration
Strabismus
Cataracts
Palsy
NLD Obstruction
Blepharoplasty

ABC ASSOCIATES, Anytown — 2010 to Present
Technician/Assistant for a cornea specialist in a large ophthalmic practice. Perform histories, vision screenings, pupil exams, and precise manifest refractions. Assist with a variety of surgical procedures. Quickly build trust and rapport and streamline processes to ensure physician efficiency.

XYZ EYE CENTRE, Othertown — 2006 to 2010
Taught customer service techniques and promoted twice within 2 months to an **Ophthalmic Assistant** for a paediatric neurology ophthalmologist performing scribing, taking histories, preparing patients for examination, and educating patients on treatment procedures.

A & Z COMMUNICATIONS, Othertown — 1999 to 2006
Recruited as a **Regional Account Manager** and promoted within 3 months to **National Account Manager**. Contributed to the company doubling in size within 10 months; maintained a 100% satisfied customer retention rate.

Equipment:

A Scans
Lasers
Tonometry
Slit Lamp
Lensometry
Keratometer
Visual Fields
Topography

Education

BSc Biology — 1998
University of the West

Certification
Certified Ophthalmic Assistant (COA)

Hillary Sanders

11 Any Avenue
Anytown AA0 0AA

in View my profile

01234 567890
OrthoSales@outlook.com

Orthopaedics Sales Professional

PERFORMANCE PROFILE

Top-producing medical device sales professional with 12+ years' experience and proven track record of surpassing sales quotas, developing new business, via effective time and territory management. Extensive orthopaedic knowledge of reconstructive, trauma, orthobiologics, hand, foot, and ankle technologies.Strong business acumen with the ability to execute the sales cycle, leading customer to action. Ability to build relationships with physicians, surgeons, and other healthcare professionals. Excellent interpersonal, cross-functional teams, networking, presentation, negotiation, and closing skills.

- Detailed knowledge and understanding of both NHS and private sector environments.
- Ability to handle customer questions and objections in a way that is consistent with product indications and sales training methodology.
- Increases territory growth by building and maintaining strong business relationships with key accounts and key opinion leaders.
- Adheres to all policies and SOPs regarding interactions with healthcare professionals, including product handling and complaints, expense reporting, sales activities, and training.
- Strong organizational and time management skills with the ability to think strategically and analytically.
- Maintains training in sales skills, product features, benefits, competitive data, and industry trends.

PROFESSIONAL SKILLS

*Strategic Sales Development	*Consultative Selling Techniques	*Post-Sale Follow-Up
*Surgical Case Coverage	*Customer Acquisition	*Presentation Skills
*Customer Solution Skills	*Maintains Sales and Product Training	*In-Service Training
*Product Demonstration	*New Production Introductions	*Policies & Procedures
*Orthopaedic Device Sales	*Customer Relationship Management	*Full Sales Cycle Skills
*Exceeds Sales Quotas	*Clinical Knowledge	*Professional Work Ethics
*Inventory Management	*Industry Trends & Territory Analysis	*Product Portfolio

PROFESSIONAL EXPERIENCE

ABC Orthopaedics, Anytown   2009 Present
Sales Representative

Manages sales territory by planning and implementing sales strategies to retain current business and converting new business in the orthopaedic sales climate.Promotes and presents company's medical-device products at hospitals, doctors' offices, surgical centres, and other healthcare facilities to raise awareness of latest medical devices offered. Provides customer base with excellent post-sale follow-up.

- Attained sales quota of £1.3M+.
- Converted new customers, resulting in increased sales of £400K.
- Increases sales growth within sensitive pricing accounts by conducting customer needs analysis to aid customer in identification of product benefits.

- Develops and maintains key customer relationships within territory.
- Manages inventory turns by implementing best strategy for utilizing inventory.

XYZ Osteologic, Anytown   2003–2009
Sales Representative

A & Z Osteonics become part of XYZ Osteologic, one of the largest agencies nationwide with a total of £60M in sales.
- Total sales £1M+ resulting in a 47% growth.
- Managed £10M territory; worked independently and as team of three sales representatives to achieve quotas and meet agency target sales goals.
- Demonstrated ability to identify and close new customers while managing existing accounts.
- Created sales strategies for territory, resulting in increased sales.

A & Z Osteonics, Anytown   2000–2003
Sales Representative

Producer of orthopaedic implants for reconstructive, trauma, and spine surgery. Hired to manage sales territory generating £6M in sales. Responsible for hospital services, including assisting current sales representatives in increasing sales by helping with customer relationship management, building relationships with new surgeons, contributing to day-to-day operations of covering cases, and setting up instruments and implants for surgeries.
- Increased sales by £26K+ for a total of £558K+ in total sales; first year 100.12% to quota.
- Established relationships with current and potential customers by establishing a reputation for strong product knowledge.
- Converted competitive business by identifying needs not met by competitors, resulting in increased sales.
- Assisted company sales representatives in achieving quotas and meeting organizational goals.

CORPORATE AWARDS / RECOGNITION

Quota Achiever: 102% to Quota (2015)   Quota Achiever: 108.9% to Quota (2012)
Quota Achiever: 101.5% to Quota (2014)   Quota Achiever: 100.12% to Quota (2011)

EDUCATION

University of London   1999
BA, Business Administration

PROFESSIONAL DEVELOPMENT
Sponsored by XYZ Orthopedics

Customer-Centric Selling   Gallup Strength Finder
XYZ Revision Training   XYZ Reconstructive Product Training
XYZ Product Trauma Training   XYZ Orthobiologic Training

Superior references available

NICOLE SILVER

11 Any Avenue ♦ Anytown AA0 0AA ♦ 01234 567891 ♦ n.silver@anyisp.com

Pharmacy Manager
Dedicated to promoting health and safety by pursuing the highest quality of pharmacist's care.

Performance Profile

GP registered Pharmacist with an outstanding record of progressive accountabilityin pharmacy and pharmacy practice settings, including retail, hospital, sales, and long-term care. In-depth knowledge of all pharmaceutical operations, as well as computerized drug distribution systems, drug utilization evaluation, complex equipment and delivery systems, emerging medications, and multi-state pharmacy regulations.

♦ A strong and trusted individual with a high standard of credibility and ethics who subscribes to a straightforward, hands-on style in getting the job done.
♦ Calm, flexible, and focused in deadline-driven, urgently-paced, and demanding environments.
♦ Superb interpersonal skills and proficiency in building and maintaining strategic business/client relationships while interfacing positively with people of all levels and backgrounds.

Professional Competencies

- Project Management
- Customer Development/Service
- Professional Presentations
- Relationship Building
- Multi-site Management

- Report Preparation
- Marketing & Sales
- Performance Improvement
- Financially Astute
- Staff Training/Development

- Technically Savvy
- Problem Resolution
- Negotiation
- Long-Term Care
- Innovation

Professional Experience

XYZ Ltd., Anytown   2004–Present
XYZ Ltd., provides a broad array of pharmacy-related services.

REGIONAL MANAGER	2014 – Present
AREA MANAGER	2011 – 2014
GENERAL MANAGER	2004 – 2011

REGIONAL MANAGER - West Division   2014 – Present
Charged with the provision of operational resources to Western Division pharmacies, which includes 47 pharmacies.
♦ Assist in division's multi-pharmacy budgeting process of £1B in annual sales and approximately three million dispensed prescriptions.
♦ Captured nearly £300K in annual savings by coordinating and executing stat delivery reduction initiative.
♦ Partnered with regional management to develop and execute multi-phase plan that boosted performance and profitability of pharmacy that generated £120M in annual revenue. Initiative resulted in 6% increase in revenue, 3% increase in operating profit, and multiple improvements in performance indicators.
♦ Created purchasing scorecard that identified sites needing improvement, such as inventory accounting for nearly 70% of expense. Scorecard was launched/implemented countrywide at all sites.
♦ Partner with Divisional Compliance Officer to identify regulatory goals and corresponding operational processes and best practices.

◆ Facilitate high-level, consistent patient care through provision of pharmaceuticals in challenged pharmacy sites.
◆ Collaborate with operations managers and pharmacy managers to exceed customer expectations and ultimately support customer development and sales efforts.
◆ Research, evaluate, and implement new technologies, including eMARs, CPOE, e-Prescribing, and automation.

AREA MANAGER   2011 – 2014
Accountable for multi-site, management of 5 pharmacies, 250 employees, and annualized revenue of £66M. Developed budgets and performance/financial objectives.
◆ Capably managed multi-site pharmacies to ensure financial and operational success as well as compliance with regulations.
◆ Analyzed and assisted in consolidating subsidiary acquisition, capturing additional £42M in annual revenue.
◆ Implemented hub/spoke model for pharmacies, resulting in efficiencies and significant cost reductions.
◆ Served as member of special committees, including Technician Certification committee.

GENERAL MANAGER   2004 – 2011
Managed financial and budgetary factors to achieve annual goals, ensured regulatory compliance and recruited, selected, trained, and coached all personnel.

◆ Captured £400K in annual revenue by coordinating training, implementation, and evaluation of IV programme.

University Hospital, Anytown   2001 – 2004

STAFF PHARMACIST

Education
BSc, Pharmacy, University of Anytown

Professional Development
Essentials of Business Development, Part I,
Corporate Finance,
Microsoft Office Certificate

Professional Licences
General Pharmaceutical Council

Professional Organizations / Affiliations
Royal Pharmaceutical Society (RPS)

Computer Skills
Operating Systems: Windows OS, Mac OS, OmniDX, Oasis
Software Applications: Microsoft Word, Excel, PowerPoint, Project, Access; SharePoint; eMARs; CPOE; e-Prescribing

Warren Davis

Linked in profile

12 Mountain Terrace
Butte, MT 59701

(406) 436-3851
warren.davis@gmail.com

Radiology Technician

Performance Profile

Detail-oriented and quality-focused certified Radiology Technician with hands-on experience in managing fluoroscopy guidelines and radiation safety, fluoroscopy equipment, X-ray image intensifiers, image recording equipment, and diagnostic imaging services. Outstanding patient rapport and exceptional patient satisfaction. Works cooperatively with members of the healthcare team to maintain standards for professional interactions.

- Maintains and improves high-quality, cost-effective department operations.
- Mechanical aptitude and manual dexterity while operating complicated diagnostic equipment.
- Flexible and able to perform tasks with minimum to no supervision.
- Comprehensive knowledge of methods and techniques of preparing patients for X-ray imaging.
- Good knowledge of latest X-ray equipment and standards; produces high-quality diagnostic film.
- Plans efficient patient exam workflow; good time management skills.
- Detail orientated; multitasker.
- Technology: Proficient in radiology/hospital information systems including IMPAX, Allscripts, Novius, and Virtual Radiologic.

Areas of Expertise

Fluoroscopy	Diagnostic Equipment
Radiation Safety	High-Quality Diagnostic Film
X-ray Image Intensifiers	ICU and NICU
Mechanical Aptitude	IMPAX, Allscripts, Novius, Virtual Radiologic
Patient Positioning Skills	Image Recording Equipment
Diagnostic Imaging Services	Maintain and Troubleshoot Imaging Equipment

Professional Experience

ABC Hospital, Anytown   2012-Current
Radiology Technician
- Accurately operates radiologic equipment to produce quality X-rays to diagnose and treat illness and possible injuries as directed by the radiologist.

(continued)

Warren Davis   warren.davis@gmail.com   Page 2

Radiology Technologist (continued)
- Ensures and executes physician's orders by using two point identifiers to ensure each patient receives the correct imaging procedures to eliminate unnecessary exposure and ensure the correct diagnosis.
- Determines the best method of obtaining optimal examination and regulates patient flow to keep from creating a backlog of patients, virtually eliminating the need for off-duty personnel.
- Maintains documentation requirements to ensure that technical data is entered timely and accurately.
- Accomplished the ability to work independently weekend nights caring for ER patients in a 180-bed general medical and surgical acute care facility. Performs all stats on patients and morning portables in ICU and NICU.
- Obtains patient cooperation and helps reduce patient anxiety by explaining procedures and establishing a comfortable environment.
- Consistently safeguards patients by executing radiation protection techniques through patient shielding skills and knowledge of applicable exposure to minimize radiation to patients and staff.

Education

BSC, Radiography   2012
Anytown University

Certifications/Licenses

Certified Radiology Technician   Current
HCPC Registered   Current
Member Society of Radiographers   Current

Excellent references available on request

ShaQuan Jones, RN

11 Any Avenue, Anytown AA0 0AA   s_jones@att.net

Registered Nurse

PERFORMANCE PROFILE

Compassionate healthcare professional with 14 years' experience as a registered nurse in a clinical setting providing comprehensive cardiac care. Experienced in advanced cardiac care as a nurse clinician. Provides high-quality nursing care and unsurpassed patient service.

- ✓ Uses systematic approach to nursing practice; maintains professional ethics.
- ✓ Facilitates outcome-based compassionate care to patients and families.
- ✓ Exceptional skills in written documentation and verbal communication; conflict resolution.
- ✓ Demonstrates independent critical-thinking skills and sound nursing judgment.
- ✓ Effective interpersonal and leadership skills supported by an enthusiastic team player attitude.

PROFESSIONAL SKILLS

- Clinic Management
- Telephone Triage
- Patient Evaluations
- Coordinates Services
- Focused Patient Care

- Diagnostic Assessment
- EKG/Stress Testing
- Holter/Event Monitoring
- Implantable Devices
- Procedural Tests

- Pharmacological Management
- Diagnostic Results
- Discharge Procedures
- Infection Control Standards
- Patient Education/Safety

EDUCATION

BSc in Nursing (BSN), University of Anytown   2006

LICENCES

2004

NMC Registered
Member Royal College of Nursing

Current

PROFESSIONAL CERTIFICATIONS/CONTINUING EDUCATION

Certifications

- Basic Cardiac Life Support for Healthcare Providers (BLS)   2016
- Advanced Cardiac Life Support Provider Course (ACLS)
- IV/Infusion Therapy Certification

Continuing Education

- Cardiovascular Nursing: A Comprehensive Overview   2015
- End of Life Issues and Pain Management   2010

PROFESSIONAL EXPERIENCE

ABC Hospital, Anytown   2014 – Present
Registered Nurse, Cardiology
Services include Cardiology, Cardiac Surgery, Electrophysiology, and Interventional Cardiology.

- Managed satellite outpatient clinic under the direction of more than seven cardiologists.

- Performed as nurse liaison between hospital and clinic; demonstrated effective time-management and leadership skills for maintaining daily flow of clinic operations.
- Assisted physicians with in-office procedures including EKG, Exercise Stress Testing, Holter/Event monitoring, and pacemaker evaluations.
- Scheduled inpatient procedures including Echo, Stress, Angiography, PTCA, and EP studies.
- Performed hospital inpatient evaluations and assessments including angiogram checks, sheath pulls, discharge planning, and patient education.
- Consulted with attending cardiologist to review positive findings, abnormal test results, and patient concerns.
- Provided patient education and enrollment in specialized clinics for lipids, heart failure, pacemaker, amiodarone, anticoagulation, and rehab management; patient advocate to cardiac support groups.

XYZ Clinic, Anytown   2006 – 2014
Registered Nurse, Neurology
XYZ Neurological Clinic specializes in comprehensive diagnostic testing and treatment of neurological diseases. Specialties include Adult and Pediatric Neurology, Neuropsychology, Electroneurodiagnostics, EMG and Nerve Conduction Studies, Sleep Centre, and Headache Management.

- Functioned as clinic's Registered Nurse responsible for providing individualized care to patients and families in accordance with the neurology clinic standards, policies, and procedures.
- Managed patient flow throughout the clinic and assisted providers in evaluation and treatment of neurological patients.
- Applied skilled telephone triage.
- Provided follow-up communications of lab/test results and medication management.
- Documented medical history, vital statistics, and test results in patient medical records.
- Facilitated communication between patients and physicians to ensure patient comprehension of treatment plans and compliance with healthcare regimen.
- Collaborated with other healthcare departments to facilitate patient care.

University Medical Centre, Anytown   2006
Senior Nursing Assistant, Medical/Surgical
University Medical Centre is among the most respected teaching institutions in the nation. Staffed by nationally and internationally renowned orthopaedic surgeons, it provides personalized orthopaedic care that combines excellence, service, compassion, and innovative research.

- Implemented orthopedic nursing care under the management of a "team nursing process" covering 4 to 7 high-acuity patients per shift.
- Applied understanding of mechanical principles necessary for using hospital equipment and instruments; applied knowledge of hospital recordkeeping.
- Maintained infection control standards and provided safe physical environments to assist in patient comfort and recovery; assisted with comprehensive discharge planning and patient education.

COMMUNITY/VOLUNTEER ACTIVITIES

Place of Hope and Kids Against Hunger
- Prepared and served meals for homeless shelter; disaster aid relief.

John Chen

11 Any Ave., Anytown AA0 0AA   01234 567890   **Linked** in profile

chen.hr@gmail.com

HUMAN RESOURCE ANALYST
Dedicated professional with integrity, resourcefulness, and sound judgment

Performance Summary

3 years of exceptional client service and support. Works with professionals of all levels and builds trusting relationships. Outstanding communication skills. Ability to solve problems with ease and sound judgment. Skilled in analyzing data and giving presentations. Incredibly organized, detailed orientated, and committed to producing quality work. Ability to adjust to evolving situations and shifting priorities in a calm and balanced way. Pursuing MSc in Human Resource Management.

Professional Skills

Research & Analysis	Problem Solving	Strategic Planning
Communication Skills	Organizational Skills	Interpersonal Skills
Teamwork	Leadership	Relationship Building
Presentations	Mediation	Negotiation
Administrative Support	Sales & Marketing	Newsletters & Reports

AB&C Ltd., Anytown   **2014–Present**
Property company that has a sales volume of more than £18 billion annually.
Estate Agent

Assists buyers and sellers in all price points in residential area, guiding them through the whole process of the buying and selling transaction. Works with all professionals on all levels. Anticipates and solves problems on a daily basis and strategizes on how to close the deal. Understands the delicate balance required to reach a positive outcome. Great client service, strong communication skills, and good organizational skills have been key factors to success.

- Manages the marketing and sales of residential properties, from studios to townhouses, in all price ranges.
- Analyzes data and properties and advises clients on the right investment.
- Creates presentations, a marketing plan, and a strategy for sellers.
- Educates and keeps clients updated on the real estate market.
- Negotiates the best price for clients.
- Manages the entire process of the sale of contract. Works with other parties, such as broker, other buyer/seller, real estate attorney, mortgage lender, and building management agent to close the deal.
- Maintains client relationships and builds trust. Result is repeat business and referrals.
- Manages confidential information.
- Mentors new employees and offers guidance on their transactions.

Education

XYZ Business School
MSc in Human Resource Management   *starting Autumn 2016. Expected date of graduation to be in 2018.*

Anytown College of Art & Design
BA in Film and Television

Computer Skills

Microsoft Office: Word, Excel, PowerPoint, Outlook

Community Activity

One of the organizers and leaders of Dogs on Beach. Objective was to negotiate permitting dogs on the Anytown beaches. Negotiated with council, gave presentations to interested bodies, and managed social media activities and face-to-face networking events to generate community and media support.

Veronica Kent

11 Any Ave., Anytown AA0 0AA   01234 567890   ronnie.kent@anyisp.com

Human Resources Generalist / Administrative Support
Flexible, disciplined, organized, and hardworking—the consummate small-office professional

Performance Summary
Human resources and accounts payable professional with over 15 years' administrative support experience. Recognized for outstanding discipline and leadership.

Skilled in all aspects of small-office human resources: payroll, benefits administration, accounts payable, customer service, sales support, collections, administrative support, purchasing, facilities management, event planning, and compliance.

Core Skills

- Human Resources
- Payroll Processing
- Benefits Administration
- Customer Service
- Employee/Vendor Relations
- EOC Compliance

- Accounts Payable
- Invoice Discrepancies
- Payment Processing
- Purchase Orders
- Expense Tracking
- Journal Entries
- Auditing & Compliance
- Spreadsheets/Reports

- Administrative Support
- Collections
- Bank Deposits
- Internal/External Liaison
- Property Leases
- Month/Year End, 1099s
- Event Planning

Technology Skills

- Windows 98/2000/XP/Vista
- Word, Excel, PowerPoint
- Outlook

- Corel Draw Graphics
- Digital Photo Graphics
- ACCPAC Accounting
- QuickBooks

- ADP Payroll, Time and Attendance
- Purchasing Software
- Internet Research

Accomplishments

- Reduced company liability and workers' compensation insurance costs by one-third; restructured liability insurance management programmes to facilitate savings.
- Detected fraudulent activities from utility companies and enabled company to recover £14,000.
- Assisted in the implementation of company merger by reorganizing company policies and procedures, vacation/sick time, and payroll systems.
- Employee of the year nominations 1992, 1996, 2003, and 2010.

Professional Experience

XYZ Communications, Anytown   2013–Present
Wireless audio products for the professional and semi-professional audio markets.
Administrative Support Generalist

- Support for an Independent Sales Contractor, selling products to distributors nationwide.
- Related experiences: administrative support, customer service, contracts and proposals, accounts payable/receivable, expense tracking, bank reconciliation and deposits, email, and Internet research.

Telecom Networks, Anytown   2004–2013
Independent business communications providers.
Human Resources Generalist/Accounts Payable Specialist

Managed full range of human resource services including:

(continued)

| Veronica Kent | 01234 567890 | ronnie.kent@anyisp.com |

- Payroll administration; experience includes maintenance of costs through negotiations and implementation of alternative benefits programme.
- Processed payroll for 250-employee company.
- General liability, workers' compensation, subcontractor, and payroll auditing and compliance.
- Responsible for all accounts payable functions, including monthly and yearly closeouts.
- Liaison between internal and external accounting functions.
- Processed renewals for company vehicles.
- Managed petty cash accounts, processed bank deposits, and handled expense tracking and reports.
- Administrative support, accounts receivable/backup, property building maintenance/facilities management for three facilities, sales support/marketing, and purchasing activities.

ABC Ltd., Anytown   1996–2004
Manufacturer and contractor.
Administrative Assistant

- Coordinated daily quality-control efforts between the internal planning departments and management.
- Collaborated, as a key member of the Quality Support Team, along with the production line and management team to contribute to the main business goal, "First Time Quality and Customer Satisfaction."
- Performed daily office support duties.

Education

Anytown City College, *Continued Education*
Othertown City College, *Continued Education*   2015
Othertown City College, *General Business Studies*   1997–2012
                                                                       2009

Personal

- Cancer Centre, Anytown Care support group volunteer.
- Coach and train beginning marathon runners.
- Eleven competitive marathons, seven half-marathons, 10k and 5k competitive runs.

Superior references available

Yasuo Kuniyoshi MBA

11 Any Avenue, Anytown AA0 0AA   01234 567890   ykonigoshi@anyisp.com

E-Commerce Marketing Communications

Performance Summary

20+ years' experience in brand marketing: international, corporate, and entrepreneurial cultures. Practical problem-solving skills, and a deep well of experience to meet the challenges of this fast-paced function.

Project planning and management experience in high-stress scenarios where failure is not an option and the wrong decision could deliver substantial client loss.

♦ Consultative approach to assess client needs and provide "turnkey" solutions and programmes that meet strategic goals.
♦ Strategic business sense, an uncompromising work ethic, and a burning desire to create consistently successful marketing solutions.
♦ Loyal support from clients, partners, managers, and business owners.
♦ Deep expertise in branding, management, and positioning product lines.
♦ Marketing messages that drive revenue and bring unique product "stories" to the community.
♦ MBA – Marketing.

Professional Skills

• Branding	• Needs Assessment	• Product Positioning
• Product Stories	• Strategic Rollouts	• Brand Development
• Brand Creation	• Project Planning	• Media Relations
• Brand Establishment	• Sales & Pricing	• Investor Sourcing
• Training Materials	• Sales Materials	• SEO
• Event Planning	• Event Promotion	• Charity Fundraisers
• Social Networking	• Distance Learning	• MarComm

Performance Highlights

Communications

♦ Built a packaged employee communication strategic rollout plan for *Anytown General Hospital*, partnered with senior internal HR leaders, and directed launch timeframe for new employee subscription benefit (*PepPods*, an online emergency preparedness and personal home record system).
♦ Sourced and secured a £1 million investor for *XYZ.net*. Marketed online learning management system.
♦ For *ABC Bank,* developed an interactive kiosk concept for banking clients to receive instant product and service information during peak periods. Praised by customers nationwide during rollout.

Marketing and Events Planner

♦ Created and launched the *AB&C* "*No More Excuses*" multimedia mobile phone campaign, the most successful January campaign in company history.

(continued)

Marketing and Events Planner, *continued*

◆ For *XYZ Health*, lined up musicians and artisans for children's entertainment, food and health-screening vendors, and launched direct mail campaign to the *XYZ Health Plan* members, resulting in an impressive 900-person turnout. Located creative team to design mascot *Percy's* character costume.

◆ Organized and launched a hugely successful *White Glove Car Wash* charity grand opening event, and donated a portion of the proceeds to the *ABC Foundation*

Multimedia Marketing Strategist

◆ Created the *ABC Media* public corporate identity, including the marketing language on the corporate website, trade show participation strategy, and public relations presentations.

◆ Established strong rapport with *XYZ Labs* editor who agreed to conduct an extensive product evaluation and testing, resulting in a rave product review for *ABC Media* in the *Internet Magazine.*

Gifted Leader

Developed a turnkey fundraising programme for immediate online client use complete with a fundraising micro-site, fundraising, sales, and pricing procedures, and training and sales support materials such as scripts and FAQs.

Improved the volume and quality of traffic to *XMedia* client websites from search engines via "natural" search results, raising their resulting online rank, and improving their click-through numbers.

Professional Experience

THE ABC BANK GROUP – Anytown	2015 – Present
Marketing Consultant	
ABC Media – Anytown	2010 – 2015
Director, Brand Marketing	
XYZ BANK – Othertown	2007 – 2010
Advertising Project Manager	
URBAN DESIGN – Othertown	2004 – 2007
Director of Marketing	

Education

MBA, Marketing Communications	2003
University of London	

Online Faculty at UNIVERSITY OF LONDON	2012 – Present

Develop and deliver online undergraduate courses in Marketing, Integrated Marketing Communications, Management, and Organizational Behaviour.

Excellent professional references available

Chang Apanya

Anytown AA0 0AA	01234 567890	techmarketing@gmail.com

E-Commerce Marketing

Performance Summary

Accomplished Senior Executive with a strong affinity for *technology* and a keen business sense for the application of *emerging products* to add value and expand markets.

Proven talent for identifying *core business needs* and translating into *technical deliverables*. Launched and managed cutting-edge Internet programmes and services to win new customers, generate revenue gains, and increase brand value.

Unique combination of technical and business/sales experience. Articulate and persuasive in defining the benefits of e-commerce technologies, differentiating offerings, and increasing customer retention. Highly self-motivated, enthusiastic, and profit oriented.

Professional Skills

Sales & Marketing	Business Development	Strategic Initiatives
Business Planning	Project Management	Strategic Partnerships
Contract Negotiations	Relationship Management	Emerging Products
E-Commerce Technologies	Increase Brand Value	Customer Retention
Secure E-Commerce	Internet Services	Smart Card Technology

Technical Skills

E-Commerce	Encryption Technology	Payment Products
Firewalls	Smart Cards	Stored Value
Digital Certificates	Network Security	Internet Security
Dual and Single Message	Payment Gateways	Financial Systems
Authorization	Clearing & Settlement	Java
Key Management	Public Key Infrastructure	RF Communications

Professional Experience

ABC Credit Card Anytown   2013 – Present

E-COMMERCE AND SMART CARD CONSULTANT

- Developed strategic e-commerce marketing plans for large and small merchants involving web purchases and retail transactions using a multifunctional, microcontroller smart card for both secure Internet online commerce and point-of-sale offline commerce.
- Combined multiple software products for Internet and non-Internet applications: home banking, stored value, digital certificates, key management, rewards & loyalty programme.
- PCS/GSM phone, and contactless microcontroller with RF communications without direct POS contact.

E-COMMERCE AND SMART CARD CONSULTANT, continued

- Consulted on business and technical requirements to define new e-commerce products and essential deliverables for ABC Credit Card, valued at £2.5 M, supporting and enhancing Internet transactions.
- Analyzed systems relating to the point-of-sale environment in the physical world and at the merchant server via the Internet for real-time authorization, clearing, and settlement.
- Managed projects including the requirements management system for electronic commerce products affecting core systems: authorization, clearing, and settlement. Provided expertise about business and technical issues regarding SET and the Credit Card Payment Gateway Service.

Communications Technology Ltd., Anytown   2007 – 2012

MANAGER OF WESTERN REGION CHANNEL PARTNER PROGRAMME

- Developed and maintained business relationships with customers usingclient–server software for applications and contracts involving:
  - o E-commerce and smart card technology for a variety of Internet/intranet products: home banking.
  - o EDI, stored value, digital certificates, key management, perimeter defense with proxy firewalls.
  - o Secure remote access.
- Negotiated an exclusive contract with one of the largest government and commercial contractors in the industry, projected to generate £2–£4 million over a 24–36-month period. Contract includes secure remote access, telecommuting, secure healthcare applications.

XYZ Ltd., Othertown   1998 – 2006

SENIOR SOFTWARE ENGINEER / SOFTWARE INSTRUCTOR   2007

Managed a software engineering group of 53. Developed in-house programme that saved over £150,000 in training costs for state-of-the-art communications system software development.

- o Designed new programmes and trained software engineers in object-oriented analysis and design using UML Solutions which were implemented in C++ in a UNIX environment.
- o Developed and maintained C and C++ communication software in a UNIX environment.
- o Created curriculum and course materials that reduced overall training costs by more than £150,000.
- o Coordinated and presented software training programmes.

Education & Credentials

BSc Electrical Engineering, University of Anytown, Emphasis: Software Engineering

<table>
<tr><td>11 Any Avenue
Anytown AA0 0AA
Linked in profile</td><td>## Nancy Wright</td><td>Home 01234 567890
Mobile 01234 567890
nancywright@yahoo.com</td></tr>
</table>

PR Manager • Account Director • Group Manager

Performance Profile

High-tech public relations professional with 13 years' experience, including nine, in the software, Internet, networking, consumer electronics, and wireless industries. Substantial experience in PR and strategic communications campaigns that lead to company acquisitions. Experienced in all aspects of strategic and tactical communications, from developing and managing multiple campaigns, accounts, and results-orientated teams, to developing and placing stories. Seasoned motivational speaker and freelance TV commentator.

Core Competencies

High-Tech Public Relations	Media Relations	New Business Development	Market Research
Strategic Communications	Craft & Place Stories	Team Management	Build & Lead Teams
Executive Communications	Strong Writing Skills	Budget Management	Mentor
PR Messaging & Tactics	Media Training	Account Management	Client Satisfaction
Storytelling	Multiple Projects	Project Management	Organizational Skills
Collateral Materials	Story Placement	Detail Oriented	Thought Leadership
Leadership Branding	Counsel Executives	Acquisition Positioning	PR Training
Analyst Relations	Strong Editing Skills	Pitch Media	Social Media

Strategic Public Relations Leadership

Orchestrated PR campaigns that positioned companies as both industry leaders and sound investments. Developed and directed PR campaigns for four companies that were subsequently acquired within two years of the campaigns: *ABC Technologies* (creator of the first iProduct®, acquired by *XYZ Media*), *A&B Digital Systems* (acquired by *X-Tech*), *X-Exchange* (acquired by *OEF Ltd.*), and *e-shop* (acquired by *GHI Ltd*). Proven client satisfaction demonstrated in repeat business and account growth: over a span of ten years, contracted by former *ABC* execs to serve as communications counsel for *M&N Technologies, ABC Systems*, and *OPQ Networks*.

Executive Communications Management

Executive Communications Manager for iconic executive and public speaker, *John Smith, JKL Group, Service Provider, ABC Systems* (currently *senior director* and *technology* consultant for *ABC*). Developed communication messaging, strategy, and platform skills for Director, Deputy Director and executives.

——Professional Experience——

Consultant   2003-Present
X&Y Public Relations, Anytown

Develop and deliver strategic communications. Drive all PR strategies and tactics, messaging, media training, media relations, budget management, story creation, and placement for technology clients.

- Representative clients include *ABC Networks* (former *XGame* and *NetLink client), AnySite.com* (founded by *eCompany.com* founder), and *XYZ Aviation.*

Consultant 2001–2003

A&B Public Relations, Anytown

Developed and implemented all strategic and tactical aspects of public relations for clients, including thought leadership, leadership branding, story creation and telling, media materials, stories, media relations, and publicity.

- *ABC Systems*—Executive Communications Manager to John Smith, Director of *ABC*, a highly pursued public speaker.
- *Link Technologies*—Company's first PR consultant. Repositioned obscure company, impaired by trademark dilution, into an industry leader by using market's widespread knowledge and use of *Link's* industry-standard networking software.

Marketing Manager 2000–2001

ABC Systems, Othertown

Directed internal, cross-functional marketing for *iProduct*, following ABC acquisition of *XGame* and its technology.

- Shortly after acquisition, ABC dissolved *XGame/Managed Appliances Business Unit (MASBU)*.

Public Relations Manager 1998–2000

XGame Technology Ltd., Anytown

Advised CEO Marketing Director on all aspects of PR. Developed and implemented all strategies, tactics, and stories.

- Revamped the start-up's teetering image, which was ruining *iProduct* sales. After two press tours, garnered hundreds of additional stories in all top trade and consumer media with the *iProduct Reviews* programme. Catapulted company into a leadership position in the Internet appliance industry, setting it up for acquisition. *iProduct* is now a household name.
- Managed and inspired cross-functional teams of marketing, operations, and customer service to work outside their job responsibilities to deliver excellent service to hundreds of editors beta-testing the *iProduct 2.0*.

Account Supervisor; Senior Account Executive; Account Executive 1996–1998

XYZ Advertising & Public Relations (Acquired by *C&D* in 2000), Othertown

Promoted annually for successful track record of positioning unknown companies as both industry leaders and solid investments/acquisitions. Designed and managed all PR strategy and activities for start-up, software, Internet, and networking companies. Managed teams of up to ten PR professionals.

- Repositioned, rebranded, relaunched, and reintroduced *XGame*, the *iProduct 1.0* and *2.0*, positioning them collectively as leading the nascent Internet appliance space.
- Accelerated *Netco* and its CEO out of obscurity and into undisputed leadership through media placement and top speaking engagements.
- Transformed unknown *XExchange* into a highly publicized leader in the Internet advertising arena. Placed hundreds of stories in both business and industry media.
- Launched *The Internet Shop*, landing continual coverage in all top Internet and business publications.

——**Complementary Experience**——

Motivational Speaker 1989–Present

Coach audiences on how to use the Olympic model to set and achieve goals, and succeed in business and life.

Awards & Achievements

Winner—Two national swimming gold medals plus one silver and one bronze.

EDUCATION—University of London; BA in Journalism

Bilingual   **Sarah**   *MBA*
                           Bernhardt
Anytown AA0 0AA   01234 567890   multimediasales@juno.com

ONLINE MULTIMEDIA SALES
Advertising, Communications, and Media

Performance Profile

High-performing sales professional with a 20-year track record of success with high-profile clients for *best-in-class* companies. Consistently **exceeding sales quotas**. Deep expertise in brand, management, and product lines positioning. **Gifted sales strategist and tactician,** excels in channel development.

Professional Skills

• Sales	• Telemarketing	• Email Marketing
• Recruitment & Selection	• Training & Development	• Employee Retention
• Performance Appraisals	• Separations	• Business Development
• Overcoming Objections	• Contract Negotiations	• Channel Development
• P&L	• Cost Containment	• Relationship Management
• Brand Management	• Strategic Alliance/Partners	• Diversity Strategies
• College Relations	• Employee Communications	• Sales Manuals

Excels in training and mentoring teams to outperform the competition. High level of personal and professional integrity, a passion for achieving organizational success, and a desire to always play on a winning team.

Professional Experience

ABC BUSINESS DEVELOPMENT – Anytown	2007 – Present
Account Manager	2014 – Present
National Ad Agency Channel Sales Representative	2010 – 2014
National Recruitment Sales Representative	2007 – 2010

Aggressively recruited to develop, revitalize, and nurture productive relationships with leading companies and government agencies. Packaged and sold targeted multimedia integrated talent solutions and services.

Key Accomplishments

➤ **Multimedia Campaign Development.** Offered existing clients an opportunity to expand by developing and recommending new and alternative multimedia account strategies targeted at niche and passive markets. Packaged and sold nontraditional campaigns from nonprint sources targeted to key audiences.

➤ **Product Development.** Credited with designing and spearheading the execution of a cutting-edge hotjobs.com product offering whereby keyword searches served up product-related ads along the margins of the website, generating more than £50K in incremental revenue per year.

➤ **Increased Advertiser Revenue.** Through a combination of face-to-face visits to 13–15 domestic markets, the creation of various telemarketing programmes, and email marketing campaigns, grew Advertising Unit by £10 million, an increase of 25%, representing one-third of all sales for the unit.

➤ **Sales Performance.** Consistently met and exceeded quarterly and annual sales revenue goals, up to 131% above quota.

➤ **Awards & Recognition.** Recipient of Year End Award for demonstrating a commitment to customers that is reflected in business performance, a high level of sales achievement, and customer satisfaction. Recipient of several prestigious awards including two Club Awards, three Sales Achievement Awards, two Sales Excellence Awards, and a Publishers Award for Sales Excellence.

Sarah Bernhardt   01234 567890   multimediasales@juno.com Page 2

XJOBS.COM – Anytown   1999 – 2007
Director of Client Services   2003 – 2007
Account Executive   1999 – 2003

Promoted and progressed rapidly through positions with increasing responsibility. Directed all aspects of sales, marketing, and operations functions, and managed full P&L (£10 million in revenue) for UK office.
Generated significant new client business and produced employer-branded recruitment and retention advertising campaign and execution strategies.

Key Accomplishments

> **Cost Containment.** Spearheaded key cost-containment initiatives, saving thousands of pounds, resulting in a Top 10 (out of 35) "managerial profitability" ranking for the UK office.
> **New Business Development.** Partnered with the sales channel in the design and implementation of a "business case building" sales contest, increasing revenue by £2 million.
> **Sales Productivity.** Noted for driving £1 million in new business development in one year.
> **Process Improvement.** Spearheaded from conception to implementation an employee retention initiative. Launched monthly performance appraisals (30/30's), which fostered a welcoming experience for new employees and drastically improved retention. Hired, trained, and supervised a staff of 12 account managers, and provided ongoing staff mentoring and support enabling them to grow company's client base.
> **High Expectation Client Relations.** Painstakingly researched and subsequently instituted recommended solutions to maximize customer satisfaction.
> **Employer Branding.** Partnered with senior-level Human Resources clients in the design and development of uniquely branded recruitment advertising strategies. Recommended tactical approaches for campaign execution.
> **Marketing Solutions.** Presented competitively positioned employee communication solutions and executed delivery of solutions such as collateral development, diversity strategies, university/college relations, and creative ad design to maximize employee communication programmes.

Education

Master of Business Administration
The School of Business, Anytown
Fully financed way through Business School

BSc in Marketing
Southern University

Professional Affiliation

Member – Association of MBA Graduate Professionals

Superior references available on request

CALISTA BOWMAN

11 Any Avenue., Anytown AA0 0AA   01234 567890   c.bowman@gmail.com

Sales & Customer Service

Performance Summary

Top-producing Sales professional with 12 years experience capitalizing on market opportunities and delivering first-rate results in business-to-business markets. Strong agricultural manufacturing background and robust networking skills with a talent for prospecting, understanding customer needs, and integrating relevant value propositions into solutions.

◆ Dynamic performer with the ability to open new territories, create trusted business relationships, and identify, pursue, propose, and close new business opportunities.

◆ Uses progressive selling techniques by creating innovative, value-orientated presentations and strong rapport-building skills that foster and grow enduring customer relationships.

◆ Negotiates and structures business deals with self-motivation, initiative, and the business knowledge necessary to meet the challenges of today's highly competitive marketplace.

◆ Outstanding capacity for developing and executing sales strategies and tactics that increase product awareness, market share, and profitability.

Professional Competencies

- Account Management
- Business Development
- Goal Achievement
- Conflict & Issue Resolution
- Problem Solving
- Time Management

- Strategic Planning
- Territory Development
- Market Development
- Informed Decision Making
- Merchandising / Marketing
- Dealer Training

- Networking
- Negotiating
- Agribusiness
- Communication
- Prospecting
- Presentation

Professional Experience

ABC Bearings, Anytown   2012 – Present
A total system solution provider, from bearings to seals and belts to gearboxes.
SALES REPRESENTATIVE
Built strong client relationships, cultivated and grew existing accounts while aggressively prospecting for new accounts.

◆ Grew key accounts 15% by commitment, persistence, and offering value-added training and services that resulted in becoming go-to supplier for problem resolution.

◆ Developed key account into lucrative monthly maintenance contract.

◆ Helped establish and launch new product line that delivered approximately £100Kin sales in less than one year.

◆ Coordinated and scheduled new jobs; managed interdepartmental activities of related jobs.

XYZ Supply, Ltd., Anytown   2007 – 2012
XYZ is a manufacturer of agriculture machinery, farm bins, commercial bins, livestock equipment.
AREA MANAGER
Charged with overseeing the North West sales territory. Developed a profitable multi-state territory from the ground up, selling a product line of steel buildings, grain bins, livestock equipment, and

Calista Bowman	01234 567890	c.bowman@gmail.com

tractor-related accessories, including loaders and other equipment. Accounts
included independent retail stores, large chain stores, distributors, and contractors.
- ◆ Packaged various divisions within XYZ Steel products, resulting in increased primary and add-on sales; turned new vendor leads into repeat customers.
- ◆ Captured more than £2M in new territory sales and multitude of referrals during first two years.
- ◆ Designed and launched highly successful dealer/builder programme with fabric membrane building line.
- ◆ Utilized strong network of current and former customers, locals, and local agribusinesses to develop leads and establish new accounts.

OEF Ltd., Anytown   2005 – 2007
DEF is an employee-owned company providing quality steel products worldwide.
AREA SALES MANAGER
Established and managed a money-making sales territory consisting of distributors, wholesalers,
and retailers. Product line included metal buildings, custom fabrication, grain bins, and livestock equipment.
Accounts consisted of independent retail stores, large store chains, and
distributors.
- ◆ Developed numerous top 50 accounts and two top 20 accounts that produced a combined £2.5M in sales during recessionary period.
- ◆ Formulated strategic business plan, proactively networked,and cultivated customer rapport to deliver wins that:
  - • grew territory by greater than 125% in six years;
  - • boosted sales in two territories by £3M and £1.5M respectively.
- ◆ Launched and managed dealer training programme that educated dealer network and boosted sales.

Education
University of Anytown, BSc Business and Management   2005

Certifications
- ◆ Microsoft Excel I & II Certification
- ◆ SKF Certification

Ongoing Professional Education
- ◆ Engineering Foundation training (conveyor components)
- ◆ 3D Customer Focused training process (customer service excellence)
- ◆ Numerous Manufacturing in-house training sessions and webinars

Computer Skills
- ◆ Microsoft Word, Excel, Outlook; CRM software

Pauline Zamudio

11 Any Avenue
Anytown AA0 0AA

01234 567890
techsales@anyisp.com

Technology Sales Management

Performance Summary

Strong background in sales, sales management, business development, and account management. Skilled in Enterprise Software Sales, Enterprise Content Management (ECM), Business Process Management (BPM), and Business Process Outsourcing (BPO). Increased sales by developing strong relationships with clients, staff, partners, and management from initial contact through implementation. Demonstrated talents in building name brand awareness.

- Exceptional ability to research, analyze, and translate information to diverse audiences.
- Skilled in development and implementation of marketing strategies that increase sales.
- Consultative sales, strong communication, negotiation, and needs assessment skills.
- Extensive experience selling to executives of large organizations.

Professional Skills

* Sales & Marketing	* Strategic Accounts	* Technical Sales
* Business Development	* Order Management	* Contract Negotiations
* Client Development	* Vendor Relations	* Business Process Management
* ECM	* FileNet	* Enterprise Document Generation
* Strategic Alliances	* Events	* Open Standards
* Relationship Management	* Platform Skills	* Government Programmes
* Systems Integration	* Training & Development	* Business Process Outsourcers
* Cost Containment	* Document Management	* Business Process Analysis

Performance Highlights

- Created a niche market at XYZ Solutions, providing a repeatable Business process management (BPM) solution for national financial services and mortgage industries, using XNet technologies. Project profit margin increased by 35%.
- Awarded XNet's "Innovative Solution of the Year" at XYZ Solutions for development of a repeatable Business Process Management solution in financial services industry.
- Met and exceeded quota by 103% and added four new named accounts.
- Recognized as top performer for XYZ.
- Achieved 125% quota target.

Professional Experience

XYZ Ltd., Anytown   2013 – Present

DIRECTOR NATIONALACCOUNTS

Software sales for 100% Open Standards–based Enterprise Document Generation for financial services and government programmes. Negotiates contracts with new suppliers and partners. Cultivates relationships from initial contact through implementation with partners, clients, staff, and management.

- Hired as first direct sales staff member for start-up operations, gaining four named accounts in first year.
- Organized "Lunch & Learn" programme for XNet System Consultants and integration partners to provide product education.
- Established strategic partnerships with several system integrators.

(continued)

Pauline Zamudio	01234 567890	techsales@anyisp.com	Page 2

ABC Ltd., Anytown   2009 – 2013
DIRECTOR OF SALES & MARKETING
Charged with providing sales and marketing for systems integration and professional services organization. Increased brand awareness through development of comprehensive marketing materials. Analyzed business needs and implemented solutions that drove business growth. Created new pricing model and product structure.
Provided sales and deployment of ECM and BPM solutions nationwide. Managed relationships with *XNet, optiva, and Xfax*. Implemented Business Process Analysis methodology: analyze and document customer's current processes, and how the technology could streamline these processes. Customers included: *ABC Bank, XYZ Trust, DEF Ltd., GHI Industries and JKL Commerce.*

- Awarded XNet's "Innovative Solution of the Year" for development of Business Process Management solution in financial services industry (2012).
- Exceeded quota by over 100% two out of four years.
- Earned membership in XNet's Value Partner Club (2011–2003).
- Developed and implemented new change management marketing programme, assisting companies with installation of complex technology.

DEF Ltd., Othertown   2006 – 2009
REGIONAL SALES Manager
Directed and managed sales staff throughout the UK. Oversaw and managed budget of £6.2M. Created and implemented new value-based sales process for rapid prototyping technology. Developed and installed Rapid Manufacturing Application within the aerospace industry. Provided global sales support for a number of companies. Trained sales and engineering staff members. Oversaw all regional operations, including deals and resources on a nationalbasis.Established and managed relationships with Business Process Outsourcers(BPO).
- Reduced operating costs for field operations by combining facilities.
- Facilitated professional sales training.
- Discovered highly complex application, resulting in creation of new product.
- Transformed 3D Solutions sales force from product focus to solutions-orientated focus, through process analysis, training, and ROI models.
- Grew annual sales 15% by focusing sales teams on solution sales.

GHI Ltd., Othertown   2002 – 2006
ACCOUNT EXECUTIVE
Promoted from Senior Account Executive in 1995. Provided direction and management to 14 staff members, charged with providing large enterprise document management and BPM solutions. Gained new channel partners with application providers and consulting vendors. Charged with selling £MM solutions to board executives at large organizations, in banking, aerospace and automative industries.

- Increased indirect sales channels by 100%.
- Exceeded quota by 125%.
- Achieved top sales award

Education

BSc, Business Administration • The Anytown University

CHERISE JOHNSON

01234 567890 • c.johnson@gmail.com • 11 Any Ave., Anytown AA0 0AA

APPLICATIONS ENGINEER

PERFORMANCE SUMMARY

Engineering PhD with 5+ years of experience using simulation and project R&D skills in basic and applied research on membrane and separation technologies, including membrane system design, fabrication & testing, process development and optimization, and performance evaluation for industrial chemical engineering applications. Demonstrated record of developing membrane system devices and processes with direct business application for improved performance and reliability while decreasing costs.

➢ Develops and implements innovative solutions through experimentation and modeling that improve performance, reliability, and energy requirements to meet both technical and economical goals.
➢ Strong coursework and research using CFD and Aspen HYSYS as well as hands-on fieldwork to verify simulations.
➢ Lifelong learner who actively stays current with industry developments, shares knowledge, and contributes to new science in areas of personal and professional interest.

PROFESSIONAL SKILLS

Material Engineering	Project Management	Computational Programming	Problem Solving
Process Design Engineering	Large Process Systems	Mathematical Modeling	Engineering Standards
Membrane Module Design	Flow Visualization	Simulation Techniques	Data & Numerical Analysis
Economic/Cost Evaluation	Production Scale-Up	Multiphysics Flow Modeling	Client Relations

PROFESSIONAL EXPERIENCE

UNIVERSITY OF ANYTOWN   2011–Present
GRADUATE RESEARCH ASSISTANT

While attending classes full-time, actively assist with a variety of commercially based research projects within the Chemical & Environmental Engineering Department. Support all stages of the research life cycle: hypothesizing and designing solutions, working onsite to test prototypes, collaborating with sponsors and research partners, and presenting results both orally and in writing. Additionally, serve as a mentor to new graduate students on lab processes, simulation skills, and research ideas.

Key Achievements:

▪ Successfully completed 2 main research projects and 2 side projects that led to development of new technologies and processes.
▪ Published 3 research articles in top-level scientific journals, with another 2 ready to submit.
▪ Proactively addressed technical difficulties with project partners and quickly provided solutions.
▪ Volunteered to support visiting professor with experimental design and instrument setup, spending at least 2 hours each day discussing progress, assisting with tests, and contributing to group discussions.

RESEARCH PROJECTS

Research Project: Low-Pressure Membrane Contractors for CO_2 Capture

▪ In partnership with Membrane Technology and Research, designed, built, and tested a 500 m^2 prototype low-pressure, counter-flow, sweep membrane module for use in post-combustion carbon dioxide capture
▪ Utilized CFD and PIV to evaluate design parameters: CFD to determine uniformity of flows, pressure drops, degree of counter-current flow, and CO_2 mass transfer within modules; and CT to visualize flows and mass transfer.
▪ Results will lead to development of first-of-its-kind, large-scale, membrane-based carbon dioxide capture processes that mitigate the effects of global warming while reducing energy cost by 50% due to pressure drop.
▪ Key contributor to biweekly update teleconference with research partner as well as quarterly research reports to DEFRA.

Research Project: Development of Novel Carbon Sorbents for CO$_2$ Capture
- Partnered with research team in £1.8M project to validate use of and develop process for using carbon sorbents to capture CO$_2$ in post-combustion application.
- Worked onsite at for 130 hours of field testing and functioning as an active member of the R&D project team.
- Performed parametric experiments to determine optimum operating conditions and evaluated technical/economic viability.
- System reduced CO$_2$ level from 4.5% to less than 0.05% while maintaining steady-state operation with 90% capture efficiency and more than 98% CO$_2$ purity in the product gas.

Research Project: New Static Mixing Spacer Design for Flat Sheet Membrane Modules
Designed new static mixing spacer using CFD simulation for project funded by USBR.
- Optimized spacer geometry to remove boundary layer effect and control polarization without power consumption increase.
- Conducted experimental measurements of mass transfer coefficient and pressure drop.

Research Project: Theoretical Analysis of Gas Separation Process in Polymeric Membranes
Created novel theoretical model that successfully predicted properties of Robeson upper bound.
- Prepared thin polymeric membranes using solvent casting and phase inversion technologies.
- Performed gas sorption and permeation experiments using rubbery and glassy polymeric membranes.

EDUCATION & PROFESSIONAL DEVELOPMENT

College Education
- PhD IN CHEMICAL ENGINEERING (*Expected July 2017*), UNIVERSITY OF ANYTOWN
  ~ Dissertation: "Transport Modeling and CFD Simulation of Membrane Gas Separation Materials and Modules"

- BSC POLYMER MATERIALS & ENGINEERING, UNIVERSITY OF OTHERTOWN
  ~ Senior Design: "Synthesis and Characterization of Polyurethane/Carbon-nanotubes Composite Materials by Using Electrospinning Technology"

Certifications – COMSOL Multiphysics
- COMSOL Multiphysics Intensive Training, COMSOL,
- COMSOL Multiphysics CFD Certification, COMSOL,
- COMSOL Multiphysics Chemical Reaction Engineering Certification, COMSOL,
- COMSOL Multiphysics Heat Transfer Certification, COMSOL,
- Solver Setting for Effective Analysis in COMSOL Multiphysics Certification,

Certifications – Process Design and Simulation
- Process Design Engineering Training
- Aspen HYSYS Advanced Training: Process Simulation and Modeling
- Aspen HYSYS Basic Process Simulation Training

ADDITIONAL INFORMATION

Technical Skills
- Commercial Multiphysics Simulation Software: COMSOL Multiphysics
- Process Simulation Software: Aspen HYSYS, Aspen Custom Modeler (ACM)
- Computational Programming: MATLAB, VBA, Fortran
- Analytical Techniques: PIV, GC, XRD, FTIR, TGA, DSC
- Design of Experiment Software: Design Expert, Minitab 16

International Exposure
- Fluent in Mandarin Chinese

JOHN A. CHRISTOPHER

11 Any Ave., Anytown AA0 0AA • 01234 567890 • jacla@anyisp.com

Applications
Adaptec Easy CD Creator
Adaptec Direct CD
Carbon Copy
Cc Mail
Clarify
HP Colorado Backup
MS Active Sync
MS Office Professional
MS Outlook 98 and 2003
MS Internet Explorer
NetAccess Internet
Netscape
Norton Ghost
Partition Magic
PC Anywhere
Rainbow
Reflection 1
Reflection X
Remedy-ARS
Symantec Norton Antivirus
Visio
Windows CE

Operating Systems
Microsoft Windows 2000
Microsoft Windows NT 4.0
Workstation and Server
Microsoft Windows ME
Microsoft Windows 95, 98
Cisco Router/Switch IOS
MS-DOS
UNIX

Hardware
Intel-based Desktops
Intel-based Mobile
Computers
HP Colorado Tape Backup
Cisco 2500 Series Router
Hewlett Packard Pro Curve
Switches
CD Writer

Protocols & Services
TCP/IP
DHCP
DNS
NetBEUI
Remote Access Service
WINS

Networking
Ethernet
Token Ring
Microsoft Networking

Network Architecture Specialist
Cisco Certified Network Associate

Performance Profile

Results-driven, self-motivated professional with solid experience supporting hundreds of users in multiple departments in the corporate environment. Recognized for outstanding support and services, process development, and project management. Able to manage multiple projects simultaneously and to move quickly among projects. Capable of leading or collaborating. Areas of expertise include:

- Network architectures and networking components
- Software and operating system deployment in corporate environments
- PC hardware installation/repair and disk imaging
- Troubleshoot complex operating system problems
- Call tracking, case management, solution integration

Accomplishments

- Reduced help desk calls by developing end-user training and knowledge database.
- Led migration for 3000+ client/server email accounts from HP Open Mail to MS Exchange.
- Developed data collection protocol for SSSI Natural Resource Inventory.
- Mentored teammates on technical materials and procedures.
- Built relationships to quickly resolve business critical issues.

Certifications

Technical Certification for MS Network Support Programme
CCNA – Cisco Certified Network Associate

Work History

Technical Support Engineer, ABC Technologies, 2014 – Present
Email Migration Specialist, ABC Technologies, 2010 – 2014
PC Technician, XYZ, 2012 – 2014

Education

B.Sc., Soil Science: Environmental Mgt. – University of Anytown

Award and Honors

Outstanding Services to Technical Services Division
High Quality Customer Service Award, XYZ Technical Support

John Stamos

11 Any Ave., Anytown AA0 0AA

01234 567890
cloudmanagement@gmail.com

Data Centre Engineer
Trained to anticipate and deliver customer satisfaction.

PERFORMANCE SUMMARY

17+ years' experience in data center management and technical support. Lead storage engineer at a dedicated high security site with 1300 enterprise servers for a global provider of secure financial messaging services on behalf of XYZ. Manage schedules and workload of three assistant engineers.

- Server technology and hardware replacement and upgrades: Hard Drive, CPU, RAM, etc.
- Worked across global groups ensuring worldwide redundancy/transparency for all platforms and configurations.
- Conversant in all relevant storage technologies & their business applications, adding £6M+ in new sales.
- Maintained customer main message flow availability at 99.999% for 10+ years.
- Executed incident free 6 hr CTR contract with £500K non-performance penalty for 10+ years.

TECHNOLOGY PROFILE

Hardware: Hitachi Data Systems (HDS, P9500, XP24000), HP 9000 Servers and Workstations, Itanium and Intel based Blade Servers, C-class Blade Enclosure, SN8000 B-series Brocade SAN Switches (DCX), B6200 D2D StoreOnce Backup System, 3Com switches, 3Par, and all major storage peripherals.

Operating Systems: Windows, HP UX, Brocade Fabric OS.

Applications: Remote Web Console (Hitachi Data Systems), Virtual Connect Support Utility, Brocade Fabric Manager, ICE (support ticket documentation tool), HP Common Desktop Environment, StorageWorks Library and Tape Tools (LTT), Insight Control Environment, SanXpert, Support Tools Manager (STM).

Hitachi Data Systems (HDS)	Environmental Assessment	System Security
Lead Storage Engineer	Event Monitoring Service (EMS)	Electrostatic Discharge
Preventative Maintenance	ElectroMagnetic Interference (EMI)	Disaster Recovery, Backups
C-class Blade Installation	Hardware Replacement and Upgrades	Application Support
Troubleshooting: Systems & Networks	Cabling and Testing	UNIX
Rack layout, IO Card Layout	Diagnose and Repair Systems	Technical Support
Operational Readiness Deadlines	Server Installations	Server Locations
SN8000 B-series Brocade SAN Switches (DCX)	Configured Technical Computing Solutions	Cooling System/Air Distribution

PROFESSIONAL COMPETENCIES

ITIL – Processes	ITSM - Change Management	Customer Service
ITIL - Best practices	ITSM - Customer/Business Relationship Management	Cost Management
ITSM - Capacity Management	ITSM - Reference Model - Business Assessment	Presentation Skills
Project Management	ITSM - Problem Management	Resource Tracking
Sales Support/Lead Generation	NI62 - High Level Account Development	Inventory Control
Scheduling Management	Needs Assessment/Business Analysis	New Product Training
Ability to Work Independently	Executive Relationship Development	Policy & Procedures

(continued)

PROFESSIONAL EXPERIENCE

Hardware Specialist, ABC Ltd., Anytown   2009–Current

Lead Storage Engineer for Data Systems storage platform and the primary interface with high-level customers. Leadership skills with the ability to mentor team to deliver results on time and within budget.

- Trusted advisor role: first point of customer contact for resolution of all issues.
- Proven ability to effectively coordinate with external suppliers and internal staff; works well with others in a team environment.
- Prompted repeat business and submitted leads to the sales force increasing client base.
- Increased team productivity resulting in the ability to manage a large data centre with the assistance of one other employee while reducing overtime by 50%.
- Implemented customer problem structure/flow increasing responsiveness and decreasing resolution time.
- Responsible for developing technical protocols and identifying process improvements techniques by using real-time data collection.

Field Engineer Technical Support, XYZ Ltd., Anytown   2001–2009

Conducted reactive field repairs and support for enterprise level HP servers and storage. Troubleshoot and resolved problems quickly to ensure uninterrupted operating capability.

- Provided 24/7 coverage for Government account.
- Quickly learned new products and services for generating sales leads.
- Improved processes and performance in a deadline-driven environment.
- Chosen by management to advance to permanent customer interaction role.

Pre-Sales Technical Consultant, XYZ Ltd., Anytown   1997–2001

Interfaced with technical customers to complete sales cycle and ensure that all needs of sales opportunities were fulfilled. Main contact for issue resolution related to product, pricing, and delivery.

- Configured technical computing solutions for government agencies to assist sales.
- Received and effectively assessed customer issues through meetings and other media.
- Proposed a variety of solutions with varying price points to meet customer needs.
- 100% of sales representatives under my watch achieved company sales quotas annually.

EDUCATION, PROFESSIONAL TRAINING & CERTIFICATIONS

Anytown University,   1996
B.Sc. in Business Management

Othertown Community College,   1993
BTEC Level 3 in Computer Science

HP D2D Gen 3 StorageWorks B6200 StoreOnce Install, Service, and Support	2016
3PAR InServ Storage Server Hardware Introduction	2015
HP StorageWorks VLS and D2D Solutions	2015
HIPAA Privacy and Security Awareness	2014

Mission Critical Certified Specialist

Certifying Body: Samsung

Mission Critical Assessment Specialist

Certifying Body: Hewlett Packard

Doug York

11 Any Avenue, Anytown AA0 0AA
01234 567890   doug@dougdesigns.com
Linked in profile

WEBSITE DESIGN • USER INTERFACE DESIGN • USER EXPERIENCE DESIGN

Professional Profile

UI / UX designer with 19 years of success designing user interfaces and user experiences for complex web, mobile, and cloud solutions. Trusted advisor who collaborates with business leaders and multidisciplinary teams comprised of product development, marketing, and IT professionals to create intuitive websites, streamlined user interfaces, and compelling user experiences. Fluent in Portuguese, Spanish, Italian, and English.

Professional Skills

Art Direction / Graphic Design	Web Development Project Management	Client Communications / Presentations
Website Design & Performance	Problem Identification & Resolution	Technology Assessments
Mobile & Cloud Solutions	UI Standards, Usability, Guidelines, & Specifications	Contract Negotiation & Administration
Servers / Website Security	User Interface Design & Interaction	Digital Strategy
Search Engine Optimization	Front-End Development	Storyboards, Page Layouts, & Site Grids
Website Development / Intranets	Prototype Creation & Usability Testing	Animated GIFs / Cinemagraphs
E-Commerce	Knowledge of Cross-Browser Quirks	Product Development / Content Marketing

Technology & Computer Science Skills

Design: Adobe Photoshop, Illustrator, Adobe Flash, Adobe Edge Inspect, Responsive Web Design, Usability, Accessibility
Development: HTML 5 – HTML, CSS3, JavaScript, Sublime Text 2 / Notepad++, and basic use of jQuery, PHP, MySQL; Joomla CMS Expert (Front-end development, administration, deployment, security, maintenance, and migration), Bootstrap v3
Website Performance Optimization: Server-side and client-side solutions
Browser Developer Tools: Firebug/Chrome/IE development tools
Servers: WHM/cPanel administration (advanced), Linux server administration (basic), and basic server security knowledge
Other: Adobe Premiere, Adobe Media Encoder (for DVD/Blu-ray and Web), Sony Vegas and Sound Forge, DVD Lab Pro 2, Adobe Lightroom, Adobe Acrobat Pro DC, Microsoft Office Suite (Word, Excel, PowerPoint, and Outlook), SEO, and research

Performance Highlights

➢ Proven leader in the design of practical user interfaces and user experiences for a wide range of solutions.
  – As a UI designer, provide user interface layout and design with special attention to visual appeal and interactive features. Collaborate with design teams, software application developers, network engineers, and other IT professionals.
  – As a UX designer, conduct user tests, face-to-face-interviews, and field research. Create user personas, study detailed analytics, provide design layouts, lead prototype creation, and conduct usability testing. Work closely with internal stakeholders, including marketing, brand development, product development, and product management teams to understand the businesses' functional requirements from the UX perspective.
➢ Articulate spokesperson with the ability to explain creative design concepts and user journeys to non designers. Effectively communicate project and design rationale to technical and nontechnical people at all organizational levels.
➢ Outstanding customer service skills with a proven record of maintaining client satisfaction and retention.

Professional Experience

XYZ Ltd.   Anytown
Art Director, Website Designer, UI Designer, and UX Designer   1998 – Present

XYZ is a boutique website design and development agency known for innovative design and quick turnaround.

  • Create attractive, highly functional user interfaces for websites, serving more than 200 corporate clients in UK, North America, and Europe.
  • Serve as the single point of contact with clients. Actively participate in brainstorming and design execution meetings.
  • Collaborate with clients' product groups, marketing teams, and IT staff to create and refine effective online marketing strategies for the clients' products/services.

Doug York   01234 567890 | doug@dougdesigns.com |

- Meet clients to gain an understanding of their business models, assess their needs, and derive insights about the clients' customers, including researching personas, competitive analysis, etc.
- Advise clients on the evolution of UI/UX solutions and emerging technologies. Identify and resolve issues as they arise.
- Design the user experience from concept through implementation across all online solutions, including active development on top of the chosen CMS solutio n.
- Manage overall quality of design for marketing online products/services. Deliver wireframes, information architecture, and high-fidelity comps.
- Lead the development and deployment of websites, intranet s, and other online solutions.
- Manage 3–15 people, depending on the project size.
- Provide quick turnaround on client requests and resolve issues in a timely and accurate manner.
- Exercise meticulous care in creating/maintaining detailed documentation such as user experience road   maps and style guides.

Selected Long-Term Client Projects

ABC LAND & SEA TRAVEL SERVICES – Art Director, UX Designer, and Web Developer   2008 – Present

ABC is a company encompassing 8 different business groups in 22 countries with annual revenue of £7.5 billion in 2013.

- Designed/developed 3 versions of company's website. (The newest design , which is some of my best work, has not been released yet, but it can be viewed with a confidentiality agreement.) Designed/developed 2 versions of the company's intranet.
- Serve as a trusted advisor to the client. Provide UX design services , including active development on top of the chosen CMS solutions. Perform graphic design and video editing. Engineer quick solutions to internal and external communication challenges. Deliver wireframes, information architecture, and high -fidelity comps. Manage quality assurance and product documentation. Lead the development/deployment of on line solutions (web, intranet, etc.) .

DEF–Art Director, UX Designer,and Web Developer   2013 – Present

DEF is a high-rise luxury building with exclusive space at street level. Designed by AB & Sons, Architects. The building won a sustainability award in 2015.

- Designed a captivating online presence for DEF on a par with the magnitude of the commercial real estate development. Delved deep into the architectural style of the building and worked to bring the grandeur of the client's vision for the website to life.
  - This two-phase project included creating a showcase sales website and turning the website into the building's intranet once DEF was fully rented.
  - Chose the best technological platform for the foundation of the website. Developed demo prototypes and presented conceptual design to key stakeholders.
  - Created an interface that could easily change states and developed an in formation architecture that could hold both personalities, only showing the relevant interface at each phase of the project.
  - Delivered the design (user architecture, interfaces, and user experiences) from concept to final product.
  - Created the information architecture (IA) for the content.
  - Created and maintained internal documentation (text and screencast) for the products.
  - Completed both phases of the project perfectly within budget, even with performing additional requests from the client.
- Ongoing services include art direction, user interface design, information architecture, and improving the building's website and intranet, serving detailed information to all tenants about the building's amenities and internal processes, area transportation and commerce, and tenant-specific documents such as lease renewals, etc.

D, E & F – UX Designer and Web Developer   2012 – 2015

D, E & F is one of the top 100 law firms in with more than 30 practice areas and clients in all economic sectors.

- Provided user interface design, information ar chitecture, and web development for the client.
- Worked closely with the advertising agency, art director, and the client to achieve a user interface that accurately reflects the client's brand. The project had a constrained budget and short deadline.
- Developed the company's website. Recommended the best technical solutions without sacrificing the required functionality.
- Deployed the solution with zero downtime, managed 2 developers, and completed the project on time and within budget.

Doug York   01234 567890 | doug@dougdesigns.com |

GHI Ltd. – UX Designer and Web Developer   2015 – Present
GHI is the largest privately owned chain of pawnshops in the UK.
- As an outside consultant working for an external agency, designed a concise user experience information architecture while giving the agency's junior art director a crash course on responsive web design and usability.
- Provided user interface design, information architecture, and web development of the 2014 annual report website.
- Provide ongoing design of the user experience from concept through design/implementation across all target devices, including desktop, smartphones, and tablets. Find creative solutions to difficult interaction challenges. Actively participate in design team brainstorming and sketch sessions and develop demo prototypes. Develop front end and deploy solution.

INTERNATIONAL BRANDING, LTD. – UX Designer and Front-end Developer   2012 – Present
International Branding is a global design and innovation consultancy with offices in 8 countries with locations in Paris, London, Warsaw, Hamburg, New York City, Sao Paulo, Shanghai, and Singapore.
- Work as an independent contractor. Collaborate with the clients' product groups to develop and implement user interfaces and information architecture for web and mobile applications that optimize user engagement and contribute to brand loyalty, customer retention, and website conversion (visit-to-order ratios) for retail commercial clients.
- Provide ongoing services including designing the user experience from concept through implementation. Actively participate in brainstorming and design meetings. Lead the development/deployment of online solutions (websites, intranet, among others). Create and maintain documentation for the products. Develop the front end and deploy online solutions. Provide quick turnaround on all issues and requests.

Education

B.Sc., Computer Science, Anytown University

Hobbies and Interests

PC building with focus on water cooling and quiet computing

Marc Peyton

11 Any Avenue
Anytown AA0 0AA

Linked in profile

01234 567890
marc.peyton@outlook.com

Copy Editor

Helping writers become readable and publishers profitable.

PERFORMANCE PROFILE

11+ years' experience as a copy editor, with complete grasp of grammar, syntax, flow, meaning, and cohesion, including summary analyses and full analyses, press and media releases, and commentaries. Experienced in managing technical and editorial issues, with the ability to step in when full editorial skills are required. Fastidious about style and consistency while meeting deadlines with high-quality products.

- Strong communication skills, with the ability to work independently and as part of a team.
- Manages multiple deadlines in fast-paced environments with changing priorities.
- Resolves problems by recommending solutions to ensure high-quality products.
- Manages heavy workloads and assures completion of work according to schedule.
- Reliable and available to help those in need complete jobs on time and accurately.

PROFESSIONAL SKILLS

*Excellent Editing Skills	*Copyediting	*Proofreading Skills
*Collaborative Skills	*Customer Service Excellence	*Headline Writing
*Leadership Skills	*Strong Writing Skills	*Tracking Skills
*Technically Proficient	*Project Management	*Researches Facts
*Production Layout	*Desktop Publishing	*Trafficking
*Proofreads Galleys	*Supplier Interaction	*Newsletter Creation

TECHNOLOGY SKILLS

*MS Office (MS Word, Excel, PowerPoint)	*Outlook	*Product & Software Tester
*LinX	*MS Visio	*InDesign
*Photoshop	*Illustrator	*PageMaker

PROFESSIONAL EXPERIENCE

ABC, Anytown   2006–Present
Copy Editor
A worldwide leader of financial market intelligence and one of the Big Three credit rating agencies. Publishes financial research and analysis for investors. Responsibilities include copyediting articles for grammar and house style. Article types include research updates and recovery reports. Performs summary and full analyses, press and media releases, and commentaries. Collaborates with analysts, manages workflow, resolves technical issues, and tracks projects. Strong competencies in public finance and corporate sectors.

- Honoured with 11 awards for customer focus and teamwork.
- Participated in alpha and beta testing of technology upgrades for internal software and client products, enabling employees to be more productive and resulting in improved customer experience.
- Participated in training initiatives, including individual training of new employees, contributions to instructional manual, and service on an interdepartmental committee tasked with ensuring quality of training and increasing productivity.

Assistant to Editor   2004–2006
Initially hired as a temporary worker for three days a week; hired full-time in 2005 due to excellent performance. Responsibilities included proofreading galleys and inputting corrections to galleys.
- Provided extra time and dedication to complete first edition in 2006.
- Charged with managing group completing summary analyses when editorial assistant and editorial manager were unavailable.
- Selected to provide training to temporary workers and permanent employees as needed to ensure superior performance.

XYZ Group, Ltd., Othertown   2001–2004
Editor
Initially hired as a temporary employee, then moved into permanent editing position. Responsibilities included collecting information, writing and editing articles, designing and placing advertisements, handling production layouts, working with outside suppliers including printing companies and advertisers, assisting with special projects, and providing administrative support to staff.
- Produced monthly, quarterly, and yearly publications for two professional associations and a for-profit subsidiary.
- Created the masthead for four-page newsletter for the for-profit subsidiary.
- Assisted in the transition from manual newsletter production methods to desktop publishing (PageMaker), resulting in improved services to clients.

AWARDS AND RECOGNITION

Awarded 11 ACEs (Acknowledging and Celebrating Excellence)
  *Awards recognized top-quality customer focus and teamwork, at ABC.

EDUCATION AND PROFESSIONAL DEVELOPMENT

Anytown University,   2001
BA Political Science

Othertown College   2015
HND Media and Journalism

Certificate: Digital and Graphic Design Production   2008
Relevant Coursework
 InDesign, Photoshop, Illustrator, Copyediting and Proofreading Fundamentals
Advanced Copyediting: 2007
Relevant Coursework
 Editing for Clarity
 Headline Writing for Commentaries
 Trimming Words for Tighter Writing
 Identifying, Translating, and Eliminating Jargon
 Actively Speaking: Spotting and Eliminating the Passive Voice

11 Any Avenue
Anytown AA0 0AA

Shawn Brandon

Linked in profile
01234 567890
shawn.brandon@gmail.com

Director of Planning & Materials

Performance Summary

Supply Chain Leader with 17 years' experience in planning and purchasing for organizations with a worldwide reach. Demonstrated talent in leading and managing unified teams, ensuring all company and personal goals are achieved. Technically astute, with skills in Kanban, SAP, BAAN, RetailEdge, and Microsoft Access.
Demonstrated knowledge in lean manufacturing. Substantiated history of developing and executing enterprise-wide processes and procedures that increase productivity, quality, and consistency by removing redundancies. Strategic planner with well-honed analytic and technical proficiencies; adept in worldwide business initiatives and able to excel in fast-paced, complex, and ambiguous environments.

Professional Skills

Strategic Planning	Worldwide Supply Chain	Purchasing	Inventory
Turnkey Solutions	Metrics	Lean Manufacturing	Sourcing
Forecasting	Replenishment	Project Management	Procedure Development
Kanban	Re-Order Points (ROP)	Logistics	Life-Cycle Management
Procurement	On-Time Delivery (OTD)	MRP/ERP	Negotiations
Staff Leadership	CILT (UK) Certified	SAP	BAAN

—— Key Highlights ——

➤ Drove site availability to 98% by establishing daily meetings between Site Manufacturing Managers, Planning group, and Purchasing group.
➤ Key contributor of the upgrade of the Molecular Biology Lab, providing planning and setup of new SAP plant with a very aggressive timeline.
➤ Reduced expedited expenses more than 60%.
➤ Saved £107,000 in service agreements and system cost.

—— Professional Experience ——

ABC Technologies, Anytown   2014 to 2017
Formerly the Special Division of Applied Technologies and Xsystems and joint ventures.
Director of Worldwide Planning

Selected to oversee the entire supply chain life cycle. Hired and managed 14 staff members, providing support for Worldwide planning and procurement, instrument master scheduling, indirect procurement, DC Kanban Administration, service logistics call centre, and data maintenance. Directed project initiatives for business process re-engineering and optimization. Led teams on Kaizen events.

• Reduced inventory 30%, totaling more than £9 million in one year.
• Saved £107,000 by initiating early termination of service agreement with Life Tech supply chain.
• Realized £170,000 in annual transportation savings by providing distribution planning changes.
• Increased product availability from 93% to 96%.
• Led the Supply Chain separation of ERP cloning from Applied Technologies without impact on customer service.

Shawn Brandon	0123456 7890	shawn.brandon@gmail.com

XYZ Technologies, othertown   2000 to 2014
Formerly X systems, providing instruments and consumables for life sciences.
Senior Manager, Planning   2010 to 2014

Promoted to provide planning and Worldwide supply chain management within the Consumables Group. Analyzed and resolved complex products. Managed six staff members. Partnered with Product Management and Manufacturing on prioritizing products, providing strategic resolutions to supply issues, and reduction of losses. Used visual reporting tools to create reports. Provided executives with weekly summaries on concerns with the site.

- Assisted in conversion of manufacturing group to an abbreviated time schedule, an £800,000 annual savings.
- Recognized with *Platinum Award* for leading the Supply Chain consolidation to othertown.
- Reduced turnaround time 50% and eliminated a £400,000 backlog.
- Cut overdue work orders 30% by establishing daily cross-functional meetings.
- Selected by the Director as a replacement before the purchase of X systems.

Senior Manager, Worldwide Spares Planning and Service Logistics   2005 to 2010

Provided life-cycle management of Spares Planning. Oversaw Service Logistics throughout Europe. Directed contingency strategy planning for supplier bankruptcy, which included leading organization discussions with Project Managers, Service Product Management, Finance, Senior Management, and staff to salvage product lines. Represented sites across the globe.

- Saved the company £2 million in inventory by developing alternatives to Lifetime Buys.
- Led an organization-wide programme, saving the company £1 million in revenue.

Manager of Worldwide Service Logistics and Service Inventory   2000 to 2005

Primary liaison for entire supply chain, providing process alignment across the organization and establishing territory boundaries for Europe and APAC. Streamlined process by implementing SOX-compliant Field Service cycle programme, metrics, and self-help tools for Field Engineers. Served as Service Business Operations Manager, driving optimization for 28 staff members in Service Call Centre, Service Administration, and Service Contract Administration functions.

- Reduced aging inventory by £750,000 and priority overnight shipments by 40%, with a total savings of £350,000 per year by designing and implementing self-help tools for Field Service Engineers.
- Served as a key speaker at a Worldwide Service Conference with more than 500 attendees.

—— **Volunteer Experience**——

National Dog Rescue, 2011 to Present
Animal rescue and adoption centre
Volunteer

Provided implementation and maintenance of a Point-of-Sale Inventory Management System. Created technical documentation of the inventory management processes.

—— **Education and Professional Development** ——

BSc Economics, University of Anytown

CPIM Certification, APICS/CILT (UK)

11 Any Ave.,
Anytown, AA0 0AA

Chris Eisenstein
MBA in Finance & General Management
0123456 7890   chriseisenstein@gmail.com

Electronics Manufacturing Management

Performance Profile

15+ years of electronic manufacturing services management experience involving operations, finance, supply chain, and project and materials management.
Includes 6 years managing cross-functional teams and customer relations. Skilled at evaluating complex issues, identifying key issues, creating action plans, and guiding execution. CILT(UK) certified: CPIM and CSCP.

Professional Skills

- Revenue & Profit Increases
- Cost Reduction & Cost Avoidance
- Process & Efficiency Improvement
- Customer Relationship Management
- Contract Development & Negotiation
- Team Building & Leadership
- Materials & Supply Chain Management
- P&L Management
- Metrics Management & Analysis

PROFESSIONAL EXPERIENCE

High-Tech Circuits, Ltd., Anytown   2004–Present
Business Analyst, Business Unit Financial Analyst   2015–Present

Perform extensive analysis and reporting for a business unit group of 300+ employees. Key actions and accomplishments include the following:

- Revitalized the Time Clock project, which was behind schedule. Established close interaction with offsite project manager and completed assembly, installation, and testing ahead of schedule. Recognized for contribution to efficiency improvement and more effective plant operation.
- Compiled and updated quarterly customer QBR reports using Excel pivot tables and Access database information. In addition, generated and reported quarterly bonuses for employees.

Business Unit Manager   2012–2015

Managed a challenging £25 million/year account and approximately £18 million of materials to maintain profitability. Major areas included forecasting, contract negotiations, supplier performance, financial management, and HR issues. Developed and coordinated activities of cross-functional teams. Key actions and accomplishments include the following:

- Spearheaded revision and execution of full manufacturing contract within 4 months versus expected 6–12 months.
- Grew revenue 330% in fiscal year 2006.

Business Unit Coordinator   2009–2012

Managed accounts valued at £12 million per year. Interacted with customers to ensure high satisfaction. Contributed to cost-reduction and efficiency improvements that included developing Excel macros to use purchasing and inventory data more efficiently and an Access database to track ECN changes and impact.

Planning Supervisor   2004–2009

Established rules, procedures, tools, and techniques to move plant from prototype to volume production. Managed master scheduling for multiple programmes, as well as work cell material management and metrics. Key actions and accomplishments include the following:

- Achieved smooth transfer of £30+ million programme to another facility through detailed material transactions and planning.
- Reduced excess inventory by £400,000 and increased inventory turns 20%.
- Originally earned promotion from Planner position within less than a year.

Previous positions: Planner; Accounting Manager

ABC Laminate Systems, Anytown   1997–2003
Production/Scheduling/Inventory Manager

Served as a member of Leadership Team and as Work Team coach for Shipping department. Additional actions and accomplishments include the following:

- Participated in Kaizen event that promoted continuous improvement and elimination of waste by initiating changes that included reducing product travel from 5,000 to 2,000 feet.
- Contributed to £500,000 inventory reduction and 98% on-time shipping record.

EDUCATION

MBA–Finance & General Management
Anytown University
BSc–Accounting
Anytown University

Professional Affiliations
Member, Production & Inventory Control Society

Certifications
Certified in Production & Inventory Management (CPIM): earned in less than one year
Certified Supply Chain Professional (CSCP): earned in less than 6 months

Application Competencies
Access, Visio, SAP, ERP Word, Excel (including pivot tables and macros), PowerPoint, etc.

Exemplary professional references available on request

PAT PAULSON

11 Any Avenue, Anytown AA0 0AA

0123456 7890

Linked in profile

pat.paulson@gmail.com

ENVIRONMENTAL CONSULTANT

Navigating the intersections of business, technology, and ecological systems.

Devise appropriate compliance and risk mitigation strategies when regulatory issues impact clients. Recognized for project leadership, supporting all aspects from requirements gathering and proposal development to resource allocation, implementation, and final handover. Exhibit consultative approach, giving clients one-on-one attention and making project adjustments to meet their needs.

Experienced interface for companies, concerned communities, and government agencies, including O&G, Technology, Pharma, and Ministry of Defense. Communicate technical concepts to nontechnical audiences. Demonstrate valuable technical expertise, working with ERPs, CRMs, and other databases to manage critical information.

PROFESSIONAL SKILLS

Environmental Assessment	Project Management	Health & Safety Protocols (EHS)
Air & Water Quality Issues	Proposals & Contract Administration	Client Consultation
Site Investigations & Remediation	Budgeting & Cost Control	Supplier Relations
Permitting	Cost Estimates	Training & Mentoring
Regulatory Compliance	Cross-discipline Communication	Team Leadership
Scientific Data Collection & Analysis	Continuous Process Improvement	
Field Surveying & Sampling	Quality Assurance	
Requirements Gathering	Risk Management	

TECHNICAL SKILLS

Scientific Modeling	Industrial & Financial Systems (IFS)	Technical Report Writing
isee systems STELLA	4D	Intranet Administration
PRé SimaPro Life Cycle	Microsoft Word	
Assessment	Microsoft Excel	
RERP/CRM	Microsoft Excel Solver Plugin	

PROFESSIONAL EXPERIENCE

XYZ Ltd., Anytown   2012 to Present

Leading provider of shipbuilding, ship repair and modernization, and industrial services.

Project Coordinator

Appointed to support 5 project managers with contract and change order management, materials, subcontracting, and quality assurance plans for FFP, T&M, hybrid, cost plus, and contract vehicles. Engaged with client stakeholders to understand their requirements and respond to needs. Contributed to preparing cost estimates for proposals. Secured final customer and regulatory approval for project closeout. Balanced competing priorities while juggling project schedules and budgets. Maintained supplier relationships during project life cycle.

Heavily utilized ERP (IFS) for project setup and to generate detailed project reports. Updated intranet to distribute project data; maintained customer information in CRM (Treasure Chest). Co-managed hundreds of craft workers spanning 12 unions. Interacted with various private customers and government agencies, including Maritime and Coast Guard Agency Ministry of Defence and chambers of Commerce, to coordinate multimillion-pound contracts. Supported compliance with health and safety requirements via administrative measures.

- Interfaced with Coast guard on contracts exceeding £90.8M. Delivered key support for completion of dockside availability initiative, ahead of contracted deadline.

continued

- Acquired experience analyzing and interpreting requirements and rules concerning labour.
- Facilitated timely implementation of projects and issuing of work orders by rapidly processing award packages.
- Ensured client satisfaction by integrating controls into work items (inspection test plan, QA/QC) and communicating status updates to client to address any issues and obtain approval for solutions. Integrated growth work into contracts.
- Played key role in implementing new version of ERP (IFS) to increase project efficiency and enhance reporting, conducting system test to ensure functionality and reporting accuracy before go live.
- Improved monitoring of job charges and resolution of discrepancies by assisting in development of new timekeeping system.
- Reduced redundant handling of data, errors, and project setup time through creation of templates in ERP.
- Elevated job estimate accuracy by recommending direct estimation of jobs in ERP to avoid need for data transfer.
- Drove continuous process improvement.

ABC LTD., Othertown | 2009 to 2012

Former provider of ship repair and fabrication services to government and commercial markets.

Project Administrative Assistant

Hired into permanent position following brief temporary role. Joined project execution team, performing project setup, change management, progress billing, and completion. Acted as point of contact for clients, regulatory agencies, and subcontractors. Entered specifications into ERP to develop budgets and work breakdown structure for project controls, financial management, and reporting. Contributed to bid package preparation and researched government RFPs. Prepared and submitted condition found reports for client approval. Ensured timely project completion process and reconciled financial discrepancies.

- Completed public works contracts exceeding £36M for clients at national and county level.
- Expedited project completion by streamlining data flow within estimation and project delivery processes.
- Played central role in obtaining release of funds held in retainage for public works jobs.
- Enhanced tracking/progress system to monitor public works initiatives by creating clear, scalable process for all jobs within shared spreadsheet for easy review and update by all project staff.
- Replaced extraneous, disorganized secondary archiving system with single, centralized solution to ensure that all projects followed same sequential index used during execution.

DEF DISTILLERY, Othertown | March 2004 to June 2005

Low-volume producer of premium craft spirits.

Production Specialist

Hired to participate in all phases of production, sales, and distribution (domestic/international) for premium product line. Ensured quality control of production to deliver best-in-class products. Interacted with regulatory agencies. Developed proficiency with specialized precision measuring tools. Gained exposure to material flows, water, and energy usage within production process.

- Contributed to new product development and production process innovation to facilitate efficiency while maintaining product integrity.
- Played active role in company winning coveted industry awards by contributing to creation of high-quality products.

EDUCATION

MSc in Natural Resources and Environment: Sustainable Systems (December 2013)
BSc Industrial Ecology
University of Anytown

Relevant Environmental Coursework: Water Quality Management, Water Resources Policy, Energy Markets and Policy, Statistics, Transportation Energy, Environmental Assessment, Environmental Law, Ecology, Land Use and GIS

Miranda Bradshaw

EXECUTIVE ADMINISTRATIVE & CLERICAL SUPPORT • OFFICE ADMINISTRATION • ACCOUNT MANAGEMENT

11 Any Avenue, Anytown AA0 0AA
01234 567890 miranda.bradshaw@anyisp.com

Linked in.

Executive Assistant & Office Manager
Supporting Financial Reporting, Shareholders & Board of Directors' Meetings, Leasing & Sales Activities, and Facilities Management

Performance Profile
Advanced problem-solving skills with the capability to accurately multitask in fast-paced environments. Proven track record in operations with a broad-based background. Recognized as a consistent producer driven to exceed goals and improve workplace efficiency. Highly focused multitasker with the ability to prioritize and manage timelines effectively. Advanced user of complex technology with solid background in MS Office, database management, end-user training, and updating websites; Solid foundation in all facets of business operations including administrative policies and procedures. Maintains excellent communication skills and a high level of confidentiality.

Professional Skills

Scheduling & Calendar Management	Account Management & Admin. Support	Staff Training & Supervision
Office Management & Organization	Correspondence / Presentations	Exceptional Customer Service
Project Management / Priority Setting	Confidentiality & Diplomacy	Supply Inventory & Requisitions
Sales & Marketing Support	Budget Administration & Expense Control	Meetings & Conferences Logistics
Computer Systems & Software Applications	Financial Reporting & Reconciliation	Problem Identification & Resolution
Filing, Faxing, & Mail Distribution	Project Management & Research Skills	Billing / Collections Management
Answering Multi-Line Phones	Client Relationship Management (CRM)	Supplier Relationship Management

Computer Skills
Microsoft Office Suite: Word, Excel, PowerPoint, and Outlook. Also proficient in Multi-Data Services software, Microsoft Front Page, LogMeIn software, Doc Record, BuildingLink, Basecamp, and Adobe Acrobat. Ability to streamline computerized processes.

Performance Highlights
➢ Executive Administrative Assistant skilled in implementing best practices in office management and providing administrative and clerical support for business leaders, shareholders, and sales/marketing professionals. Known for building strong business relationships across a variety of industries, taking initiative to solve problems within the realm of responsibility, and keeping the office running smoothly.
➢ Highly organized and pragmatic Office Manager who achieved significant cost savings for office supplies by negotiating with suppliers and monitoring office supply budget. Skilled in the design/implementation of business process improvements. Created the company's physical filing system, organizing 10,000+ files. Coordinated the launch of the company's MDS software, created user manuals, and trained over 80% of the office staff.

Professional Experience

ABC PROPERTIES LTD.	ANYTOWN
Account Manager	2014 – Present
Executive Assistant and Office Manager	2013 – 2014
Administrative Assistant	2011 – 2012

In business since 1985, ABC provides professional property management services for Anytown's most prestigious long- and short-term rental properties.

Account Manager
• Manage the daily operations of a £135,000 portfolio consisting of 9 residential and commercial property accounts, including building staff supervision for this mid-sized property management firm with 150 accounts. Interface with maintenance staff. Communicate board priorities and concerns. Provide onsite presence with residents and staff. Handle client concerns and requests to ensure their satisfaction with property management services.

- Ensure that the properties are maintained in compliance with building regulations. Approve and monitor building renovations to ensure that contractors are properly licensed and insured. Schedule and file all necessary inspections of physical plant and equipment. Clear open violations, as needed. Provide computerized work order tracking.
- Cultivate business relationships with qualified, licensed service professionals. Analyze and audit all service contracts annually. Bid out all contracts for best price and coverage. Provide owners with multiple bids for large contracts.
- Work with the board of directors to create an annual operating budget to keep properties operating profitably. Prepare performance-based analyses (budgets, forecasts, revenues, operating cost analyses, and probability assessments).
- Prepare monthly financial reports, quarterly and year-end financial statements, and balance sheets with breakdown of deposits and disbursements by property. Provide accountant with all necessary financial reports for year-end reporting and tax preparation.
- Leverage extensive industry knowledge, range of professional experience, and advanced communication skills to take initiative in situations before they become problematic. Predict the needs of managers/clients prior to their requests.

Executive Assistant & Office Manager
- Provided office management. Ensured effective and efficient administrative and clerical support for 5 executives. Supported executives in the management of rentals and commercial properties.
- Provided executive support to CEO and CFO. Booked meetings for CEO and CFO. Prepared reports and presentations for board meetings and took meeting minutes. Reserved conference rooms, scheduled presentations, confirmed attendance, prepared agendas, and compiled/distributed meeting minutes.
- Created sales package customized to each building. Reviewed each sales/leasing package to ensure accuracy and completion. Coordinated the closing process of apartments. Generated £25,000 per month in commissions.
- Ensured entire portfolio met deadlines for property registration.
- Created and revised systems and procedures by analyzing operating practices, recordkeeping systems, forms control, office operations, budgetary, and staffing requirements.
- Managed computer systems/software. Created a user guide for the client management software (MDS).

Administrative Assistant
- Executed a diverse range of administrative tasks. Read, researched, composed, and distributed correspondence (memos, letters, and reports), addressed internal/external communications, and brought critical issues to the attention of executive leaders. Anticipated the needs of executives and took proactive measures to keep office running smoothly.
- Created spreadsheets, charts, and financial reports for board meetings and presentations regarding the financial status of clients' accounts and properties. Processed and reconciled invoices and expense reports. Followed up on invoicing/collections matters relating to suppliers and clients.
- Managed executives' calendars in Microsoft Outlook. Handled appointment scheduling, travel arrangements, and meeting logistics for property owners' meetings and industry conferences. Represented executives by attending meetings in their absence and serving as the executive's spokesperson.
- Devised a physical filing system integrated with the company's client management software for easier file retrieval.

Education
BSc Marketing and International Business, University of Anytown

Languages
English and Spanish (Written and Spoken Proficiency)

Community Involvement / Volunteer Activities
Treasurer Anytown Community Association
volunteer : Green Impact Committee

Scott Simon

11 Any Ave., Anytown AA0 0AA   0123456 7890   ssimon@anyisp.com

INSURANCE ADJUSTER/INVESTIGATOR

Performance Profile
INSURANCE ADJUSTER/INVESTIGATOR

Logical and analytical approach to identifying and resolving situations with high potential for conflict. Organized and creative, with solid approach to comprehensive information gathering.

Police-trained investigator, superior questioning and analytical skills, experienced in negotiations, and ability to develop trust and open communication.

Calm under pressure. Committed to applying a trained and seasoned detective's skills to the insurance profession.

Core Competencies

- Investigative Techniques
- Courtroom Representation
- Risk Assessment
- Needs Assessment
- Witness Questioning
- Incident Documentation
- Report Writing
- Conflict Resolution
- Legal Compliance
- Negotiating
- Safety Principles
- One-on-One Training

Professional Training

- Police Science
- Reconnaissance
- Photography
- Crisis Evidence
- Investigation Techniques
- Surveillance
- Family Violence
- Public Relations
- Security
- Accident Investigation
- Child Abuse Rape
- Communication Skills

Police Service

Anytown   2006 – 2017
- **Detective Inspector CID (Anti-Fraud)**
Anytown   2003 – 2006
- **Detective Sergoant CID (Anti-Fraud)**
Anytown   2000 – 2003
- **Police Officer**
Othertown   1998 – 2000
- **Police Officer**

Education

- **MSc, Leadership and Organizational Change**   2014
Anytown University
- **BSc, Criminal Justice**
Pfeiffer University, Charlotte, NC   2007
- **Information systems security coursework**   2009
Othertown Community College

Superior references available upon request

Mary Cassat

11 Any Ave.,
Anytown AA0 0AA

01234 567890

mcassat@anyisp.com

HOSPITALITY MANAGEMENT
Operations / Sales / Marketing

Performance Profile

10+ years' progressive experience in hospitality management. A track record of delivering *measurable revenue and profit contributions*. Team building and leadership strengths with proven ability to hire, train, and motivate top-performing teams. Organized, with the ability to multitask in a fast-paced environment and respond quickly and effectively to problems, thrives on challenges. *Foreign language:* Spanish.

Core Competencies

➢ Revenue Optimization	➢ Cost Containment	➢ Recruitment & Selection
➢ Staff Development	➢ Team Building	➢ Operations Management
➢ Spanish	➢ Time Management	➢ Policy & Procedures
➢ Customer Service	➢ Productivity Growth	➢ Accounting/POS Support
➢ Brand Integrity	➢ Client Relations	➢ Inventory Control
➢ P&L	➢ Turnover Reduction	➢ Problem Solving
➢ Payroll	➢ 250 Covers Daily	➢ Liquor Inventory
➢ Scheduling	➢ 300 Pre-theatre	➢ Cash Reconciliation
➢ Food Cost Reduction	➢ Purchasing	➢ Administration
➢ Training Manuals	➢ POS Systems	➢ Marketing/Advertising

PROFESSIONAL EXPERIENCE

ABC RESTAURANT, ANYTOWN	Present
Assistant General manager	2015–Present
Administrative Manager	2012–2015
Bartender	2010–2012
Waitness	2010

Assistant General manager   **2015– Present**

Day-to-day food and beverage operations of £5+ million fine dining establishment that averages 250 covers daily. Train, manage, and mentor cross-functional team of 60+, ensuring highest standard of customer service and brand integrity.

| Mary Cassat | 0123456 7890 | mcassat@anyisp.com | Page 2 |

Supervise food & beverage inventories, manage costs and maximize profitability, monitor safe handling best practices & procedures, prepare sales and labor forecasts. P&L accountability and Payroll responsibility. Accounting & POS support.

- Orchestrated scheduling initiative that minimized overtime, captured **10% increase in productivity, and reduced payroll by over 10%.**
- Hired, trained, and supervised cross-functional front and back-of-house staff of 60 with minimum turnover; **achieved impact ratio over 100%.**
- Generated mystery shopper **score of 90+% annually.**
- **Slashed food cost by over £150,000** annually.
- Organized liquor perpetual inventory, streamlined daily procedures, **cost reduction of 2%.**

Administrative Manager   2012–2015

Promoted after nine months to initiate and manage administrative affairs for new location including daily cash and credit reconciliations, employee file maintenance, accounts payable, office administration, benefits administration, new employee processing, etc.

- Achieved 95% or better on all audits.
- Appointed as administrative trainer; trained six managers.
- Authored Positouch Procedural Guide for use at all locations.
- Designed employee file initiative that was adopted for use company wide.
- Implemented side work, floor plan, and scheduling charts to organize restaurant opening.
- Responsibility for implementing HASAW.

Bartender   2010–2012
Waitress   2010

XYZ RESTAURANT othertown   2006–2009

Shift Supervisor / Bartender / Server

Advanced to shift supervisor with responsibility for opening / closing, scheduling staff, maintaining inventory, purchasing, reconciling cash drawer, etc., for busy City Centre restaurant.

- Gained valuable experience in all aspects of restaurant operations.
- Developed "spotter" system to eliminate theft that has been implemented by other establishments throughout the area.
- Increased sales through "door to door" advertising programme.

EDUCATION

UNIVERSITY OF ANYTOWN
BA Humanities

Professional Development / Certifications
Service Training
Servsafe, FMP (Food Management Professionals) Certified Trainer

Professional Affiliations
Member, BPW UK (Business and Professional Women UK)

Computer Skills
PC and Macintosh: Word, Excel, Databases, POS Systems (Positouch, Squirrel, Micros), Restaurant Magic

11 Any Avenue, Anytown AA0 0AA	**Jean Saint Laurent**	0123456 7890 j.saintlaurent@gmail.com

Insurance Underwriter ~ Insurance Investment

Charter Insurance Professional & Investment Operations Certified

Performance Summary

Six years of experience in providing investment reporting, transaction processing, and client reporting. Contributed to continuous process improvement by streamlining the delivery of new workflow procedures. Recognized for outstanding work ethic, leadership, and financial services expertise through job promotion within the first year of employment. Maintained dealer agreements, created detailed reports, and reviewed documents during opening of new accounts. Reduced costs through analytical research of market prices.

——Professional Skills——

* Client Reporting Analysis	* Portfolio Administration	* Strategic Analysis	* Negotiations
* Renewals	* Risk Management	* Pricing Analysis	* Data Analysis
* Regulation Compliance	* Training & Mentoring	* Partnership Development	* Relationship Management
* Business Development	* Process Improvement	* Issue Resolution	* Communications
* Client Administration	* Conflict Resolution	* Report Development	* Fluent in French

——Professional Experience——

ABC Investment Advisors, Anytown
A leading investment management firm with oversight of more than £100M in assets for high net-worth clients.
Underwriter & Compliance Analyst   2010 – Present
Provided employee training with a focus on accurate and on-time reporting. Reviewed documents for opening new accounts and completion. Managed dealer agreements, memberships, and registrations. Served as a liaison between Bermuda Monetary Authority and the Bermuda Investment Advisory Services while maintaining compliance with legislation. Reviewed and updated terms of agreement attached to forms, ensuring forms reflected changes in product offerings.

- Partnered with Investment Managers to maintain up-to-date information and remain in compliance with the Monetary Authority while adhering to Customer due diligence requirements.
- Researched all client files to enhance requirements using industry-accepted Anti-Money Laundering(AML) database.

Investment Valuations Analyst   2008 – 2009
Provided development and analysis of investment reports, valuations, and statements, while ensuring accuracy of daily transaction imports. Performed market analysis of prices on equities, bonds, and derivatives. Created a comprehensive pricing file to maintain inventory of all holdings. Partnered with the Portfolio Management Team in report development.

- Spearheaded initiative to enhance procedures and improve operational efficiency through auditing of performance measurement calculations, client valuations, and system integrity.
- Selected to resolve complex system problems and implement new strategies and solutions, saving the company revenue lost during system outages.
- Reduced subscription cost 10% annually by negotiating prices with supplier on software.
- Key member of team that improved business processes and contributed to development of new application system.

XYZ Financial Services, Anytown   2004 – 2008
A provider of comprehensive financial services, investment management, research and training, and investor services with
£250million assets under custody, £2million under management, £9billion in revenue, and more than 20,000 employees.
Business Reporting Analyst   2006 – 2008
Reported directly to the Senior Director of Investor Services, providing drafting and review of business case, business
requirements, and functional specifications documents. Identified and resolved a variety of issues, ensuring quick resolution
of complex problems. Assisted with defining and reviewing client requirements from a fund accounting and investment
operations perspective.

- Key contributor in completing a comprehensive data conversion to bring in-house recordkeeping for numerous
  banks within Europe. Ensured project was completed on time and in adherence to service obligations.
- Improved overall ability to design effective systems by creating business requirements and functional specifications
  documents.
- Identified discrepancies between legacy presentation and internal system requirements by performing Gap Analysis.

Investment Manager and Custody Associate   2004 – 2006
Selected to provide outstanding support on client settlement inquiries. Reconciled cash and stock, providing reports of
assigned funds to ensure accuracy of accounting records. Communicated with internal and external clients. Provided daily
servicing of multiple funds under management by investment managers and clients. Served as a liaison between clients or
investment managers on management of portfolios, ensuring on-time completion of tasks. Monitored corporate actions,
income and dividend receipt, and overdue payments. Worked on special projects, including international tax reclaims and
user acceptance testing.

- Hand picked as a member of a newly formed team which was created to centralize tasks, including cash and stock
  reconciliation, account opening and closing, client billing, and reporting.
- Recognized for streamlining the completion of tasks by identifying the need and creating solution to reduce invoice
  redundancy and completion time.
- Improved cross-functionality and enhanced staff training by creating comprehensive manual on procedures and
  daily tasks.

——Education & Certification——

BSc Accountancy
University of Anytown

Postgraduate Certificate-Banking and Finance
University of Anytown

Chartered Insurance Professional
Insurance Institute of Canada, Toronto, Canada

Chartered Life Underwriter
The Risk Management Society

Investment Operations Certification
Advanced Certificate in Operational Risk
The Chartered Institute for Securities and Investment, London, England

——Affiliations——

Insurance Institute of Canada, Member

Association of British Insures, Member

11 Any Avenue
Anytown AA0 0AA

Shawn Brandon

Linked in profile
0123456 7890
shawn.brandon@gmail.com

Logistics Management

Performance Summary

Supply Chain Leader with 18 years' experience demonstrating consistent professional growth through achievement in planning and purchasing for global distribution. Demonstrated talent in leading and managing unified teams, ensuring company goals are always achieved. Technically astute, with skills in Kanban, SAP, BAAN, and Microsoft Access. Demonstrated knowledge in lean manufacturing. Experienced with development and execution of enterprise-wide redundancy elimination that increases productivity and improves quality. Strategic planner with well-honed analytic and technical proficiencies; adept in globe-spanning business initiatives and excels in the complex, time-sensitive world of logistics.

Professional Skills

Purchasing	Inventory	Strategic Planning	Worldwide Supply Chain
Lean Manufacturing	Sourcing	Turnkey Solutions	Procedure Development
Project Management	Metrics	Forecasting	Replenishment
Logistics	Life-Cycle Management	Kanban	Re-Order Points (ROP)
MRP/ERP	Negotiations	Procurement	On-Time Delivery (OTD)
SAP	BAAN	Staff Leadership	CILT (UK) Certified

—— Performance Highlights ——

➢ Drove site availability to 98% by establishing daily meetings between Site Manufacturing Managers, Planning group, and Purchasing group.
➢ Reduced expedited expenses more than 60%.
➢ Saved £107,000 in service agreements and system cost.
➢ Key contributor of the upgrade of the Molecular Biology Lab, providing planning and setup of new SAP plant with a very aggressive timeline.

—— Professional Experience ——

XYZ Technologies, Anytown   2014 to Present
Division of Applied Technologies.
Director of Worldwide Planning

Selected to oversee the entire supply chain life cycle. Hired and managed 14 staff members, providing support for Worldwide planning and procurement, instrument master scheduling, indirect procurement, DC Kanban Administration, service logistics call centre, and data maintenance. Directed project initiatives for business process re-engineering and optimization. Led teams on Kaizen events.

• Reduced inventory 30%, totaling more than £9 million in one year.
• Saved £107,000 by initiating early termination of service agreement with Life Tech supply chain.
• Realized £170,000 in annual transportation savings by providing distribution planning changes.
• Increased product availability from 93% to 96%.
• Led the Supply Chain separation of ERP cloning from Applied Technologies without impact on customer service.

ABC Technologies, Othertown   1998 to 2014
Providing instruments and consumables for life sciences.
Senior Manager, Worldwide Planning   2009 to 2014
Senior Manager, Worldwide Spares Planning and Service Logistics   2006 to 2009
Manager of Worldwide Service Logistics and Service Inventory   1998 to 2006

Senior Manager, Worldwide Planning   2009 to 2014

Promoted to provide planning and Worldwide supply chain management within the Consumables Group. Analyzed and resolved complex products. Managed six staff members. Partnered with Product Management and Manufacturing on prioritizing products, providing strategic resolutions to supply issues, and reduction of losses. Used visual reporting tools to create reports. Provided executives with weekly summaries on concerns with the site.

- Assisted in transitioning manufacturing group to an abbreviated time schedule, an £800,000 annual savings.
- Recognized with *Platinum Award* for leading the Supply Chain consolidation to Othertown.
- Reduced turnaround time 50% and eliminated a £400,000 backlog.
- Cut overdue work orders 30% by establishing daily cross-functional meetings.
- Selected by the Director as a replacement before the purchase of Systems.

Senior Manager, Worldwide Spares Planning and Service Logistics   2006 to 2009

Provided life-cycle management of Spares Planning. Oversaw Service Logistics throughout Europe. Directed contingency strategy planning for supplier bankruptcy, which included leading organization discussions with Project Managers, Service Product Management, Finance, Senior Management, and staff to salvage product lines. Represented sites across the globe.

- Saved the company £2 million in inventory by developing alternatives to Lifetime Buys.
- Led an organization-wide programme, saving the company £1 million in revenue.

Manager of Worldwide Service Logistics and Service Inventory   1998 to 2006

Primary liaison for entire supply chain, providing process alignment across the organization and establishing territory boundaries for Europe and APAC. Streamlined process by implementing SOX-compliant Field Service cycle programme, metrics, and self-help tools for Field Engineers. Served as Service Business Operations Manager, driving optimization for 28 staff members in Service Call Centre, Service Administration, and Service Contract Administration functions.

- Reduced aging inventory by £750,000 and priority overnight shipments by 40%, with a total savings of £350,000 per year by designing and implementing self-help tools for Field Service Engineers.
- Served as a key speaker at a Worldwide Service Conference with more than 500 attendees.

Previous experience as *Manager of Worldwide Logistics Service and Senior Logistics Planner at Cyber Technologies | Production Control Manger, Purchasing Supervisor, and Senior Buyer at DEF.*

Volunteer Experience

National Dog Rescue, Anytown   2011 to Present
Animal rescue and adoption centre
Volunteer

Provided implementation and maintenance of a Point-of-Sale Inventory Management System. Created technical documentation of the inventory management processes.

—— Education and Professional Development ——

BSc Economics, University of Anytown

CPIM Certification, APICS/CILT (UK)

JOSE SIERRA

Linked **in** profile

11 Any Avenue, Anytown AA0 0AA 0123456 7890/ jose_sierra@gmail.com

PROCUREMENT / LOGISTICS / MATERIALS MANAGEMENT

7 years of experience within a warehouse operation, as well as prior positions with the Royal Marines. Earned a Bachelor of Science in Business Management. Received "Employee of the Year" award with current employer.

➢ Skilled in communicating and building relationships effectively with both suppliers and partner organizations.
➢ Excellent planning, scheduling, and task management background within challenging environments.
➢ Record of success in improving team performance through training and reducing problems.

PROFESSIONAL SKILLS

❑ Logistics & Transportation	❑ Materials Requirement Planning	❑ Team Building and Leadership
❑ Inventory Management	❑ Cost Reduction and Avoidance	❑ Quality and Safety Assurance
❑ Escalated Problem Resolution	❑ Regulatory Compliance Issues	❑ Process Simplification/Redesign

PROFESSIONAL EXPERIENCE

XYZ Retail Ltd., Anytown   2010–Present
Safety & Security Officer

Ensure highest level of security, safety, and protection within a warehouse operation with over 200 employees. Communicate with internal and external customers, routing calls to the appropriate individuals. Enforce safety guidelines and regulations, documenting all pertinent events and alerting management. Identify accident trends to aid with adjustment of training methods. Report directly to the Security Supervisor.

Selected Accomplishments:

■ **Awarded Employee of the Year, 2017** for overall exemplary performance. Recognized for maintaining 7 years of perfect attendance.

■ **Oversaw zero security incidents** and lost-time accident events through strict adherence to rules and procedures.

■ **Reduced accidents within the division** by reviewing accident reports and adjusting training methods to address critical need areas.

■ **Frequently worked alone as the sale security officer on duty,** earning highest level of trust to complete tasks with zero supervision or follow-up.

Royal Marine Corps   2006–2009
Vehicle Director/Commander

Promoted to supervise team of 16–20 in day-to-day activities, with group including Light-Armoured Vehicle Drivers and Gunners. Delivered training on safety, weapons, and tactics. Evaluated team members to determine combat readiness.

Selected Accomplishments:

■ **Trained unit that had the highest proficiency scores** In the entire company (measured by Light-Armoured Gunnery Skills Test scores), as well as ranking as the most physically fit unit company wide.

■ **Initiated new training methods and improved existing ones** to strengthen team capabilities in core areas.

PROFESSIONAL DEVELOPMENT

B.Sc. in Business/Organizational Management, 2010: University of Othertown
Diploma: Science in General Education: Anytown Community College

Tina Turner

11 Any Avenue, Anytown AA0 0AA   0123456 7890   tturner@anyisp.com

Meeting Planner
Conferences · Events · Fundraising · Golf Tournaments

PERFORMANCE PROFILE

14 years' experience in all aspects of event planning, development, and management. Multi-task with strong detail, problem-solving and follow-through capabilities. Demonstrated ability to manage, motivate, and build cohesive teams that achieve results.

PROFESSIONAL SKILLS

- Event management
- Conferences & Meetings
- Logistics
- Database Management
- Team Management
- Budgets
- Excel
- MS Project

- PACs
- Special Events
- Meetings & Workshops
- High-Net Donors
- Planning/Organization
- Negotiations
- PowerPoint
- Publisher

- Associations
- Fundraisers
- Tours & Competitions
- Supplier Management
- Contracts
- Access
- Outlook
- MeetingTrak

PERFORMANCE HIGHLIGHTS!

Planned and coordinated government, association, and private conferences, meetings, events, and fundraisers: all conference activities, workshops, meetings, tours, and special events. **Saved £72,000 on most recent meeting.**

Meeting Coordination

Negotiated hotel and supplier contracts. Prepared and administered budgets. Arranged all on-site logistics, including transportation, accommodations, meals, guest speakers, and audiovisual support.

- Coordinated 18 annual workshops for Public Health England.
- Coordinated 2004 National Conference on Smoking and Health (2,000 participants).
- Organized 6,000-participant national annual conferences.
- Coordinated Global Scholarship Pre-Conference Training.
- Developed and supervised education sessions at XYZ's 2001 National Convention.
- Directed XYZ's National Seminar Series.
- Developed, promoted, and implemented XYZ's National Certification Programme
- Managed logistics for a Regional Training programme in Brussels.

Fundraising

Coordinated fundraising events. Supervised major-donor relationships. Team player in the development and implementation of membership and retention programmes.

- Coordinated 2 golf tournaments
- Spouse programmes
- Parties

Continued

| Tina Turner | 0123456 7890 | tturner@anyisp.com | Page 2 |

EVENTS MANAGEMENT HIGHLIGHTS

- Public Health England : Action on Smoking & Health
- Tobacco Control Training & Technical Assistance Project
- Department of Health: Children, Youth and Families
- Medicines and Healthcare products Regulation Agency
- National Centre for Health Statistics
- British Medical Association
- Housing & Urban Development
- XYZ National Seminar Series
- XYZ 1998 & 1999 National Conventions

PROFESSIONAL EXPERIENCE

XYZ Events ■ Anytown   2013–Present
Senior Conference Specialist
■ ABC, Anytown   2008–2013
Senior Conference Coordinator
CONSTRUCTION ASSOCIATION ■ Othertown   2003–2008
Coordinator of Education Programmes
NATIONAL ASSOCIATION OF WELDERS ■ Othertown   2001–2003
Assistant Coordinator of Education Programmes

EDUCATION

Othertown University
BSc Exercise Physiology   2001

Diploma in Fundraising - Institute of Fundraising ■ 2015
Event Management Diploma ■ 2007

Professional Affiliations
Member : Institute of Fundraising

Blake Neal

11 Any Avenue
Anytown AA0 0AA

Linked in profile

0123456 7890
blake.neal@gmail.com

Merchandiser

PERFORMANCE PROFILE

Results-driven merchandiser with 3 years' experience in major metropolitan market, gained while working full-time. Provides organizational support to the merchandising team using organizational and analytical skills, while keeping up with current industry trends to support brands and achieve financial goals. Experienced in sales events and product placement to promote merchandise. Committed to learning and continuous development. BA of Fashion Technology.

- Demonstrates communication, interpersonal, planning, problem-solving, and coordinating skills.
- Teams with internal departments to develop product lines.
- Detail-orientated, flexible, fast learner with multifunctional skills.
- Ability to work independently and within team-based environments.
- Proficient at producing weekly and monthly sales reports and formulating conclusions.
- Ability to work with the different roles of cross-functional teams and understand how they relate to the merchandising role.
- Strong financial skills and business acumen.
- Excellent verbal and writing skills, organizational skills, and the ability to multitask and prioritize multiple projects in deadline-driven environments.
- Strong PC knowledge, specifically Excel.

PROFESSIONAL SKILLS

*Merchandising & Retail	*Financial Research & Analysis	*Sample Quality Control
*Business Recommendations	*Sample Administration	*In-Store Visits
*Updates Stock & Weekly Sales Reports	*Buying Trends Analysis	*Special Projects
*Monitors Deliveries and Samples	*Coordinates Flow of Merchandise	*Database Management
*Merchandising Technical Skills	*Best Practices	*Microsoft Excel
*Purchase Orders & Reorders	*Sales, Margins, & Inventory Analysis	*Budget Management

PROFESSIONAL EXPERIENCE

ABC Ltd., Anytown   2013– Present
Merchandiser
ABC stores have been operating in Anytown since 1952 and rank among the top 5 men's retail stores in the UK. Selected to perform merchandising tasks including: line planning, creating and updating sales inventory reports, sales performance, margin, markdown analysis, and mannequin placement.
Managed store communications and coordinated with vendors for ITEM masters, deliveries, and samples.
Responsible for setting up new items in company database.

- Managed merchandise selection and buying for the largest scarf sales event of the year in coordination with buyer, resulting in 110% of target sales for 2015 promotions.

(continued)

- Assisted buyer in merchandise selection, maintenance, and distribution of purchase orders, and managed OTB with planning team to ensure smooth execution of sales events.
- Conducted in-store visits to ensure the implementation and execution of seasonal plans.
- Successfully revamped scarf category in the accessory department, introduced new product sub-categories, built supplier relationships, redesigned floor plans, and increased visibilityof accessory categories, resulting in a significant increase in sales.
- Worked with suppliers on tight timelines, resulting in successful fill rate at new store openings.
- Revamped accessory category and introduced new products to fit customer purchasing trends, resulting in increased sales.

XYZ Events Management, Anytown   2012–2013
Event Coordinator

XYZ Events Management focuses on events, retail, grooming, and image management. Selected to manage business development of new personality development programmes. Managed market research, parent interviews, and business plan preparation, resulting in management approval to launch new programme.

- Developed and managed relationships with strategic business alliances including retailers, and established brand with marketing partners.
- Developed new cross-business products and launched service enhancements to ensure a scalable and sustainable business model.
- Created business plans and managed launch of new products by supervising a team of sales and operations executives, resulting in the highest earning potential within one year.
- Launched new service enhancements, providing opportunities for cross-selling and developing existing infrastructure, resulting in doubling of revenue earnings.
- Coordinated events to collect target data, resulting in creation of new source of data to reach targeted customer base.
- Managed BTL to ensure increased participation during children's painting exhibition event. Resulted in establishment of XYZ's credibility in creating and managing events for children.

EDUCATION

Anytown University   2012
BA Fashion Technology
Awarded Best Innovative Project for 2012 Graduation Project

- Received coverage by national newspaper,
- Graduation Project Details: Designed 3 season washable silk scarves for men

Superior reference available

Walter Stuempfig

11 Any Avenue., Anytown AA0 0AA   0123456 7890   wstuempfig@anyisp.com

---

MULTIMEDIA MANAGEMENT

Multimedia Communications & Production ♦ MIS Management
A combination of technology management and creative multimedia skills.

Performance Review
Uniquely qualified management professional for a digital media technical production position with a distinctive blend of hands-on technical, project management, and multimedia communications experience. Offers a skill set that spans interactive digital technologies, broadcast, radio, and print media.

Proven leader with a strength for identifying talent, building and motivating creative teams that work cooperatively to achieve goals. Highly articulate with excellent interpersonal skills and a sincere passion for blending communications with technology.

MIS Capabilities

• Systems Management	• Needs Analysis	• Strategic Planning
• Systems Configuration	• System Testing	• Systems Upgrades
• P&L	• Budgets	• Project Management
• Supplier Management	• LAN/WAN	• Telecom Integration
• Multimedia	• Network Security	• Workflow Applications
• Technology Acquisition	• System Maintenance	• Technology Integration
• Resource Planning	• Recruitment & Selection	• Performance Reviews

Multimedia Management Capabilities

• Multimedia	• Television	• Radio
• Account Management	• Client Relations	• Market Research
• Multimedia Production	• Creative Design	• Multimedia Communications
• Communications	• Cross-Functional Teams	• Multimedia Presentations
• Photographers	• Videographers	• Copywriters
• Scriptwriters	• Graphic Designers	• Artists
• Musicians	• Talent	• Animators

PROFESSIONAL EXPERIENCE

ABC Ltd., Anytown	2004–Present
DIRECTOR OF MIS	2014–Present
ASSISTANT DIRECTOR OF IT/ COMMUNICATIONS	2012–2014
CORPORATE COMMUNICATIONS OFFICER	2008–2012
ASSOCIATE	2004–2008

Advanced rapidly through series of increasingly responsible positions with UK division of European investment group. Initially hired to manage market research projects, advanced to plan and execute corporate communications projects, and in 2014, assumed responsibility for spearheading the introduction of emerging technologies to automate the entire company.

Current scope of responsibility is expansive and focuses on strategic planning, implementation, and administration of all information systems and technology. Lead technical staff members, manage budgets, select and oversee Suppliers define business requirements, and produce deliverables through formal project plans.

Manage systems configuration and maintenance, troubleshoot problems, plan and direct upgrades, and test operations to ensure optimum systems functionality and availability.

Continued

Walter Stuempfig   0123456 7890   wstuempfig@anyisp.com   Page 2

Technical Contributions

- Pioneered the company's computerization from the ground floor; led the installation and integration of a state-of-the-art and highly secure network involving 50+ workstations running on 6 LANs interconnected by V-LAN switching technology.
- Defined requirements; planned and accelerated the implementation of advanced technology solutions, deployed on a calculated timeframe, to meet the short- and long-term needs of the organization.
- Orchestrated the introduction of sophisticated applications and multimedia technology to streamline workflow processes, expand presentation capabilities, and keep pace with the competition.
- Administered the life cycle of multiple projects from initial systems/network planning and technology acquisition through installation, training, and operation. Saved hundreds of thousands in consulting fees by managing IS and telecommunication issues in-house.

Business Contributions

- Created and produced high-impact multimedia presentations to communicate the value and benefits of individual investment projects to top-level company executives. Tailored presentations to appeal to highly sophisticated, multicultural audiences.
- Assembled and directed exceptionally well-qualified project teams from diverse creative disciplines; collaborated with and guided photographers, videographers, copywriters, scriptwriters, graphic designers, and artists to produce innovative presentations and special events.
- Performed market research and analyses to determine risks and feasibility of multiple investment projects valued at up to £150 million. Developed and recommended tactical plans to transform vision into achievement.

XYZ Advertising Anytown   1996–2004

DIRECTOR OF ADVERTISING

DEF Advertising, Anytown   1994–1996

ADVERTISING ACCOUNT EXECUTIVE

GHI Communications, othertown   1992–1994

PRODUCER

Early career involved a series of progressive creative and account management positions spanning all advertising mediums: multimedia, television, radio, and print. Worked directly with clients to assess complex and often obscure needs; conceptualized and developed advertising campaigns to communicate the desired message in an influential manner.

Achievement Highlights

- Designed, wrote, produced, and launched advertising campaigns that consistently gave clients a competitive distinction. Developed a reputation for ability to intuit and interpret clients' desires and produce campaigns that achieved results.
- Recruited and led creative teams consisting of graphic designers, artists, musicians, cartoonists, animators, videographers, photographers, and other freelancers and third-party creative services to develop and produce multimillion-pound advertising campaigns.

EDUCATION & TRAINING

BSc Broadcast Production, Anytown university
Continuing education in Marketing Research and Broadcast Production
School of Visual Arts, Anytown

Arshile Gorky

11 Any Avenue
Anytown AA0 0AA

Mobile: 0123456 7890
Home: 01234 567890

agorky@anyisp.com

Operations Management
Operations/ Project Management • Staff Training & Management • Safety Initiatives

Performance Profile
2 years experience in water park operations with a broad range of business, organizational, and interpersonal skills. Natural leader, able to develop strong, easy working relationships with management, staff, and the general public to ensure positive, high-quality guest experiences.

Professional Skills
• Outstanding track record of strategic contributions in visioning, planning, strategizing, and accomplishment of a range of business-related initiatives, with significant success in developing emerging concepts into full-fledged, high-performance realities.
Offer a valuable blend of leadership, creative, and analytical abilities that combine efficiency with imagination to produce results. Proven success in planning, directing, and coordinating staff activities to maximize cost options.

Professional Experience

XYZ Ltd., Anytown

Assistant to the Operations Manager
Recruited, following a productive four-month lifeguard internship, to contribute to the ongoing success of this popular water park attraction. Performed a variety of management-level functions and team-building training for staff, and developed key organizational systems to standardize strategic functions.

• Spearheaded, developed, created, and implemented a Water Park Evacuation Operations Report, coordinating all strategic safety and evacuation information.

Lifeguard Internship
Served as one of 8 lifeguards at water park.
Patrolled recreational areas on foot or from lifeguard stands. Rescued distressed people using rescue techniques and equipment. Contacted emergency medical personnel in case of serious injuries.
Key Contributions:

• Saved several lives in backboard and other types of rescues and resuscitations.
• Received many commendations for performance above and beyond the call of duty.

Education

BA, Business Administration

Marquis White

11 Any Avenue, Anytown AA0 0AA
01234 567890 m.white@gmail.com

Linked **in** profile

Paralegal

Performance Profile

Highly organized paralegal known to uphold ethical standards of the legal profession, exercising discretion and maintaining a high level of confidentiality. Proven ability to thrive in a fast-paced environment through advanced multitasking skills.

Professional Skills

- Self-starter with the ability to work independently in all aspects of litigation. Works well under pressure.
- Strong interpersonal skills with the ability to communicate effectively with all levels of employees, executives, outside counsel, and state agencies.
- Demonstrated success in problem-solving skills dealing with complex, ambiguous situations with diplomacy and tact.
- Highly organized with strong attention to detail and the ability to work effectively with tight deadlines.
- Outstanding research, writing, and proofreading skills.
- Proficient in Microsoft Office, Excel, PowerPoint, Outlook, LEXIS/NEXIS, Lender Processing Services (LPS), and Team Connect.
- Strong knowledge of legal terminology, legal documents, practices, and procedures.

Areas of Expertise

Research and Analytical Skills – Legal Document Preparation – Reasoning and Deductive Skills – Self-Motivated – Detail Orientated – Multitasker – Editing/Grammar – Technology – Sound Judgment and Logic – Ability to Meet Deadlines – Accuracy – Problem-Solving Skills–Dependable – Flexible

Professional Experience

AB & C Anytown   2014–Present
Litigation Paralegal
Creditors' rights law firm with cases nationwide. Litigation practicehandlingsecured transactions, fraud, contract law, real estate transactions, debt collection, and commercial and residential leases. All legal work at the appellate level is handled by the litigation department. Selected to reorganize the firm's litigation department.

- Promoted to paralegal for lead litigation counsel.
- Successfully increase client satisfaction with the progress of litigation files resulting in additional referrals and new business.
- Assist with marketing and setting up new clients by drafting client bulletins and assembling materials for potential new clients.
- Manage and execute the progression of litigation casework to yield the best outcomes for clients.
- Draft and prepare legal pleadings, motions, briefs, discovery, affidavits, and settlement agreements.
- Maintain complex docket schedule. Make travel arrangements and schedules to ensure all parties are available when needed for conferences, court appearances, and depositions.
- Trial and deposition preparation including examination and preparation of evidence.
- Manage hourly billing approval, invoicing, and auditing litigation files with little supervision.

(continued)

XY & Z, othertown   2011–2014
Litigation Paralegal
Creditors' rights firm handling foreclosure/bankruptcy/loss mitigation, and eviction cases. Highly ranked law firm Member of the Mortgage Bankers Association and Legal Financial Network. Hired as entry-level paralegal to be trained for complex litigation work.

- Sole paralegal at the firm to successfully manage large volumes of discovery work for the firm's litigation cases.
- Assigned to complex litigation sub-team (consisting of head litigation counsel and senior litigation paralegal) after only one year of employment with the firm.
- Ensured legal documents were processed in a timely manner to comply with deadlines.
- Composed and revised legal documents for attorneys including general correspondence and court filings.
- Effectively drafted and responded to interrogatories, requests for production, and requests for admissions.
- Adeptly scheduled appointments and conferences.
- Skillfully performed as a liaison to ensure timely and full communication.
- Productively drafted complaints, answers, motions, briefs, oppositions, and replies.

Education

Diploma in Paralegal Studies   2010
NALP Approved Programme

- **Relevant Coursework:** Legal Research and Writing, Principles and Practice of Litigation, Applied Legal Research and Litigation, Family Law, Estate Law, Tort Law, Intellectual Property Law, Civil Law and Procedure, Criminal Law, Administrative Law, and Contract Law.
- NALP Licence to practice

Internships

Member of the National Association of Licenced Paralegals.

Anneke Tso

11 Any Avenue
Anytown AA0 0AA

Mobile : 0123456 7890

atso@anyisp.com

Director of Recruitment

I offer process development, service delivery, and enhanced profits.

Performance Profile

Talented and forward-thinking senior recruitment leader with proven track record of success turning around company performance by distilling and managing processes, enhancing organizational structure, and developing skilled self-managed teams.

The "go-to" person for diverse organizational and process-related challenges. Confident and passionate individual with a mission to create best in class recruiting departments through comprehensive use of marketing tools and cutting-edge sales practices.

Professional Skills

Project Implementation	Sales and Marketing	Onboarding/Referral Programmes
Process Reengineering	Recruitment Metrics	Role Competency Design
Training and Development	Financial Analysis	Workforce Planning
Turnaround	Sourcing Channels	Strategic Planning
Disbursed Management	Advertising	Proposal Generation
CRM	Performance Metrics	Tracking Systems
Strategic Planning	EOC compliance	Contracts

Professional Experience

A & E Ltd., *Anytown*   2014 to Present
Leader in Recruitment Process Outsourcing
Recruitment Manager

Sourcing strategies to support the strategic, operational, and business plan for the company. Influence senior business executives on strategy, resources, hiring forecasts, and capacity planning. Establish and oversee maintenance of effective candidate sourcing channels and both internal and external CV-tracking systems to speed the process of identifying qualified applicants and tracking effectiveness and efficiency metrics.

- Assist with proposal generation, implementation, training, and daily oversight of key account service delivery teams, overall delivery of key account results, and the management and nurturing of client relationships to deliver the highest caliber client results.
- Provide feedback to management and clients regarding workload and accomplishments, ensuring accuracy of data and thorough completion of assignments.

X & Y CONSTRUCTION, Ltd., *Anytown*   2010 to 2014
Top 100 Design/Builders in the UK
Recruitment Manager

230-person recruiting function. Report directly to CEO. Provided strategic direction and tactical follow-up on all levels of recruitment process re-design.
- Managed the internship programme and volunteered to represent student construction organizations establishing a future flow of qualified construction management graduates.
- Improved the applicant experience by instituting full life-cycle recruiting to the company.
- Spearheaded company-wide skills matrix to aid in succession planning and resource management.
- Partnered with IT to create and launch career site.
- Orchestrated a comprehensive employee retention process overhaul.
- Established a 30-60-90 new employee review process, introduced menter system and re-engineered new hire employee orientation procedures, reducing communication breakdowns and ensuring employees' complete preparedness for first day of employment.

DEF AIR, *Othertown*   2002 to 2010
A low-cost airline
Recruitment Manager

Hired to develop and implement recruiting function for a start-up airline to support 2,000 employees. Assisted with the creation and management of a £1M advertising budget. Presented detailed and comprehensive reports and analyses on staffing metrics including attrition, programme results, time-to-fill, and recruiter performance.
- Exceeded 2004-headcount targets by 20%, employing 2,000 external and 500 internal employees.
- Board approval for the implementation of an applicant microsite, which significantly increased the performance of the baggage handler screening process.
- Rebuilt recruitment & selection cycle with EOC regulations.
- Conducted quarterly internal audits to ensure compliance.
- Created a robust Employee Referral Programme (ERP) that propelled referrals to 13% resulting in lower cost-per-hire for hourly airport employees.
- Implemented behavioural interviewing with recurrent training for managers.

GHI RECRUITMENT   1996 to 2002
Global staffing company
Technology Recruiter

Juan Hernandez

11 Any Avenue., Anytown AA0 0AA   juan.h@gmail.com   in View my profile   0123456 7890

Regulatory Change Management

Performance Profile

Regulatory Change Agent with seven years of experience in Line of Business Mortgage Servicing and Escrow Services at XYZ's corporate headquarters, providing project management, technical writing, and escrow records management for a total portfolio valued in excess of £300 million.

Professional Skills

Diversified Financial Services	Operations Excellence	Strategic Planning & Project Mgmt.
Company & Industry Research	Lean Six Sigma (DMAIC & 5S)	Change Management
Business Analysis	Technical Writing & Communications	Stakeholder Management
Business Performance Metrics	Business Policies & Procedures	Impact Assessment
Portfolio Management	Process Design & Improvement	Problem Identification & Resolution
Escrow Services & Recordkeeping	Productivity Optimization	Exceptional Customer Service
Federal & State Mortgage Regulations	Workflow Analysis	Leadership & Team Building
Regulatory Change & Compliance	Job Roles & Organizational Structure	Training Design & Facilitation

Computer Skills

DAPTIV, MSP, SharePoint, Visio, Minitab, Quality Companion, Banking Mainframe, XNET, Client Product Implementations through BPM Portal, Agiletics Escrow Software, Escrow PINNACLE web module, People Soft Finance Work Bench, Microsoft Office: Advanced Excel, Word, PowerPoint

Performance Highlights

➢ Business Process Analyst who has led 140+ change initiatives in the past two years, which resulted in highly effective business processes/procedures and operations/technology improvements in mortgage servicing practices.

➢ Change Agent skilled in evaluating effects of federal/state banking and mortgage servicing regulations on operations performance; translating the magnitude and type of change required; and offering pragmatic, actionable recommendations to assure regulatory compliance.

➢ Group Leader who collaborates with Technical Writing Team to create project deliverables such as project descriptions, project timelines, communication plans, mitigation plans, risk assessments, post implementation support plans, etc. Able to remain calm under pressure and produce high-quality written documents/reports under extremely tight deadlines.

Professional Experience

XYZ Bank, Anytown   2008 to Present
Senior Mortgage Adviser   2012 to Present

Report directly to Assistant Director. Serveas a liaison between Compliance, Legal, and Risk to proactively manage change in the business unit. Lead projects involving investor/insurer, regulatory changes, and mortgage servicing processes.

• Review and analyze internal and external regulatory reports. Evaluate the potential impact of regulatory, compliance, and financial decisions. Make recommendations to management for planning and decision-making purposes to ensure compliance with changes to applicable regulations. Deliver the change effort; define the scope; monitor the progress; and create communications to ensure effective implementation and measure adoption.

• Coordinate and conduct annual review of policy/procedure analyses with assigned lines of business. Collaborate with department leaders to address gaps in processes and provide updates to investor/insurer and regulatory announcements.

• Provide action plan tracking and status reporting to management and partners. Confirm that changes are communicated effectively and that employees affected by change are receiving the necessary training.

• Delegate and manage 1–5+ supporting technical writers' workloads on larger writing initiatives, which requires time management and multitasking. Review documents to ensure adherence to mortgage servicing and corporate style guides. Maintain project documents on Daptiv and SharePoint.

• Create functional requirements documents and analyze impacts for investor/insurer and regulatory changes.

Selected Accomplishments:
- – Led 150+ change initiatives in the past two years.
- – Authored 90+ technical documents including policies/procedures and reference guides.
- – Maintain over 100 policies/procedures and reference documents for assigned lines of business on SharePoint system.

Team Leader, Escrow Services Group   2010 to 2012
- Oversaw records management for total portfolio valued at £300 million.
- Led a customer service group that provided customer support for multiple escrow products (e.g., landlords, solicitors, property owners, and pre-needs clients).
- Conducted weekly team meetings, oversaw production team and project management team. Monitored productivity, coached production team in daily work and new procedures, resolved errors and/or problems, collected and compiled data for middle and senior managers.

Selected Accomplishments:
- – Lean Six Sigma Green Belt Project. Implemented DMAIC (which stands for define, measure, analyze, improve, and control) to reduce impact of Escrow Services interest check process on Escheat Department's volume by 30% and reduced Escrow process cycle time, which increased production capacity by 52%, taking it from 48% to 100%.

Customer Service Representative   2008 to 2010
- Processed clients' deposits and withdrawals. Monitored transactions for accuracy. Resolved discrepancies.
- Handled client calls and managed book of business for clients' web accounts.
- Processed client forms and participated in manual month-end statement preparation and mailings.
- Handled returned mail such as interest statements.
- Performed research and implemented process improvement projects.

Selected Accomplishments:
- – **Escrow Services Archive Project (2010)**–Implemented Lean Six Sigma 5S (which stands for sort, set in order, shine, standardize, and systematize). Decreased the number of filing cabinets needed in the department from 11 to 8, streamlining recordkeeping and making it easier to access client files.
- – **Escrow Services Archive Project (2008)**–Implemented Lean Six Sigma 5S to decrease the types of documents stored in filing cabinets to daily work files. All other files are now stored electronically, increasing the speed in locating client files.

Education
Certificate in Mortgage Advice and Practice (CeMAP)

MA in Music Performance University of Anytown
BA Music Education University of Anytown

Certifications / Professional Development
Mortgage Servicing Certification, 2016
Certified Lean Six Sigma Green Belt, 2015
Enhancing Leadership Presence, 2014
Efficient Business Communications, 2013
Leadership Communications Essentials, 2012
Certified Lean Six Sigma Yellow Belt, 2011

Excellent Business References Available Upon Request

JAMES MARTIN

11 Any Ave., Anytown AA0 0AA

 View my profile | 01234 567890 | james.martin@anyisp.com

SENIOR REGULATORY COMPLIANCE

11+ years of compliance experience in banking capital markets, brokerage and investment firms, and insurance sector, ensuring strict adherence to legal and financial regulations to alleviate risk exposure, facilitate smooth audits, and enable company profitability. Adept at maintaining overview of company operations to monitor, investigate, and ensure fulfillment of regulatory obligations and alignment of compliance policies. Advise key decision makers on regulatory and compliance requirements to aid in development of strategic solutions that support new programmes.

Registered investment adviser whose wide-ranging expertise spans the Financial Services and Market Act, Commodity Futures Trading Commission/National Futures Association Municipal Securities Financial Conduct Authority, European Banking Authority, EU Regulatory Reform and the Financial Policy Committee

PROFESSIONAL SKILLS

Regulatory Compliance	Staff Development	Anti-money Laundering (AML)
Legal Analysis	Team Leadership	Customer Due Diligence
Risk Assessments	Account Surveillance	Training & Development
Controls	Mediations/Arbitrations	
Negotiations	Performance Management	
Due Diligence	Fiduciary Responsibility	

PERFORMANCE HIGHLIGHTS

- Played pivotal role in alleviating AML concerns through automation of new international account forms,
- Thwarted reputational and financial damage of firm by uncovering and remediating adverse practices among select financial advisors via conducting surveillance on personal trading and researching patterns.
- Increased volume of licensed support staff through implementation of Series 7 training programme as well as raised number of certifications held by financial advisors by offering incentives and training programme for office staff.

PROFESSIONAL EXPERIENCE

ABC Bank | Anytown   2007 – Present
Regulatory Compliance Manager   2012 – Present
Appointed to ensure branch adherence to internal and regulatory agency requirements as well as to provide guidance on trading strategy policies, including options, commodities, derivatives, and structured investments. Monitored office activities, from trading to complaint resolution, liaising with senior compliance executives.

continued

- Spearheaded smooth transition of million-pound wealth management teams from competition to ABC platform.
- Bolstered office productivity by analyzing product profitability, helping financial advisors better understand products to increase their payout.
- Championed 1st successful internal audit with no significant findings, examining recordkeeping, trade tickets, correspondence, structured investments, trading activity, and client activity to ensure compliance.
- Fostered numerous strategic business relationships, forging alliance between Anytown College of Education and branch office for summer intern programme as well as proposing partnership between XYZ Bank and Financial Advisers

Financial Adviser   2007 – 2012
Managed portfolios for more than 100 clients, facilitating financial seminars and providing financial planning expertise for individual, institutional, and nonprofit clients.

EARLIER CAREER

Bank of othertown | **Compliance/Quality Control Manager**   2005 – 2007

EDUCATION

BA Business Administration: University of Anytown
Law Coursework (18 months): University of Anytown

PROFESSIONAL LICENSES

- ICA Professional postgraduate Diploma in Governanace, Risk &Compliance

- ICA Professional postgraduate Diploma in Financial Crime Compliance

PROFESSIONAL AFFILIATION

India Exports, Ltd., Executive Assistant to Executive Director, Mentor

Superior references available upon request

ANN JOHANSEN

01234 567890 • A._Johansen@anyisp.com • 11 Any Ave., Anytown AA0 0AA

CHEMICAL ENGINEER

Performance Summary

Entry-level chemical engineer seeking to combine advanced coursework and hands-on experience in waste/water treatment into a challenging career solving practical problems and contributing to useful products within the oil and gas industry. Big-picture thinker who maintains the ability to analyze and troubleshoot the smallest aspect of raw ingredients, processes, and other external forces to identify problems and improve output. Thorough understanding of laboratory operations and active contributor to improving daily operations. A determined problem solver with a strong commitment to success, an obsessive desire to produce quality work, and a need for self-improvement.

➢ Readily uses spreadsheets, industry-standard software, and other tools to identify efficient processes, optimize unit operation, and determine how changes in input will affect output.
➢ Demonstrated capability of translating theories learned in class such as troubleshooting equipment, costing personnel resources, and process design into "real world" application.
➢ Actively pursues additional knowledge of environmental field and regulations, from technical and practical perspectives.
➢ Willing to relocate—willing to travel.

PROFESSIONAL SKILLS & ABILITIES

Laboratory Operations	Process Flow Diagram	Continuous Improvement	Problem Solving
Regulatory Compliance	Automatic Process Control	Input & Product Costing	Project Management
Quantitative Analysis	Process Design & Modeling	Data Analysis	Engineering Reports

PROFESSIONAL EXPERIENCE

Anytown water, Anytown   2015–Present
Employed at wastewater treatment plant handling 11M gallons of wastewater daily and serving a population of 72K people.

LAB TECHNICIAN

Collect water samples from 3 waste/water treatment plants in the city and conduct tests to ensure exit streams comply with limits set by DOE. Tests include total suspended solids (TSS), mixed liquor suspended solids (MLSS), total solids (TS), fecal coliform, ammonia nitrogen, biochemical oxygen demand (BOD), settability, carbonaceous biochemical oxygen demand (CBOD), pH, dissolved oxygen (DO), and total residual chlorine (TRC). Perform grease trap inspections at local businesses and record waste transported to disposers. Responsible for calibrating equipment in waste/water laboratory on a regular basis, primarily pH and DO meters.

▪ Enhanced future data access by compiling laboratory test results during several months and storing them in a shared computer.
▪ Added an additional level of confidence to laboratory testing by creating spreadsheets for waste/water test calculations.
▪ Optimized time and resource use by collaborating with supervisor and co-workers to prioritize and efficiently divide activities.
▪ Regularly conducted discharge monitoring report quality assurance (DMRQA) tests to ensure quality of laboratory testing methods.

EDUCATION & PROFESSIONAL ACTIVITIES

University of Anytown
▪ BSc ENGINEERING, CONCENTRATION IN CHEMICAL ENGINEERING
   Senior Project: Add pre-acidulation step to process of manufacturing tall oil soap at Paper Mill.
   — *Team determined that adding carbon dioxide in a pre-acidulation step would lower pH of tall oil before being sent to sulfuric acid reactor and reduce amount of system sulfates.*
   — *Created Levenspiel plot to illustrate reactor size required for task and material reactor should be made of.*
   — *Utilized Stokes' Law to determine dimensions of settling tanks in the process.*

Certifications
▪ Waste Water Treatment Operations

Technical Skills
▪ Windows Operating Environments, Honeywell OS, Pro II, Simulink, MATLAB, LinkoFOG, Microsoft (Word, Excel, PowerPoint)

Trevor Dixon

11 Any Avenue
Anytown AA0 0AA

0123456 7890
trevor.designs@gmail.com

Entry-Level Fashion Design Assistant

PERFORMANCE SUMMARY

Multilingual, multicultural professional with background in organizational management and design-manufacturing-to-market cycle. Excellent listening and communication skills, backed with the academic rigour of both visual arts and business degrees. Consistent track record of anticipating needs and preferences. Fluent English, French, and German and a strong desire to grow in the Fashion Industry.

- Highly organized, proactive, and detail orientated with the ability to multitask without losing focus.
- Ability to work in fast-paced, collaborative environments with critical deadlines.
- Strong interpersonal skills with the ability to work both independently and in team environments.
- Capable of thnking on my feet and have a strong sense of urgency.
- Excellent communication (written and verbal), interpersonal, presentational, and follow-up skills.
- Software Applications: Microsoft Suite (Excel, Word, PowerPoint, Outlook) and InDesign.

PROFESSIONAL SKILLS

Exceptional Client Satisfaction	Client Hosting	Fashion News & Trends
Administrative Skills	InDesign	Social Networking
Scheduling	Data Entry	Multilingual
Organizational Management	Visual Design	File & Record Management
Fabric Selection	Travel Arrangements & Logistics	Multicultural
Tailoring & Clothing Design	Performance Improvements	Vendor Negotiations
Project Management	Financial Planning/Budget Management	Merchandise Sourcing
Marketing Captions/Headlines	Strong Market Research Abilities	Contract Creation/Execution

PROFESSIONAL EXPERIENCE

XYZ, Rome, Italy   2015–Present
Designer, PR and Marketing Manager
Selected to provide initial watch design for female line; sketched and graphically designed. Direct creation of prototype including collaborating with engineers, orchestrating final product development, negotiating budgets with CEO and cngineers, and serving as liaison for translations from French to German. Promoted for successful track record of positioning start-up company as an industry leader and solid investment partner.

- CEO approved designs; negotiations with materials suppliers and engineers are in process.
- Helped consolidate slogan "Accessorize Me" for a line of scarves to maintain the company as an industry leader in luxury accessories.

ABC Ltd., Brooklyn, NY   2013–2015
Assistant to Print Management Consultant
Local full-service printing firm, specializing in delivering high-quality printing services at wholesale prices. Volunteered for position to start a career in the USA. Responsible for computer work, updated client list, designed layouts, scheduled client appointments, vendor communications, logistics, and coordinated deliveries to clients. Met clients to discuss marketing material design options.

- Successfully promoted full line of print management services to potential clients.

(continued)

(continued)
- Expedited order placement and product delivery to prevent downtime.
- Generated new business through networking.
- Turned a request for wedding invitation cards into a complete wedding-logo printing package, generating increased revenue for the company.

EDUCATION

Anytown College of Art & Design   2015
MA, Fine Arts

Anytown University   2012
BSc. Business Administration

PROFESSIONAL DEVELOPMENT

Life and Art   2012
Sponsoring Organization:Museum of Fine Arts

Marketing HNW Individuals   2010
Sponsoring Organization: Anytown College

JAKE COHEN

11 Any Ave., ♦ Anytown AA0 0AA   ♦ 0123456 7890 ♦ jake.cohen@outlook.com

ACCOUNT MANAGER
PERFORMANCE PROFILE

Entry-level, high-potential self-starter conversant with client-needs strategies and professional work experience in Sales. Collaborates effectively across all professional levels to build relationships and generate sales. Uses consultative solutions-selling techniques by creating value-orientated presentations based on client knowledge coupled with in-depth product understanding and natural rapport-building skills that foster enduring customer relationships. Technology adept.

PROFESSIONAL SKILLS

♦ Account Prospecting	♦ Marketing Plan Development	♦ Social Media
♦ Problem Resolution	♦ Relationship Building	♦ Product Knowledge
♦ Customer Service	♦ Presentation	♦ Goal Achievement
♦ Sales Strategy & Support	♦ Survey Analysis	♦ Negotiation
♦ Communication	♦ Market Research	♦ Leadership

EDUCATION

BA, Communication, Organizational & Marketing Communication   2016

PROFESSIONAL EXPERIENCE

ABC Insurance Group, Anytown   May–August 2016
Marketing & Business Development Specialist Internship
ABC Insurance is a specialty property and casualty insurance company with a niche orientation and focus on the transportation industry.
♦ Charged with managing an agency base to grow product lines, renew existing accounts, and add new business. Proactively prospected for new accounts with agents and clients.
♦ As collaborative partner, forged and nurtured new client relationships.

DEF, Anytown   January–May 2015
Sales & Marketing Internship
DEF is a leading manufacturer and distributor of sustainably resourced natural products for the consumer, professional, commercial, and construction markets.
♦ Successfully managed territory of customers through daily communication and order execution.
♦ Built and maintained relationships with key accounts via interpersonal relationship selling.
♦ Made sales calls to new business prospects, which led to increased sales.

JKL Ltd., Anytown   May–August 2014
Sales & Marketing Internship
JKL Ltd. is a full-line £300M per year steel service centre.
♦ Communicated daily with customers to generate sales and build lasting relationships.
♦ Developed and implemented sales strategies aimed at revenue growth.
♦ Processed steel orders and followed through with customer for seamless on-time delivery.
♦ Tenaciously negotiated carrier freight rates, which decreased transportation costs.

Zoe Blake

Linked in profile

11 Any Avenue
Anytown AA0 0AA

01234 567890
zoe.blake@gmail.com

Accounting / Finance

Performance Profile

Energetic and team-spirited 2016 accountancy graduate seeking opportunity to contribute to an organization's goals and objectives. Accurate, precise, and ethically responsible in all work-related assignments. Quick learner with an eagerness for learning and expanding accounting capabilities. Proven ability to identify problems and implement creative solutions.

- Graduate with proven analytical and critical thinking skills.
- Disciplined with a desire to succeed as evidenced by working 20 hours per week while attending college full-time.
- Exceptional skills in written documentation and verbal communication.
- Effective interpersonal and leadership skills supported by an enthusiastic, team player attitude.
- Foreign Language—proficient in Chinese.
- Technology: MS Word, Excel, PowerPoint, Access, Database, and Adobe Photoshop;

Professional Skills

- Customer Service Skills
- Accounts Payable
- Accounts Receivable
- Budget Forecasting

- GAAP
- Inventory Analysis
- Bookkeeping
- Journal Entries

- Financial Presentations
- Management Skills
- Cost Control
- Market Research

Education

BSc. Accounting and Finance, University, of Anytown   2016
Relevant Course Work: Intermediate Accounting I, Intermediate Accounting II, Accounting Theory, Accounting Principles, Income Tax, and Auditing.

Activities

Volunteer Income Tax Assistance (V.I.T.A.)
Prepared income tax returns for small business and non-profit organisation

Experience

University of Anytown   January 2014—Current
Students Manager, Dining Services
- Calculate weekly payroll for all employees.
- Conduct store management as well as accounting and financial presentations for daily business performance to enhance use of funds.
- Supervise daily sales operations and training of new employees to maintain quality and efficiency.

Student Employee   January 2012—December 2014
- Provided high-quality customer services and efficiently carried out monetary transactions.
- Assisted with opening and closing accounting procedures for Coffee Shop

Student Worker, Rivers Centre   January 2010—December 2012
- Arranged services to meet a large portion of the leisure, recreational, conference, and meeting needs on campus.
- Managed procedures of business conferences and banquets for campus needs.
- Successfully promoted student-faculty interaction and learning outside the classroom environment.

JOEY HUANG,

11 Any ave., Anytown AA0 0AA
huang.acupuncture@gmail.com

0123456 7890
LinkedIn Profile

BAAB QUALIFIED ACUPUNCTURIST

* Mind, body, and spirit healing through the application of traditional acupuncture. *

Acupuncturist experienced in Classical Five-Element Acupuncture with broad background in psychotherapy and coaching. Sensitive, intuitive practitioner dedicated to restoring clients' physical, emotional, and spiritual wellness. Thoroughly evaluate clients to accurately diagnose, formulate treatment plans, and provide effective treatments while encouraging healthy lifestyles. Ethical and compassionate; natural relationship builder committed to cultivating trusting alliances with clients and colleagues. Uphold policies, procedures, and standards, including Professional Standard Authenity regulations.

PROFESSIONAL SKILLS

History Taking/Physical Exam	Treatment Evaluation	Team Collaboration
Diagnostics	Treatment Modification	Regulatory Compliance
Treatment Plan Development	Documentation/Records	Ear Acupuncture
Acupuncture Needling	Client Education	Clinic Management
Moxibustion	Client Counselling/Coaching	Public Speaking

TREATMENT EXPERIENCE

Arthritis	High Blood Pressure	Chronic Bladder Infection
Neuralgia	Arteriosclerosis	Infertility (Men & Women)
Sciatica	Anemia	Sexual Dysfunction
Plantar Fasciitis	Asthma	Candida
Back Pain	Irritable Bowel Syndrome (IBS)	Chronic Fatigue
Tendonitis	Constipation	Epstein-Barr Virus
Stiff Neck	Food Allergies	Multiple Sclerosis (MS)
Headaches/Migraines	Gastritis	Smoking Cessation
Sprains	Abdominal Bloating	Drugs
Muscle Spasms	Diabetes	Alcohol
Sinusitis	Dermatological Disorders	Anxiety
Sore Throat	Irregular Menstruation	Insomnia
Hay Fever	Endometriosis	Depression
Dizziness	Menopause Symptoms	Stress

Comprehensive list of treatment experience available on request

PROFESSIONAL EXPERIENCE

Anytown College of Traditional Medicine   2013 – 2016

Student Acupuncturist
Provided 900+ hours of comprehensive acupuncture treatments for this nonprofit academic institution. Conducted comprehensive intakes, including physical exams, dietary assessments, and medication/herb interaction evaluations. Formulated traditional acupuncture diagnoses, facilitated client education, and researched client medical histories. Developed treatment plans and performed acupuncture needling and moxibustion.

continued

Provided lifestyle coaching, maintained practitioner/client relations, and liaised with supervisors to evaluate treatment results. Assessed integrative healthcare options and provided referrals. Recorded client progress in accurate, concise manner reflecting assessments, interventions, and treatment plan modifications.

➢ Consistently received positive client evaluations; encouraged by supervisors to consider specialization based on excellence in treating complicated cases.
➢ Provided case management and collaborative healthcare for client with advanced multiple sclerosis (MS).
➢ Mentored new students on course, providing support from a learner's viewpoint.
➢ Improved accessibility to and interest in college library by writing comprehensive marketing materials to promote library's collection and researching and developing 12 colour posters illustrating several acupuncture collections.

Anytown Clinic | Acupuncture   2012 – 2013

Acupuncturist

Provided National Acupuncture Detoxification Association (NADA GB) ear acupuncture treatment to clients suffering from stress, insomnia, and other conditions. Provided client management, ensuring warm, accepting, and comfortable clinic atmosphere.

EDUCATION

Professional Licentiate in Acupuncture
Anytown College of Traditional Medicine
Accredited by the British Acupuncture Accreditation Board

PROFESSIONAL ASSOCIATIONS

Member British Acupuncture council (BAcC)

PRIA GAPUR

11 Any Ave., Anytown AA0 0AA | 01234 567890 | PATTY.G@OUTLOOK.COM

ACTUARIAL ANALYST
RESEARCH & ANALYSIS • PROBLEM SOLVING • FINANCE • RISK ANALYSIS

Performance-driven analyst nearing completion of an MSc. In Actuary Science, seeking the opportunity to apply finely honed analytical skills, statistical techniques, and mathematical methods to assess and minimize risk within a dynamic actuary position. Exemplary ability to research, gather, and examine data to determine risk factors to assist in decision-making efforts. Strong ability to complete multiple tasks in a deadline-driven environment. Excellent financial modelling abilities; leverages advanced Microsoft Excel skills including pivot tables, formulas, and Vlookups to compile and organize large data sets. Solid foundation in actuarial valuations, costing, and projections. Astute problem solver with comprehensive knowledge in economic and business functions coupled with a drive to exceed expectations.

- Uses big-picture understanding of finance and maths to assess financial cost of risk.
- Expertise performing statistical analysis within a team, developing premiums and benefits for life insurance products.
- Associate of the Society of Actuaries (ASA) designation (Feb 2016).

Professional Skills

- Planning & Analysis	- Finance/Accounting	- Data Research & Analysis
- Risk Analysis/Management	- Actuarial Science	- Actuarial Models
- Financial Analysis	- Probabilities/Statistics	- Financial Reporting

EDUCATION & PROFESSIONAL CERTIFICATIONS

MSc. in Actuarial Science - University, of Anytown
BSc. Accounting & Management - University, of Anytown
Certified Actuary

EXPERIENCE

Analyst Intern, **XYZ Life Insurance Co., Ltd.**, New Delhi, India   May 2016 – July 2016
- Collaborated within a team of 5, contributing strong analytical skills and financial acumen to develop premiums and benefits for new insurance products.
- Used a range of computer applications and methodologies to conduct detailed analysis of life insurance products.
- Constructed dashboard using Excel functions such as PivotTable and VBA based on current client data.

Financial Intern, **Bank of ABC**, Bangalore, India   May 2015 – Aug 2015
- Efficiently and accurately prepared financial statements by creating Excel models to analyze financial data.
- Conducted in-depth database analysis to identify trends, build reports, and present findings.
- Worked with and supported Account Managers in the analysis of client information.
- Liaised with banks on loan activities and performed international transfers.

Mathematics Tutor, **University,** of Anytown   Jan 2012 – May 2012
- Delivered tutoring on Advanced Calculus and Linear Model course.
- Monitored and assessed student performance and formulated tactics to assist them in increasing their abilities.

AFFILIATIONS

Member: International Actuarial Association
Member: Society of Actuaries

COMPUTER TECHNOLOGY

Word, Excel, Access, PowerPoint, Outlook, VBA, SAS, MATLAB

JEAN MONARSKI

11 Any Ave., Anytown AA0 0AA   jean@anyisp.com   01234 567890

Accountant

Performance Summary

Chartered Accountant with three years accounting experience.Good listening skills harnessed to an analytical mind with the business knowledge to understand what is going on behind the numbers. Analysis of sales data recently led to optimization of product availability and price, which resulted in inventory turnover increase of 11%.

Professional Skills

- Accounting Discrepancies
- Sales Analysis
- Accounts Receivable
- Forecast Sales & Pricing
- Financial Analysis
- Inventory Replenishment

- Website Maintenance
- Customer Relationship
- Journal Entries
- Contract Development
- Negotiation
- E-commerce Technologies

- Consultative Selling
- Data Evaluation
- Logistics
- Purchase Orders
- GAAP UK

Professional Experience

ABC Ltd., Anytown   2014 – Present
Accountant

ABC imports fishing equipment directly from foreign manufacturers and distributes to individual consumers and secondary distributors.

- Negotiated contracts with a major fishing retail chain to expand market reach that resulted in strategic business alliances with retailers in Saitama, Tokyo, and Hyogo through distribution of fishing equipment imported mainly from the United States and Poland.
- Accounting journal entries and preparation of balance sheet for tax return with proper application of tax regulations.
- Launched and developed original fly fishing rods through cooperation with a manufacturer in China and negotiated contract to reduce cost down to competitive range that could compete against much larger and long-running business entities.
- Track and improve sales levels and trends and determine stock replenishments for maximization of sales and minimization of product obsolescence to protect limited working capital.
- Maintain open lines of communication between manufacturers and customers to expedite product orders and for fast problem resolution.
- Cooperation with an outsourced inventory warehouse, to automate sales order process and to facilitate inspection of defective items to protect sales opportunity.

Education

BSc. Economics–University of Anytown   2013

References available on request

MALIK DRAYTON

01234 567890 • m_drayton@gmail.com • 11 Any Ave., Anytown AA0 0AA

ENTERPRISE SECURITY ENTRY LEVEL
IT Security & Privacy ~ Enterprise Risk ~ Information System Risk ~ Business System Analysis

PERFORMANCE SUMMARY

Innovative, approachable IT professional who draws on advanced education, hands-on experience, and a collaborative approach to bring awareness and support to an enterprise-wide approach to security and risk management. Experienced in addressing infrastructure security issues such as data integrity, authentication, and confidentiality to ensure compliance with customer expectations, industry standards, and legislative requirements. Identifies IT and operational risks, threats, and vulnerabilities by applying forensics and research, documenting business implications, and developing systems, processes, and solutions to mitigate/manage risk throughout business. Bilingual, English and Arabic; EMEA culture conversant.

➢ Uses proven methodologies and tools, proper system design, and effective processes and controls to guard against poor-quality data and security threats.

➢ Works independently or within a challenging and collaborative team environment that supports debate and discussion in a service-orientated approach to risk management.

PROFESSIONAL SKILLS & INTERESTS

Enterprise Risk Management	**Network & Data Security**	**Security Policies & Standards**	**Project Management**
Operating System Security	**E-commerce Security**	**Industry Best Practices**	**Gathering Business Needs**
Security & Risk Analysis	**IT Law & Trends**	**Firewall Fundamentals**	**Client Presentations**
Digital Forensics	**System Development**	**Problem Solving**	**Analytical Thinking**

TECHNICAL EXPERIENCE

UNIVERSITY OF ANYTOWN   2013–2016
SYSTEM DEVELOPMENT & PROJECT MANAGEMENT
Supported staff in operations of graduate/undergraduate courses Developed projects from initiation to closure to meet deliverable deadlines, despite full schedules. Created proposal reports, scope statements, team contracts, schedules, progress reports, and resource assignments. Assumed responsibility in staff absence. **Major Projects:**

Windows Server & Linux Virtual Installation
- Provided recommendations and documented challenges regarding future requirements in complete report containing snapshots.

Virtual Networking
- Led individual/class lab projects preparing virtual environment, creating internetwork, installing 3 virtual machines, developing subnet inside internetwork that included sub-netting and routing, and implementing simple DNS infrastructure over internetwork.
- Demonstrated #2 machine could perform a "Man in the Middle Attack," such that if hosts were in switched Ethernet environment, #2 could eavesdrop on communication between #1 and #2 machines, deny service, and stop communication between 1 and 2.
- Configured routing protocols while monitoring subnets and SMTP configuration for possible issues.

Bitcoin Authentication
- Independently researched and mastered bitcoin authentication, then recommended safe environments for use.
- Created comprehensive paper on bitcoin use, reliability, weaknesses, and possible audit transactions.

Risk Management
- Conceptualized idea for project to increase awareness of ways publicly available information can be used to formulate non- or low-tech security breach, gaining access to corporate tech that provided competitive edge.
- Directed 4-student team in creating and managing lab environment; created management-level report highlighting threats.

E-commerce Infrastructure
- Reviewed web application vulnerabilities and studied e-commerce site behavior under normal and peak conditions.

ISO 9001 Compliance Audit

- Led effort to create proposal for ISO compliance in Russian Multicultural Learning Center to prepare for bidding process on government contract for military training.
- Authored 106-page document that outlined phases of proposed project (proposal reports, scope statements, team contracts, schedules, progress reports, and resource assignments) as well as examining all aspects of ISO compliance.

ABC AIRLINES • Anytown   2010–12
IT PROJECT ANALYST TRAINING, ORACLE APPLICATIONS
Entry-level position providing exposure to a variety of functions and projects, with a focus on operating Oracle-based systems within company's IT Department. Read manuals for Oracle add-ons applications and examining features that they offer in addition to the compatibility with rules and regulations.

EDUCATION & PROFESSIONAL ACTIVITIES

- Msc. INFORMATION SYSTEMS SECURITY MANAGEMENT, University of Anytown
  ~ Thesis Research & Publication: "Disaster Recovery for Mid-Sized Businesses." Provided effective and financially feasible disaster recovery/business continuity framework and implementation template where mid-sized businesses can proactively prevent disruptions and react to interruptions of vital operations.
- Bsc. BUSINESS : MANAGEMENT INFORMATION SYSTEMS, of Othertown University

CERTIFICATIONS
- Awarded: COBIT 5 Implementation & COBIT 5 Foundation, XYZ Security Training
- In Progress: Certified Information Systems Security Professional (CISSP), Certified Information Security Manager (CISM), Project Management Professional (PMP), Informational Technology Infrastructure Library (ITIL)

PROFESSIONAL AFFILIATIONS
- Member: Information Systems Audit and Control Association (ISACA)
- Member: Project Management Institute (PMI)
- Member: Institute of Electrical and Electronics Engineers

TECHNICAL SKILLS
- Operating Systems: Windows Server 2008/2012, XP, Vista; UNIX, Linux Ubuntu, Fedora, Kali, BackTrack
- Software: MS Office Suite, Visio, Microsoft Project, Single Point Sign-In, VMware
- Networking: TCP/IP, DNS, DHCP, Ethernet, SMTP
- Hardware: Servers, Hubs, Routers, Switches, PCs

Jayana Stewart

11 Any Ave., Anytown AA0 0AA | 01234 567890 JStewart@gmail.com

Entry-Level Mechanical Engineer

Performance Profile

High-potential recent graduate who is prepared to meet the expectations of new and challenging assignments through a strong work ethic and the motivation to do whatever it takes to get the job done. A self-starter with an established ability to balance competing demands without compromising quality or productivity.

- Bilingual communicator (English/French) with strong interpersonal skills and a strong team orientation.
- Energetic, ambitious, and well organized with solid problem-solving skills and a proven ability to focus on detail, plan, prioritize, meet deadlines, and deliver first-rate work.
- Successfully executes day-to-day initiatives requiring flexibility and think-on-your-feet abilities.
- Confidently interfaces and establishes rapport with diverse groups of people at all levels.

Professional Competencies

• SolidWorks	• Autodesk Inventor	• Machine Shop
• Bandsaw & Drill	• Water Jet Cutter	• Communication
• Modelling/Fabricating Robots	• Manufacturing	• 3D Printer
• Analytical	• Mill & Lathe	• Detail Orientated
• Bilingual English/French	• Critical Thinking	• Problem Resolution

Education

Bsc. Mechanical Engineering, University of Anytown 2016

Mechanical Engineering Projects

Senior Design Project

- Member of six-person mechanical engineering team honoured with 2nd-place award in competition against 22 other teams.
- Key role on team that designed and built autonomous vehicle that navigated through predesigned course and delivered payload from start to finish. Primary accountabilities included drawing, machining, and parts assembly.
- Delivered presentation on robot fabrication and programming process to peers and professors.

Manufacturing Processes Project

- Built mechanically functional handheld video game console using aluminum plates, tactile switches, 3D printer, CNC mill, and EDM.
- Used 3D printer to create buttons and majority of console body.
- Employed sander to create smooth finish on console's aluminum plates.

Jayana Stewart | Page Two

01234 567890 | JStewart@gmail.com

MATE ROV competition, 2015 (USA)
Built Underwater Unmanned Vehicle (UUV) using lathe, bandsaw, and drill.

Internship Experience

ABC Industries, Anytown, 2014–Present
An international manufacturer of protection tape, PVC electrical insulating tape, masking tape, OPP packing tape, PVC duct and pipe-wrapping tape.

Research & Development Department
Employed various methods, including quality-control processes, to test combinations of natural and synthetic rubber for efficacy of adhesive properties under various temperatures and conditions.

Quality Control Department
Studied and used various methods of quality control to ensure products met predetermined requirements; properties examined included tensile strength, shear adhesion, and electrical resistance.

Electrical & Mechanical Department
Used SolidWorks to modelmachine parts.

Computer Skills

Microsoft Word, Excel, PowerPoint; MATLAB; SolidWorks; Autodesk Inventor; LabVIEW; C++; Java

Languages

Fluent in English and French, verbal and written language.

Excellent references available on request

Kris Cohen, RN

11 Any Ave., Anytown AA0 0AA   0123456 7890   Rcohen@gmail.com

Registered Nurse,

Performance Summary

Reliable and team-orientated RN, experienced with post-surgical and long-term care. Demonstrates strong clinical competencies and knowledge in nursing. Motivated and thrives in a fast-paced environment; flexible with scheduling needs.

- Responsible for assessment, planning, and implementation of patient care.
- Communicates well with patients, family, and healthcare professionals.
- Able to delegate tasks while maintaining accountability.
- Applies analytical thinking skills to identify, prevent, and solve patient-related problems and family concerns.

Education

University of Anytown   2015
Bsc. Nursing
 Member: Royal College of Nursing
Basic Life Support (BLS)
Advanced Cardiac Life Support (ACLS) certifications

Professional Nursing Skills

Physical assessment	Medication administration
Urinary catheter insertion	Pain management
Intravenous (IV) therapy	Nasogastric intubation
Gastrostomy tube feeding	Diabetes management/teaching
Vacuum-assisted closure (VAC) wound care	Specimen collection
Peripherally inserted central catheter (PICC) dressing change	Colostomy/ileostomy care
Medical Surgical Nursing, 144 clinical hours	

Professional Experience

XYZ Health— Anytown   2016–Present

Registered Nurse

Provides patients with highest level of safe nursing care in a 123-bed skilled nursing facility. Receives new patients and executes body checks to assess physical condition upon admission. Initiates IV start and IV therapy and administers medication as ordered by physicians. Communicates the patient's change of condition to physician in SBAR format. Diverse responsibilities include:

- Maintaining narcotic control, including correctly signing, counting, and cosigning wastage.
- Supervising certified nursing assistants for patient care assignments.
- Providing treatment of surgical wounds and setting up wounds (VAC) for wound care.
- Preparing discharge documentation and reconciled medication list to patient upon discharge.

Linked **in** profile

Regina G. Livingston   Linked **in** profile
11 Any Ave., Anytown AA0 0AA ♦ 0123456 7890 ♦ rgivingston@gmail.com

Entry-Level Sales Associate

Performance Summary

High-potential business professional with a solid track record of delivering sales and customer service excellence to expand customer base and grow bottom-line performance. Finely honed ability to engage customers and build strong relationships. A self-starter with well-developed initiative and the ability to balance competing demands without compromising quality or productivity.

♦ Enthusiastic, optimistic, and personable with a genuine desire to provide outstanding service.
♦ An eager learner who quickly integrates new knowledge and skills into job performance to contribute, grow, and excel.
♦ Professionalism, loyalty, and teamwork with a high standard of ethics; subscribes to a straightforward, hands-on style in getting the job done.
♦ Works productively and independently in varied environments with minimal direction and supervision.

Education

BA, Political Science, Anytown University   Dec 2016

Professional Competencies

♦ Retail Sales	♦ Customer Service	♦ Problem Resolution
♦ Adaptable & Flexible	♦ Communication	♦ Analytical Thinking
♦ Well Prepared & Organized	♦ Time Management	♦ Disciplined Work Ethic

Professional Experience

ABC Ltd., Anytown   Summer 2016
ABC is a chain of 1,060 mid-range department stores in nationwide.
Sales Associate

Charged with greeting and delivering first-class assistance to customers, asking questions and listening to shoppers' needs, then providing options and advice on meeting those needs.
♦ Performed sales functions and operated electronic cash registers.
♦ Maintained selling-floor presentations and restocking as needed.
♦ Ensured fitting rooms were ready for customers by promptly clearing merchandise and returning it to selling floor. Maintained neat and well-organized work area.
♦ Conducted loss prevention, inventory control, and compliance procedures.

XYZ's, Anytown   Summer 2014 & 2015
XYZ's, topped the list of the five fastest-growing restaurant chains in the U.K
Cashier

♦ Assisted in opening and closing store to ensure restaurant was welcoming, well organized, and prepared for service in morning and clean and secure in evening.
♦ Handled cash transactions and trained new cashiers on electronic cash register system.
♦ Managed customer complaints, resolving issues to ensure happy customers and repeat business.

Anytown Extracurricular Activities

♦ Women's football team
♦ Regular volunteer at North Anytown Food Bank
♦ Student Mentoring Programmes

Technical Skills

Microsoft Excel, PowerPoint, Word, Access, and Publisher

Languages

Spanish

Community Service

♦ North Anytown Food Bank
♦ Anytown Community Garden
♦ Toys for Tots Toy Library
♦ First Aid Training – St John Ambulance
♦ Prince's Trust Project

Regina G. Livingston

11 Any Ave., Anytown AA0 0AA

rgivingston@gmail.com

0123456 7890

Entry-Level Sales Associate

High-potential business professional with a solid record of delivering sales and customer service excellence to expand customer base and grow bottom-line performance. Finely honed ability to engage customers and build strong relationships. A self-starter with well-developed initiative and the ability to balance multiple competing demands without compromising quality or productivity.

◆ Enthusiastic, optimistic, and personable with a genuine desire to provide outstanding service.
◆ An eager learner who quickly integrates new knowledge and skills into job performance to contribute, grow, and excel.
◆ Professionalism, loyalty, and teamwork with a high standard of ethics; subscribes to a straightforward, hands-on style in getting the job done.
◆ Works productively and independently in varied environments with minimal direction and supervision.

Education

BA Political Science, University of Anytown 2016

Professional Competencies

◆ Retail Sales
◆ Adaptable & Flexible
◆ Well Prepared & Organized

◆ Customer Service
◆ Communication
◆ Time Management

◆ Problem Resolution
◆ Communication
◆ Disciplined Work Ethic

Professional Experience

ABC Ltd., Anytown

Summer 2016

ABC is a chain of 1,060 mid-range department stores nationwide.

Sales Associate

Charged with greeting and delivering first class assistance to customers, asking questions and listening to shoppers' needs, then providing options and advice on meeting those needs.
◆ Performed sales functions and operated electronic cash registers.
◆ Maintained selling floor presentations and restocking as needed.
◆ Ensured fitting rooms were ready for customers by promptly clearing merchandise and returning it to selling floor. Maintained neat and well-organized work area.
◆ Conducted loss prevention, inventory control, and compliance procedures.

XYZ's., Anytown

Summer 2014 & 2015

XYZ's topped the list of the five fastest-growing restaurant chains in the UK.

Cashier

◆ Assisted in opening and closing store to ensure restaurant was welcoming, well organized, and prepared for service in morning and clean and secure in evening.
◆ Handled cash transactions and trained new cashiers on electronic cash register system.
◆ Managed customer complaints, resolving issues to ensure happy customers and repeat business.
◆ Cleaned lobby and bathrooms, meeting restaurant's high standards. Restocked supplies.

Brian Cooper
11 Any ave., Anytown AA0 0AA

0123456 7890   Conservation11579@gmail.com

Geographic Information Systems (GIS)

Performance Profile

Entry-level **Geographic Information Systems** professional with multiple certifications covering GIS, **environmental safety**, and **rescue** measures. Self-motivated, disciplined with a desire to succeed-time. **Advanced problem - solving** and **multitasking** skills for fast-paced environments. Experience coordinating city planning departments, and subcontractors during planning and building phases of projects.

- Accurate **field notes** using **multiple software** applications.
- Solid **cost assessment** analysis skills.
- Advanced analytical and **problem-solving skills.**
- Proven background in leading **GIS** teams.

Professional Skills

- Project management
- Research analysis and reporting
- P&L management
- Disaster preparation and recovery
- Word, Excel, PowerPoint
- Windows XP, MAC OS
- Arc GIS, Arc INFO, Arc Catalog

- GIS Map interpretation and analysis
- Environmental resource management
- Team-building and leadership skills
- Land use planning
- Excellent time management skills
- Plan and develop business proposals
- Business development

Professional Highlights

- **The Urban Scene:** Analysis of urban lifestyles, **land use** and design, population trends, and utilization of urban life spaces.
- **Map Interpretation and Analysis:** Interpretation of maps with emphasis on critical analysis, scale, and projection.
- **Geographical Analysis: Advanced quantitative techniques** used by geographer in analysis of spatial phenomena. Emphasis on **multivariate statistical methods** for geographical analysis using statistical software.
- **Land Use Planning:** Issues and responses concerning **land use, coastal zones, environmental resource management**, planning parameters for residences, industrial areas, and urban and regional revitalization.
- **Hazards and Risk Management:** Broad overview of hazards and disasters (natural or technological), emphasizing the physical and social dynamics that interact to produce hazard, the spatial and temporal distribution of various hazards, disaster preparation, and loss reduction.

Education & Training

BSc, Geography Anytown University,   2014
Areas of emphasis: GIS, natural resource management

Intermediate GIS, GIS cartography and base map development, GIS in environment technology.
Anytown Community College ,
GIS Certification   Completion date: 2013

Excellent references available

KENNETH DERBY

11 Any Ave., Anytown AA0 0AA   0123456 7890   ken.derby@live.com

Linked in profile

ANALYTICS PRODUCT MANAGER

PERFORMANCE PROFILE

Nineteen years' combined product management and data analytics expertise with recent success in mobile/web applications for XYZ . Possess broad understanding of data analytics specialty area, remaining abreast of market trends and requirements while ensuring cutting-edge use of big data to deliver measurable business value for customers. Conceptualize and realize best-in-class customer experiences by scrutinizing user analytics and data to steer decision making.

Build and direct collaborative cross-functional teams known for successfully launching products, despite involvement of complex hardware, software, and back-end components. Design targeted product stories, fine-tuning concepts for technical and non-technical audiences. Collate and prioritize stakeholder requirements, ensuring clarity during product development.

PROFESSIONAL SKILLS

Product Management	Analytics Solution Design	Business Requirements Gathering
Enterprise Network Security	Cross-functional Team Leadership	Communication and Collaboration
Online Media and Publication	Software and Hardware Design	Mobile Devices and Applications
Technical Marketing	Product Marketing	Partner/Stakeholder Management
Cloud Computing	SCRUM Methodology	B2C and B2B Social Networking
Project and Programme Management	Media Advertising	Database Design

TECHNICAL SKILLS

Google Analytics	Adobe Analytics Suite	comScore
Localytics	Websense	Visual Revenue
Tableau	Oracle	Microsoft Access/Excel
SQL	Weka	Orange
JMP Pro	Microsoft Business Intelligence	SharePoint

PERFORMANCE HIGHLIGHTS

◇ **Product Management** – Supported delivery of over £1B in annual revenue through analysis and interpretation of big data to enact forward-looking business decisions for XYZ Business Intelligence solutions.

◇ **Data Analytics** – Transformed data-driven strategic planning and development across XYZ applications and content properties by implementing Adobe Analytics tool.

◇ **Technology** – Developed and produced cloud-based, AI-recommended technology that was presented at global technology conferences in 2006 and 2007.

◇ **Product Management** – Yielded £150M+ in annual revenue and captured 13% market share in security appliance segment via strategic positioning of software security solutions based on industry trends and customer needs.

PROFESSIONAL EXPERIENCE

XYZ Technology – Anytown	2005 – Present

Technology company.

Senior Product Manager/Planner, Analytics	2012 – Present
Senior Programme Manager, Entertainment Video and Sports	2008 – 2012
Senior Product Planner,	2005 – 2008

KENNETH DERBY

0123456 7890 ken.derby@live.com

Senior Product Manager/Planner, Analytics 2012 – Present
Promoted to oversee cross-organizational product management of XYZ Business Intelligence solutions. Drive strategic direction
of XYZ portal and optimization of content experience to boost user engagement by delivering real-time analytics. Facilitate monthly
business reviews. Discover revenue-generating opportunities by executing data analysis to align advertisers and user
base. Envision and implement market share maximization strategies to strengthen Internet ranking. Supervise 2 contract employees.
❖ Contributed to £1B+ in annual revenue by using big data to make strategic business decisions.
❖ Embedded positive change to data-driven strategic planning and development spanning XYZ applications and content
    properties through introduction of global Analytics solution.
❖ Enabled forecasting of impact of future product releases, mitigating negative performance effects, by coordinating forward-
    looking planning process.
❖ Set foundation for £36M in projected advertising revenue through formulation of 3-year search strategy.
❖ Yielded £10M in annual revenue through conceptualization and implementation of customer-targeting strategies.
❖ Elevated global audience 20% within 30 days of designing and launching process to track Facebook engagement, establishing
    Facebook as high-growth source of traffic.
❖ Defined requirements and shepherded project to deliver global analytics solutions to align with business strategy,
    lower costs, and unify reporting.
❖ Shrank engineering expenses 20% via creation of predictive models to determine business impact of design modifications.
❖ Enabled settlement of £500K from £14M in music industry payment litigation after defining legal cost mitigation solution

Senior Programme Manager, Entertainment Video and Sports 2008 – 2012
Appointed to optimize user experience, boost search transfers, and fuel competitive market growth by delivering in-depth product
and user insights. Drove vision and strategy to amplify revenue, market share, and customer satisfaction. Discovered opportunities
for and built business plans to capture cost savings, outsourcing as appropriate.
❖ Laid groundwork for Entertainment's new XYZ property through in-depth examination of market data; since its
    launch, it has delivered over £250M.
❖ Captured £500K cost savings by envisioning revenue growth strategy and business plan content development.
❖ Spearheaded interdisciplinary team that delivered inaugural social integration.
❖ Earned 3 performance awards for strategy and insight, prolific output, and cross-company collaboration.

Senior Product Planner 2005 – 2008
Brought onboard to oversee long-term strategy and vision, value proposition, and customer advocacy. Determined market and
product requirements for 5 distinct product and service offerings.
❖ Delivered new cloud based AI recommended technology, that was presented at World Conference Keynote.
❖ Originated several million in global revenue through delivery and management of 4 advanced recommendation services
❖ Actualized and directed Entertainment's integration.
❖ Conveyed strategic recommendations for 3 confidential initiatives after conducting extensive due diligence.

ABC Enterprise Solutions | Othertown 2002 – 2005
Multinational communications and technology.
R&D Product Manager
Challenged to oversee product life cycle for integrated partner product line, from development strategy to sales support and
customer satisfaction. Drove analysis of new customer market opportunities to expand existing business and security product line
into enterprise mobile solutions. Elicited future product requirements from customers and remained abreast of industry trends.
Monitored weekly P&L and channel inventory for all regions to maximize marketing programs. Assessed M&A targets to optimize ROI
and secure strategic intellectual property.

KENNETH DERBY

0123456 7890   ken.derby@live.com

❖ Contributed to £150M+ in annual revenue, coupled with 13% market share in security appliance segment, through strategic management of software security solutions product line.
❖ Played influential role in closing premier reseller partners, by designing product solution compatibility.
❖ Minimized customer attrition and maximized contract renewal through creation of feature prioritization tool.
❖ Advocated and launched 2 new product lines leveraging £3M development budget.
❖ Piloted development of security products.
❖ Facilitated effective negotiation of OEM deals through establishment of margin/forecasting tool.

DEF Laboratories, Computer Division	Othertown	1999 – 2002

Communications & technology.
Senior Technical Marketing Manager
Designated to establish and lead competitive benchmark testing lab and 3-member team. Conducted sales engineering team training on new products, competitive positioning, and customer deployment procedures. Crafted clear, concise customer sizing guides for enterprise products.

❖ Augmented sales 5% by envisioning and introducing technical marketing programme based on competitive landscape.
❖ Substantially elevated product sales via conducting and documenting highly detailed competitive analysis.

EARLIER CAREER

JKL Ltd., Anytown **– Technical Designer/Product Manager**   1997 – 1999

EDUCATION

Msc. Predictive Analytics (in progress), University, of Anytown
BSc. Information Systems Management, University of Anytown

PROFESSIONAL ACCREDITATIONS

Check Point Certified Security Administrator (CCSA) and Check Point Certified Security Expert (CCSE)

ONGOING PROFESSIONAL EDUCATION

❖ Executive and Media Communication Training,
❖ VoIP Mobility Training
❖ Six Sigma Training

Superior references from world-class companies available

Jen Ellis

11 Any Ave., Anytown AA0 0AA   01234 567890   jellis@gmail.com
Linked **in** profile

Branch Manager

Performance Profile

Branch Manager & Loan Officer with 12 years of experience managing branch banking and lending activities, improving business processes, and leading a team of financial services professionals who generate approximately £9 million in loans each year.

Professional Skills

Asset Preservation & Loss Prevention	Regulatory Compliance	Verbal & Written Communications
Loan Applications & Processing	Requirements Elicitation	Lead Generation / Prospecting
Credit Administration / Credit Analysis	Financial Statements & Financial Audits	Customer Accounts Setup
Credit Quality / Credit Scores	Data Entry & Database Management	Customer Relationship Management
Banking Products & Financial Services	Strategic Business Planning	New Business Development
Mortgage Lending & Underwriting	Economics, Accounting, & Finance	Staff Training & Supervision
Asset Management / Portfolio Valuation	Statistical Analysis & Market Trends	Teamwork & Collaboration
Loan Reviews, Approvals, & Closings	Spreadsheets, Flat Files, & Databases	Exceptional Customer Service
Documentation for Funding	General Ledger Accounting	Cross-Selling Opportunities

Performance Highlights

- Strategic Business Leader who uses financial data and market trends analysis to drive business decisions.
- Credit Administrator proficient in interviewing clients, gathering financial information, processing loan applications, analyzing and interpreting credit quality for loan approval or denial, and closing asset-based loans.
- Compliance Resource for fair lending and responsible banking laws.
- Loan Manager with knowledge and experience in asset management/valuation, working with distressed properties and reviewing collateral reporting packages comprised of accounts receivable, inventory reports, sales journals, cash receipts registers, accounts payable listings, and other financial reports.

Professional Experience

ABC Bank, Anytown   2010 to Present
Branch Manager / Assistant Branch Manager

Promoted from Assistant Branch Manager to Branch Manager in July of 2012. Serve in a business development and sales role. Offer personal and real estate loans as well as credit insurance. Generate £9 million in loans each year, provide exceptional customer service, and build strong customer relationships.

- Recruit, hire, train, supervise, and evaluate performance of branch employees working in lending and loan collection.
- Monitor and direct loan activities. Analyze and deter risks associated with personal and property loans. Perform due diligence and conduct thorough credit risk assessments to provide an accurate risk profile and portfolio analysis pertinent to sustaining portfolio value and branch growth.
- Meet clients to determine loan needs and discuss rates, terms, and underwriting requirements. Assist clients in loan application process. Analyze loan applicants' financial data to determine credit worthiness, including income, property valuations, credit report, credit history, etc.
- Oversee customer service activities, loan presentations, collection of outstanding loan payments, and provide troubleshooting for a high-volume call centre.

(continued)

Notable Achievements:
- Awarded "Branch of the Month" for July 2010 and September 2011.
- Personally received "Branch Manager of the Month" on numerous occasions in past 7 years.
- Increased employee productivity and cultivated a positive workplace environment by facilitating employee training and job shadowing for new bank employees and bank managers. Trained new employee and coached staff to optimal performance.
- Increased lending activities by 10% across loan staff by auditing staff performance against job requirements and instituting structured collection and solicitation procedures, which increased sales and reduced losses.
- Branch was recognized in top 20% for deterrence of losses, through the introduction of delinquency controls.

XYZ, Anytown   2004 to 2010
Investigative Supervisor

Built a successful, full-service investigative firm that offered consulting services to insurance companies, large organizations, solicitors, and private citizens. Directed a team of investigators handling concurrent caseloads of fraud, security, and other criminal cases. Conducted formal and adhoc meetings with team members to gather information and maintain positive investigative outcomes.
- Conducted initial client needs assessments to properly analyze clients' situations and recommend solutions.
- Performed case reviews and managed ongoing investigative activities such as surveillance, interview, data collection, etc.
- Advised clients on asset security, fraud awareness, and theft prevention. Also investigated and reported on workers' compensation and insurance fraud cases for clients.
- Performed background checks for clients vetting new employees. Researched applicants' criminal and credit/financial histories. Verified accuracy of gaps in employment. Verified identity of candidates in certain instances. Provided business clients with the necessary information to develop a safe and reputable work environment.
- Conducted facility security audits, discussed security measures with security guards and other onsite staff. Audited each building structure and access points to identify weaknesses and security risks. Reviewed and advised on evacuation plans/procedures and other emergency response preparedness measures.
- Established internal business operating procedures and company policies.
- Oversaw budget administration, new business development, team management, and administration of case reports. Established new client accounts and negotiated service contracts.
- Oversaw accounting and finances. Managed accounts receivable, accounts payable, and payroll. Led the collection of contract payments. Maintained invoice records and statement balances. Monitored expense records to ensure case budgetary restraints were met. Collaborated with an outside accounting firm to file business and personal taxes.
- Worked closely with claims examiners, customer service reps, outsourced suppliers, and other third parties involved in the data verification process.

Education

BA Criminal Justice – Anytown of University

Professional Development Courses

Coaching for Results | Advanced Selling | Sales Management
Leadership, Exercising Influence in the Workplace | Branch Management, Analytics, and Profitability

Raffaela Zanotti, CPA

11 Any Avenue
Anytown AA0 0AA

Linked [in] profile
01234 567890
r.zanotti@att.net

Client Services Manager

PERFORMANCE SUMMARY

Twelve years' experience with a global management consulting firm delivering value through improving business processes, reducing costs, and increasing profitability for a wide range of clients across diverse industries including pharmaceutical, manufacturing, retail, technology, healthcare, life sciences, and telecom companies. Leader with a proven track record of managing all phases of client service, including sales, proposal development, project delivery, team management, and executive relationship management.

- Strong GAAP and financial statement presentation skills.
- Manage client service teams, plan and execute business process reviews, and manage budgets.
- Active client communications to manage expectations, meet deadlines, and lead change efforts.
- Act as a primary contact for board executives during projects.
- Manage multiple concurrent engagements to ensure direction and address issues.

PROFESSIONAL SKILLS

Regulatory Compliance	Internal Controls	Sales & Proposal Development
Financial Statement Analysis	Business Review & Assessment	GAAP
Risk Assessment	Strategic Development & Training	Capital Budgeting
Business Process Improvement	Engagement Team Management	Planning, Budgeting, & Forecasting
Plan & Execute Client Engagements	Metrics & KPI Development	Executive Client Relationships
Process & Policies Development	Staff Planning	Organization Design

PROFESSIONAL EXPERIENCE

ABC Consulting Group, Any town	2005–Present
Manager	2010–Present
Senior Consultant	2007–2010
Consultant	2005–2007
Manager	2010–Present

Global management consulting firm focused on clients with a variety of business problems, including establishing strategy, organization design, and change management, and improving operations to grow business, increase efficiency, and manage risk. Manage day-to-day project activities for multiple client engagements.

- Designed and executed process improvements for annual and long-range strategic and planning processes aligning financial planning with operational forecasts; reduced planning cycle by two months.
- Improved management reporting by eliminating unnecessary reports and creating consistent information across reports. Established new metrics and KPIs focused on key decision-making results.!
- Developed agendas for three new CFOs to help with prioritizing initiatives and evaluating direct reports, and created plans to help guide their first 180 days in office.
- Relocated an underperforming national accounts support center. Staffing realignments, training, and process improvements resulted in increased customer satisfaction and £1M annual savings.

-continued-

Raffaela Zanotti   r.zanotti@att.net   Page 2

(Professional Experience, continued)

Senior Consultant   2007–2010
Responsible for leading individual pieces of larger/complicated client engagements. Worked with clients and subject matter experts to identify areas for improvement and created recommendations. Developed material and assisted in conducting client meetings and workshops.

- Assessed client's current process to close, consolidate, and report financial results, and created a new process that reduced the amount of analysis at month's end, resulting in a timesaver of four days.
- Made improvements to the Accounts Payable (AP) process through technology enhancements and updated employee training, resulting in a 30% reduction in backlog of invoices, and a reduction in staffing.
- Redesigned global chart of accounts across business units and geographies, reducing number of accounts from 5000+ to 2000. Eliminated reporting redundancy, and created consistent analysis and reporting.
- Developed strategy for CFO and finance department to reduce costs and improve efficiency through a shared service center, improved treasury operations, and timely and accurate reporting to management.
- Performed market sizing and assessment study for client looking to grow customer base across Europe Study focused on researching market size and trends, resulting in a successful strategy to grow sales.

Consultant   2005–2007
Served in a variety of engagements to collect data and information to perform current state assessments and trend analysis for clients. Reviewed industry standards and developed new processes, structures, and created client deliverables.

- Implemented a financial review program for 60 facilities to collect month-end data, review performance trends, and monitor internal controls.
- Established a shared service center by relocating accounting process from individual locations, resulting in reduced costs, increased efficiency, and scalability to accommodate projected business growth.
- Assisted client struggling with regulatory demands. Implemented internal controls and compliance programme, preventing client's stock from being delisted.
- Developed a training programme to accompany new budgeting and planning system and process. Delivered live training to 40+ global users who executed a successful planning cycle on the new system.
- Assisted company implementing new SAP (ERP) by adjusting current AP, AR, and General Accounting practices for the new system. New processes resulted in standardization and improved efficiency.

EDUCATION & PROFESSIONAL LICENSES

University of Anytown   2003
MSc of Accounting

University of Anytown   2002
BSc, Accounting and Finance

Chartered Certificate Accountant   Active

PROFESSIONAL ORGANIZATIONS

The Association of Chartered
Certificate Accountants(ACCA)

Elise Petit

11Any Avenue

Anytown AA0 0AA

Linked in profile

0123456 7890

e.g.petit@gmail.com

Controller

PERFORMANCE PROFILE

Certified Management Accountant (CMA) with 18+ years of progressive full-cycle accounting and managerial experience. Results-driven leader with a proven track record that reflects strong business acumen, financial development skills, strategic planning, financial reporting skills, and a demonstrated commitment to organizational growth. Skilled in analyzing existing operations and implementing cost-effective systems, strategies, and processes to improve organizational performance and profitability.

- Extensive knowledge of accounting, budgeting, and cost-control principles.
- In-depth knowledge of preparation of financial reports and analysis of financial data.
- Streamlines financial operations to maximize performance and profitability.
- Strategic business planning and analysis, including identification of operational business issues, risks, and opportunities.
- Solid interpersonal skills and cross-functional team interactions combined with leadership abilities.
- Comprehensive knowledge of accounting reporting and automated financial systems.
- Strong organizational and project management skills; ability to manage multiple projects, set priorities, and meet deadlines.

PROFESSIONAL SKILLS

*Forecasting & Budget Planning	*GAAP UK	*CMA
*Full-Cycle Accounting	*Financial Planning & Analysis	*Variance Analysis
*Leadership & Mentoring Skills	*Policies & Procedures	*ERP Systems
*Audits & Taxation	*General Ledger	*Inventory Control Programmes
*Cost Controls	*Bank Reconciliations	*Journal Entries
*Balance Sheet & Income Statement	*Foreign Exchange Transactions	*Capital Leasing
*Systems Administration	*Client Collection Schedules	*ACCPAC
*Daily Operating System Updates	*Accounts Payable (A/P)	*Sales Commissions
*Accounts Receivable (A/R)	*Sage MAS (ERP system)	*Excel
*Project Management	*Internal Controls	

PROFESSIONAL EXPERIENCE

ABC, Anytown

Senior Accountant

2002–Present

Industry leader with annual revenue of £80M. Company installs and maintains industrial conveyor belt systems. Responsible for final adjusting journal entries, financials, financial statement analysis, and GL account reconciliations. Managed payroll for the entire company that has grown from 100 employees to over 250 employees in the past decade. Prepares year-end working papers and communicates with external auditors for annual audits.

- Streamlined payroll reporting for improvement of tracking working hours of hourly staff.
- Delivered semi-monthly payroll on time for 12 years, meeting all deadlines.
- Accomplished a proven track record of delivering timely financial statements, consistently meeting corporate deadlines.
- Assisted in the transition from UNIX-based system to ERP operating system.

(continued)

| Elise Petit | e.g.petit@gmail.com | Page 2 |

(Professional Experience, continued)

OEF, Anytown   1999–2002
Inventory/Purchasing Supervisor and Project Manager
International company with 75+ employees with locations in Canada, the UK , and Australia. Produces vehicle engine additives. Designed inventory control programme to track production and control inventory levels.

- Negotiated with suppliers to locate optimum suppliers based on cost, customer service, and delivery times, resulting in cost savings.
- Effectively communicated with other departments to ensure proper inventory level control procedures were established and regulated, saving the company money in excess inventory.
- Conducted daily operating systems updates and weekly bonus procedures for sales representatives.

XYZ Services, Othertown   1998–1999
Accountant and Accounts Receivable Administrator
National company with revenues in excess of £12M specializing in replacing goods for insurance claims. Effectively administered payroll for company with 60+ employees. Prepared monthly financial statements through trial balance using ACCPAC.

- Developed a series of spreadsheets for easier reporting and tracking of company information, resulting in better analysis of financial information.
- Effectively administered payroll for 55 non-executive employees.
- Collected accounts receivables with a monthly average of £1M and approximately 40% of payables up to £500K monthly.

EDUCATION

University of Othertown   1998
Bsc.Accounting

PROFESSIONAL DEVELOPMENT & CERTIFICATIONS

Level 1 – Payroll Administrator Certification   1997

Level 2 – Payroll Administrator Certification   2003

Superior references available

Teresa Mamalakis

11 Any Avenue
Anytown AA0 0AA

0123456 7890
t.mamalakis@gmail.com

Director of Financial Planning & Analysis

**I streamline processes to reduce expenses, increase sales,
and provide necessary metrics for strategic decision making.**

PERFORMANCE PROFILE

15+ years' experience with financial planning and analysis, ranging from financial services, manufacturing, and retail distribution, to global corporate reporting; backed by a proven track record in high-growth, multinational companies. Exceptional knowledge of accounting concepts, standards and practices, and fiscal planning. Strong financial acumen and extensive understanding of business drivers. Exhibits professional standards of integrity and ethics in all transactions. Solid academic background in finance.

- Demonstrates extensive knowledge of financial assessments and identifies key metrics critical to business performance.
- Excellent analytical thinking, innovative, problem-solving, and organizational skills with strong attention to detail.
- Excellent interpersonal and communication skills with the ability to work with cross-functional teams.
- Effectively interfaces with all levels of financial and IT management teams.
- Strong leadership skills with an emphasis on teamwork, innovation, and integrity.
- Exceptional communication and presentation skills with the ability to deliver strategic messages to senior leadership.
- Works with complex concepts, analyzes data, and makes recommendations for increased productivity.
- Solid judgment skills, with the ability to work in fast-paced and challenging environments and consistently meet deadlines.

FINANCIAL PLANNING SKILLS

*Data Analytics & Profitability Analysis	*Reporting Skills	*Strategic Planning
*Identifies Opportunities & Risks	*Financial Acumen	*System Process Improvements
*Fiscal Planning	*Negotiation Skills	*Latest Estimates
*Presentation Skills	*Rolling Forecast	*Profit & Loss Statements
*Accounting Concepts, Standards, & Practices	*Forecasting & Budgeting	*Financial Modeling
*Expense Control	*Balance Sheet	*Cash Flow
*Best Practices	*Management Consulting	*Project Management Skills
*Inventory Control: FIFO & LIFO	*Capital Budgeting	*Depreciation
*Activity-Based Costing	*Cost of Sales	*Product Cost Control
*Assisted in Sales Presentations	*Project Costing	*Net Income

TECHNOLOGY SKILLS

*MS Word, Excel, Access, Outlook, & PowerPoint	*SAP	*Oracle Essbase
*Hyperion Planning	*FI/CO	*Business Warehouse (BW)
*Strategic Enterprise Management (SEM)	*Microsoft Project	*AS400
*Business Planning & Consolidation (BPC)	*VAI-S2K	*Quick View
*Advanced Business Application Programming (ABAP)	*Apple OSX	*VBA

(continued)

PROFESSIONAL EXPERIENCE

ABC Associates, Anytown   2015–Present
Senior Manager of Financial Planning
£250M domestic leader in sales of retail and wholesale tobacco products. Selected to manage £60M of stock inventory throughout company. Charged with revamping receiving process for warehouse and retail locations. Prepares annual business plans for retail, wholesale, and Internet businesses. Prepares annual sales and expense budgets with quarterly latest estimate updates. Interacts with management team on strategy and forward-looking business plans.

- Conducts annual physical inventory, routine cash, and payroll audits throughout company.
- Decreased inventory by £10M to reach optimum inventory levels.
- Realigned assortment with sales patterns, resulting in a savings of approximately £400K annually.
- Reduced aging inventory by 50% +, down from £750K to less than £350K, reaching acceptable levels.
- Partnered with IT to develop in-house aging report; monitoring of inventory was elevated from annual to monthly review.
- Re-engineered budget process by engaging stakeholders to participate in process, resulting in improved accuracy and obtainable long-range plans.
- Developed bottom-up approach to planning sales, budgeting expenses, and exposing critical risks. Reduced expense budget by £3M (10%).
- Reduced time, expense, and labuor while improving accuracy of physical inventory by partnering with IT to enhance inventory control system and implement the use of barcoding and scanners. Reduced staff needed for physical inventory count, from 20 to 6 employees.
- Reduced shrinkage, theft, and shortages at store locations by partnering with internal security manager to increase the number of security cameras. Reduced shrinkage by more than £100K annually.

DEF Consulting – Anytown   2012–2015
Consultant / Business Analyst
Business process improvement services; ranked in the top 10 of Enterprise Performance Management (EPM); £2M in sales. Hired to develop and implement finance models to integrate with Hyperion planning software. Created functional specifications, according to the needs of local Regeneron team. Participated in sales presentations with potential clients to assist in new business development efforts.

- Financial process liaison between technical team and client requirements.
- Developed month- and quarter-end financial reports for board of directors.
- Created rolling forecast and 5-year strategic planning initiatives.
- Integrated complex client planning model templates to work in new environment, resulting in accelerating the migration period from 9 to under 6 months.
- Developed bottom-up approach for budgeting and planning to identify opportunities and risks; engaged managers and cross-functional channels for accountability for budgets and sales targets.
- Discovered significant risk in payroll expense by implementing a time-management tool, which tracks by projects, resulting in a reduction in payroll costs by £1.2M over a 12-month period.

LKL Ltd., Anytown   2004–2012
Manager – Strategic Planning and Analysis   2006–2012
Senior Retail Accountant,   2004–2006

Manager – Strategic Planning and Analysis   2006–2012
Hired to power the company budgeting and planning effort, including wholesale, retail, Internet, and mail order. Forecasted sales, cost of sales, stock assortments, and budgeting expenses. Produced monthly P&L statement, cash

-continued-flow statements, and balance sheet. Reported financial results and recommendations for improvements to senior management.

- Responsible for preparation of consolidated business plans and forecasts including retail and wholesale divisions and 40 retail boutiques.
- Built consolidation reports for upper management, saving the company £29K in consulting fees.
- Reduced maintenance costs by creating national accounts with suppliers for lighting costs for retail boutiques. Replaced local suppliers with variable costs, saving the company £500K.
- Reduced rent expense by £2.4 million in 24 months by implementing a comprehensive review of leases, exposing overpayments, late fees, and percent of rent being erroneously paid to landlords.

Senior Retail Accountant,   2004–2006

Hired to oversee and manage financial operations for 40 retail boutiques, including expenses, budgets, and variance to plan analysis. Produced monthly P&L and cash flow statements, and balance sheet. Reported financial results to senior management with recommendations for improving results.

- Conducted physical inventory for retail boutiques with an inventory value of £1M per store and warehouse inventory of £20M.
- Implemented internal physical inventory programme using in-house-developed software rather than outside suppliers, resulting in savings of £80K per year.
- Coordinated with IT department to develop POS software to reduce credit card chargebacks, resulting in a savings of £100K in lost sales per year.
- Reduced expenses by 17% for retail boutiques by developing a second version of P&L highlighting managers' controllable expenses and tying incentive bonuses to net income. Resulted in a 3.4 million reduction in controllable expenses over a three-year period.

MNO, othertown   2000–2004

Senior Business Manager

Product company. Hired for budgeting and financial planning department. Responsible for tracking sales and expense performance of 260 boutiques. Created pro forma models to analyze potential new store locations and acquisitions.

- Streamlined planning process by implementing strategy to allocate resources strategically rather than functionally, tying performance to budget targets, and reduced expenses by approximately £3M over 12 months.
- Reduced payroll expense by £2.1M over 12 months across 260 store locations by tying payroll hours to sales and empowering managers to meet goals.

PQR Companies, Othertown   1998–2000

Financial Analyst   2000

£84B international financial services and insurance products firm. Hired to perform financial reporting, month-end close, and overall expense variance analysis. Managed forecasting and budgeting.

- Reported financial results in preparation for IPO.
- Developed access database to track performance of mortgage-backed securities for proposed marketing.
- Effectively managed P&L reporting for all domestic profit centers.

(continued)

1999–2000

Senior Financial Analyst
Global alternative asset management firm; £2.8B in sales. Responsible for P&L reporting on Northeast and Southeast regional profit centres.
- Instrumental in merger and acquisition support as a member of due diligence team with primary responsibility for acquisition models.
- Analyzed takeover targets, created pro forma statement and models, and performed analysis.

1998–1999

Planning Analyst
International producer and seller of fine jewelry and luxury goods. Hired to prepare business plans for all domestic retail locations totaling £3.8B in sales. Charged with analyzing and reporting key indicators, including sales, expenses, and profit margins. Responsible for identifying areas within retail chain for reduction of expenses.
- Reduced payroll expense by £1.1M across 65% of boutiques.
- Re-engineered budget and planning efforts by including stakeholders for responsibility of stores' success, resulting in increased probability by +5.5% over the following six months.

XYZ Bank, Othertown   1993–1998
Manager
Global diversified financial services and products firm; £68B in sales. Hired to contribute to month-end close process, supporting three business offices. Created expense variance reporting for monitoring expenses, planning sales, and managing general accounting support. Produced long-range forecasts with monthly update for three business offices.
- Revamped intercompany reporting for three business offices, resulting in elimination of duplicate entries, reducing the time to close.
- Reduced expenses by £120K for three major sales offices by implementing new expense controls.
- Assisted in increasing annual sales by creating a monthly query identifying high net worth individuals (HNWI). Monthly report was utilized to target and cross-sell existing as well as other products.

EDUCATION & CERTIFICATIONS

University of Othertown   1990
BSc International Finance

SAP Certification; Cost Management and Controlling Certification; Certified Microsoft Office Professional

Superior references available

Kathy Miller

11 Any Avenue
Anytown AA0 0AA

Linked in profile

01234 567890
Kmiller@verizon.net

Director National & Global Accounts

PERFORMANCE PROFILE

Exceptional pharmaceutical sales record, backed by rigorous academic training and including 10 years in National & Global Accounts. Experienced as National Account Analyst in the venture capital industry and National Account Consulting, providing a unique background and analytical skills necessary to consistently outperform sales quotas, develop new business, build strong customer relationships, and effectively manage sales teams. Exceptional skills in all stages of the sales cycle and strategic planning.

- Builds and nurtures long-term customer relationships with executive-level decision makers; easily develops rapport with management, physician opinion leaders, and clinical staff.
- Knowledgeable in healthcare marketplace, including competition, industry regulations, trends, customer
- needs, and pricing.
  Strong contract development, negotiating, and implementation (pull-through) skills.
- Leads the planning process for new product launches for managed care and commercial payers.
- Excellent written and oral communication skills; delivers high-impact presentations.
- Multitasker with the ability to manage multiple projects simultaneously in fast-paced environments with changing requirements and priorities.
- Manages strategic planning process, prepares forecasts, and develops growth strategies.
- Cross-functional team leadership skills with CAMs, RAMs, marketing, field sales, and customers.

BUSINESS DEVELOPMENT SKILLS

*Develops Strategic Business Plans	*Excellent Analytical Skills	*Profit Margin Enhancement
*Fiscal Responsibilities	*Efficient Resource Allocation	*Forecasting & Budgeting
*Ensures End-User & Patient Access	*Negotiations & Contracting Skills	*Executes Pull-Through
*Ensures Physician Reimbursement	*Identifies Industry Trends	*Managed Care
*Long-Term Customer Relationships	*Healthcare Provider Relations	*Identifies Customer Needs
*Customer Advocate	*Product Launch Strategies	*Business Acumen
*Policies & Procedures	*CRM Applications	*Performance Metric Reporting

SALES MANAGEMENT SKILLS

*Sales Management	*Leadership & Mentoring Skills	*Budget Accountability
*Hires & Trains Managers	*Sales Training & Development	*Reporting Procedures
*Contract Pull-Through Procedures	*Establishes Best Practices	*Assist Field Sales
*Quota & Incentive Plan Development	*Identifies Policies & Procedures	*Compensation Plans
*Industry Guidelines	*Regulatory Compliance	*Customer Relations

PROFESSIONAL EXPERIENCE

ABC Tech, Anytown   2014–Present
Director National Accounts
Hired to develop contracting strategies supporting the launch of a new product and build relationships with decision makers at commercial organizations, Group Purchasing Organizations (GPOs), and disease state opinion leaders in oncology marketplace.

- Researches and analyzes competitive information regarding the oncology marketplace to assist in reaching company's goals and objectives.
- Collaborates with scientific and marketing team members, including external advertising and consulting agencies to create customer-oriented messaging.
- Developing early-stage contract template designed to optimize product uptake, providing end-users with product access for appropriate patients by partnering with payers and GPOs.

DEF, Anytown   2010–2014
Biopharmaceutical National Account Analyst and Consultant
Venture capital and consulting service for organizations with novel human therapeutics and medical devices. Hired to consult start-up organizations regarding the establishment or improvement of national account departments. Provided strategic analysis and guidance for selling into disease-specific marketplaces. Guided organizations to incorporate policies and procedures, enabling start-up companies to maximize profit margins while complying with industry guidelines and government regulations.

- Successfully assisted in the establishment of national account departments at four start-up organizations.
- Instrumental in the establishment of a national accounts department for a major pharmaceutical organization to support the launch of a surgical device.
- Researched and analyzed market conditions for pharmaceuticals and medical devices designed to treat numerous disease states and facilitated successful product launches.

HIJ, Anytown   2006–2010
Senior Clinical Specialist
Hired to increase sales volume, market share, and profitability of a mature drug. Analyzed the marketplace and collaborated with key opinion leaders as well as innovative overseas healthcare providers to formulate a strategic plan to increase product uptake. Collaborated across multiple organizations to gain commitment and resources to increase sales and medication-related patient outcomes. Participated in the administration of phase IV research.

- Influenced positive changes to reimbursement policies (step edits) at commercial payers.
- Established relationships with global disease state opinion leaders, marketing personnel, a nationwide patient advocacy group, and select local chapters to research and perform strategic marketplace analysis.
- Instrumental in building pilot programme for the introduction of continuous quality improvement (CQI) tactics into pulmonary disease management, including a patient/family educational component focused on benefits of compliance.
- Advanced pilot programme into a national initiative resulting in increased sales. Turned around 80% of territories performing below quota, resulting in 90% of territories reaching quota within six months of implementation.
- Pilot programme increased medication-related patient outcomes by 14%.

KLM, Anytown   2000–2006
Account Manager
World's largest biotech organization providing drugs for unmet medical needs. Hired to build relationships with executive-level decision makers to assist in managing £225M in product sales at 14 corporate accounts and 3 national accounts. Led contract negotiations, monitored compliance, and conducted internal/external business reviews quarterly. Identified growth obstacles, created solutions, and motivated product stakeholders to participate in co-branded initiatives developed to aid each party in achieving its goals.

- Provided internal contract pull-through efforts by collaborating with marketing personnel, regional managers, district managers, and sales representatives.

(continued)

- Influenced external contract pull-through efforts by building strong relationships with senior management and key opinion leaders at accounts.
- Signed 100% of annual customer contracts prior to due date.
- Exceeded expected profit margins annually by negotiating contracts using.
- Developed programme increasing from 56% to 77% the national number of patients who experienced therapeutic results
- Selected as national account/corporate account trainer.

Regional Accounts Manager   1998–2000
Promoted from previous position as district sales manager (1996–1998) within two years. Supported the national "Plan of Action" by collaborating with national account managers and coordinating the pull-through process for joint initiatives. Negotiated contracts, monitored contract compliance, and led the pull-through efforts for co-branded product initiatives. Conducted regular internal and external business reviews each quarter; managed £180M insales.

- Converted £2.3M account from competitor's product.
- Created pilot programme for sales initiative to increase appropriate product use and medication-related patient outcomes, resulting in increased number of patients in target range from 59% to 78%.
- Successfully completed contracting process on time annually, resulting in uninterrupted sales.
- Exceeded required profit margins at contracted accounts and exceeded sales quota annually.

District Sales Manager,   1996–1998
Responsibilities included supervising eight representatives and one clinical nurse specialist marketing biotechnology to key executives, physicians, local payers, distributors, and regulatory agencies. Hired and trained new staff while developing existing personnel to improve business acumen. Managed £36M in annual sales.

- Exceeded sales quota and objective each year.
- Oversaw contracting efforts with 194 healthcare providers, ensuring uninterrupted business.
- Instrumental in successfully reopening contract efforts with group purchasing organizations.
- Committee member of advisory board focused on strategies to provide end-userand patient access.

Professional Sales Representative,   1991–1996
Provided pull-through for mandated contract sales and marketing initiatives. Marketed cutting-edge recombinant DNA human therapeutics to subspecialty physician practices.

- Led the district in sales 3 of 5 years, including the results generated by academic sales territories.
- Negotiated contracts and oversaw implementation at 36 oncology and dialysis clinics

(continued)

EDUCATION

University of Anytown   2010
MSc. Pharmacy

University of Anytown   2002
MSc. Pharmaceutical Management

University of Anytown   1990
BSc. Management

PROFESSIONAL DEVELOPMENT

Cultural Intelligence: Facilitator Training, 2013
Understanding Changes in Healthcare Reform, 2013
Biopharmaceutical Sales and Marketing in Today's Multicultural Environment, 2012
Healthcare Reform and Its Effects on Providers, 2011
Emotional Intelligence: Motivating Customers and Co-workers, 2011
Transformational Leadership in the Medical Setting, 2010
Large Account Management: Collaborating Within and Across Organizations, 2010
New Frontiers in Healthcare: Rare Disease Management, 2009

PROFESSIONAL CERTIFICATIONS

Certified Medical Representative

Nationally Certified Paramedic

Specialty Training Received:
- Advanced Cardiac Life Support
- Pre-Hospital Trauma Life Support
- Pediatric Advanced Life Support
- Neonatal Transport Specialist

PROFESSIONAL ORGANIZATION/AFFILIATIONS

International Women in Leadership Association
National Association of Sales Professionals

(continued)

PUBLICATIONS

Miller, K. (n.d.). Cultural Intelligence and Leadership: A Study of Pharmaceutical Leaders in India. *International Journal of Marketing Management* 2015.

GLOBAL EXPERIENCE AND CULTURAL DIVERSITY AWARENESS

Performed consulting and research at Indian nanotechnology pharmaceutical organization (Delhi, Agra, Una, India).

International liaison for key opinion leaders: Essen, Germany; Rotterdam, Netherlands; Istanbul, Turkey; Turin, Italy; Toronto, Canada.

International Business Conduct Training: Germany, India, and China.

United States Department of State: Global Leadership Programme.

International Centre of Indiana: International Leadership Event Host.

Extensive travel and business experience in Europe and Asia.

DARCY BINGLEY

11 Any Ave., Anytown AA0 0AA | 0123456 7890 | d.bingley@gmail.com

DIRECTOR OF STRATEGIC ALLIANCES & BUSINESS DEVELOPMENT | ACCOUNT EXECUTIVE | SENIOR MANAGER

Driving innovation, fueling growth, and eliminating waste while introducing energy-saving and sustainability solutions for multinational and government clients.

Energy consulting executive who positions organizations for success via long-term sustainability plans, state-of-the-art solutions/products, and streamlined business processes. Natural relationship builder adept at cultivating and maintaining mutually beneficial partnerships with high-tech, manufacturing, and government clients. Evaluate client needs to formulate strategic energy-saving and sustainability plans, leveraging industrial process and industry expertise to navigate and influence energy policy decisions, curb energy consumption, and reduce energy costs.

Solutions-focused innovator known for pioneering design and launch of groundbreaking software products that provide clients with transparent energy consumption data and support continuous process improvement across quality, throughput, waste, costs, and sustainability. Skillfully identify, secure, and execute complex, multimillion-pound initiatives, ensuring completion within strict time, budget, and quality requirements. Passionate about protecting environment for public enjoyment.

PROFESSIONAL SKILLS

Business Development	Business Partnering	Cost Control
Account Management	Lean Manufacturing	Operations Management
Client Relationship Development	Budget Management	Team Building & Leadership
Strategic Business Planning	Needs Assessment	Proposal Development
Product Development & Launch	Investment Analysis	Negotiations
Project Management	Business & Financial Analysis	Renewable Energy
Process Re-engineering	Forecasting & Modeling	Regulatory Compliance

PERFORMANCE HIGHLIGHTS

➢ Drove new and existing business developing and promoting enterprise software package/maintenance module for smart buildings that was deployed across 73 facilities; energy dashboard module is forecasted to launch across 34 additional facilities, generating energy-saving opportunities for clients.

➢ Identified more than £6M in utility/gas savings for clients while generating equal amount of revenue through management of programme focused on identifying natural gas energy savings for industrial clients.

➢ Increased facility runtimes 25% and reduced waste 15% for manufacturing plant via optimizing process improvements, earning recognition as Process Engineering Expert.

➢ Currently in strategic partnership with government to achieve 30% energy consumption reduction.

PROFESSIONAL EXPERIENCE

ABC Tech Systems, Anytown   2008 – Present

£32M+ consulting firm specializing in commissioning and energy efficiency. Entered into strategic partnership with XYZ (Japan) in 2013, providing sustainability and energy efficiency consulting for multinational companies.

DIRECTOR – TECHNICAL SERVICES

Advanced to oversee vertical line of business focused on building systems integration while managing firm's largest account. Monitor market and identify trends to propose new product/technical solutions, attract new clients, and secure new accounts, managing all aspects of project life cycle for long-term, high-calibre initiatives. Lead 10-member team in ensuring customer satisfaction and retention.

DIRECTOR – TECHNICAL SERVICES, continued

Formulate business/corporate strategies for key accounts. Collaborate with senior staff to cross-sell products, driving overall company growth. Deliver presentations on integrated building systems at industry conferences.

➤ Consistently maintained between £3M and £5M in profits of existing accounts (25% of company revenue), delivering average 12% EBITDA, through cultivating solid, mutually beneficial alliances with clients.
➤ Personally generated 10% of all company-wide sales and played pivotal role in delivering 20% revenue growth within new and existing accounts.
➤ Established company standard for number of energy site audits executed within 60 days after spearheading on-time, on-budget delivery of £800K government project with 50 site locations in 60-day timeframe.
➤ Secured £500K+ in sales from enterprise software solution tool for energy and facility management.
➤ Developed and implemented key performance metrics for multimillion- pound projects, tracking profit margins, budgets, and forecasted revenue for initiatives.

DEF Ltd., | Anytown   2007 – 2008
Middle-market food manufacturing company. Sold to Quality Food Company in 2010.

PROJECT & PROCESS ENGINEERING MANAGER – PRODUCT DEVELOPMENT & ENGINEERING

Required to streamline and optimize existing processes in order to drive profitability and growth. Proposed solutions to key decision makers, developing and presenting financial models to gain authorization on required capital funds. Designed solutions based on statistical process control models. Controlled project budgets of up to £5M. Participated in board meetings and weekly meetings with CFO.

➤ Played integral role in transforming highly manual processing plant into automated, efficient facility, increasing yield 50%, cutting costs 50%, reducing waste 10%, and enabling plant to meet 6-month product launch deadline and high customer demands.
➤ Enhanced product quality while driving development of new products and managing capital projects valued at up to £5M.
➤ Contributed to developing sustainable packaging practices and processes to meet client's sustainability goals through partnership with supply chain staff to inspect packaging materials.

GHI Ltd., | Othertown   2004 – 2007
Largest exporter of wines from Europe.

SENIOR PROCESS ENGINEER – CORPORATE ENGINEERING

Brought onboard as trusted adviser, incorporating Lean Six Sigma principles to spearhead capital projects and process improvement initiatives at European wine producers. Liaised between operations, satellite wineries, and corporate engineering in development of projects, formulation of project budgets(up to £25M), and proposal of forecasted results. Served as active participant on committee, bringing sustainable practices to wine producers. Supervised 2 control technicians in delivery of various projects.

➤ Optimized critical wine-making processes, achieving 25% throughput increase, accelerating processing time, and enhancing product quality through institution of rigorous statistical process control and Six Sigma–based principles.
➤ Strengthened communication between corporate engineering and satellite wineries by engaging company owners, corporate, and local winery teams, introducing company-wide operations consistency.

JKL Logistics, | Othertown   2000 – 2004
                                                                            (continued)

Specialty electronic-grade chemical manufacturing firm serving multinational clients.

PROCESS & RELIABILITY ENGINEERING MANAGER
Hired as staff engineer and earned promotion to manager within 2 years after applying analytical approach to process design and developing processes to meet demanding customer requirements. Directed day-to-day operations for 24-hour chemical processing facility, ensuring that operations were maintained, yielded necessary throughput and quality, and met strict customer standards. Supervised up to 8 staff and indirectly managed 70+ employees across shifts. Ensured safe operations, mitigating risk exposure to plant personnel and nearby community.

➤ Enhanced processing efficiency while sustaining product quality by spearheading process engineering efforts.
➤ Realized 25% reduction in unplanned maintenance downtime and improved product quality by as much as 1,000% through coordination of processing plant transformations and capital projects.
➤ Formulated hundreds of SOPs to address stringent quality and compliance standards within 6-month period while managing plant's largest division.

EARLIER CAREER

XYZ Group| RESERVOIR ENGINEER – OPERATIONS & ENGINEERING | 1998 – 2000

EDUCATION

MBA, Business Administration & Entrepreneurship
Othertown University
MBA, Business Administration & Finance
Othertown University
MSc, Chemical Engineering
University of Anytown
BSc, Chemical Engineering
University of Anytown

EXTRACURRICULAR ACTIVITIES

➤ Member of the UK Ballroom Dance association & Dance UK
➤ Competitive ballroom dancer, regional champion, social dances, and current champion, Foxtrot

References available upon request

Patrice Evans MBA

11 Any Ave., Anytown AA0 0AA
01234 567890 patrice.evans@anyisp.com

DISASTER RECOVERY & BUSINESS CONTINUITY PLANNING • INTERNAL CONTROLS

Linked in.

Disaster Recovery and Business Continuity Planning Coordinator

Professional Profile

➢ Business Continuity and Internal Controls professional with strong accounting experience across diverse industries, including mass media, manufacturing, software development, and financial services.

➢ Director of Policies and Controls skilled in developing and implementing enterprise-wide business continuity and disaster recovery strategies and solutions. Expertise in business continuity planning, analysis, implementation, training, exercises, and continuous process improvements to ensure the safety of employees and the protection of intellectual property and essential resources, functions, and business services.

Professional Skills

Business Continuity Management (BCM)	Financial Accounting	Leadership & Teambuilding
Business Continuity Planning (BCP)	Financial Analysis & Reporting	Communications & Presentations
Business Impact Assessments (BIA)	Risk Mitigation Strategies	Incident / Crisis Communication Programme
Internal Controls Management	Project Management	BCM Awareness & Training
Business Process Mapping (BPM)	Resource Allocation	Supplier Relationship Management
Crisis Management / Disaster Recovery (DR)	Process Improvements	Analytical & Problem-Solving Skills
Policies, Procedures, & Systems Development	Productivity Optimization	Creativity, Integrity, Initiative, & Drive

Computer Skills

Proficient Microsoft Office Suite: Word, Excel, PowerPoint, Access, and Outlook, Microsoft Office 365, Visio, and Project. PeopleSoft Financials, SharePoint, and Essbase.

Performance Highlights

• Director of Policies and Controls at ABC who championed and influenced the inclusion of business continuity and disaster recovery protocols into functional strategies for this global media company with £1 billion in annual revenues.
   – Collaborated with technology team to develop a business continuity wiki application on the Company intranet. Managed essential informatics for senior management and response team during a crisis or incident.
   – Led the development and implementation of a new Vendor Portal application, which led to a reduction of 3 FTEs from a staff of 6, yielded £142,000 in annual savings, and reduced the average time from 2.5 weeks to 4 days.

• Finance Manager at DEF Products, who joined this startup company and established the company's initial accounting system and internal controls. Directed and coached staff members in setting up accounts payable, order entry, customer services, purchasing, and payroll functions. Successfully led migration from ISO 9002:1994 to ISO 9001:2000, resulting in the company being the first producer to attain this quality certification.

Professional Experience

ABC GROUP, Anytown   2003 – 2016
Privately held global mass media company with portfolio of industry-leading print, video, and digital brands

Director, Policies & Controls	2011 – 2016
Senior Manager, Policies & Controls	2008 – 2011
Manager, Accounting	2003 – 2008

continued

Director, Policies & Controls   2011 – 2016
Reported to Managing Director. Managed business continuity, ensuring that all departments within Accounting
Services maintained processes and procedures that were cost effective, efficient, and deterred fraud.

- Collaborated with IT and senior business leaders to create the initial Business Continuity Plan for ABC Group.
- Created a checklist that helped guide the response team, created testing protocols, and established a steering committee and core team.
- Led and facilitated corporate response efforts for designated incidents/crisis situations. Monitored and evaluated BCP tests and reported findings to management.
- Chosen to lead newly formed supplier Controls group that provided oversight of all suppliers, monitored changes to existing information, and prevented fraud in a master file containing almost 200,000 suppliers. Managed the business/technology team charged with developing and implementing the £70,000 portal application, which came in on time and 7% under budget, which saved £5,000.

Senior Manager, Policies & Controls   2008 – 2011
Selected to lead newly created Policies & Controls group that ensured all accounting services departments had adequate policies
and internal controls in place for all critical business processes.
- Coordinated all business continuity planning (BCP) efforts company wide.
- Collaborated with auditors on Internal Controls audit report and contributed accounting expertise to special projects in conjunction with the brands and corporate groups.
- Created and developed "The Business Director Policies & Controls Guidelines" Document. With the Managing Director coauthored and co-presented "The Business of Content" presentation series, which was delivered to over 250 employees.
- Saved the company £120,000 by reducing headcount by 2 FTEs.

Manager, Accounting   2003 – 2008
Led accounting team that captured and reported financial information for the company's digital, and intercompany operations.
- Integrated digital company's accounting into ABC Group. Learned accounting practices and integrated them into ABC's , performing monthly accounting close and related balance sheet analysis.
- Performed account analysis, reviewed staff work (journal entries and account analysis), and handled ad hoc requests
- Trained and mentored 6 staff accountants.

DEF PRODUCTS, Anytown   1999 – 2003
Specialty chemical manufacturer and distributor chemicals used by diverse industries such as automotive (OEM) parts and food processors.

Finance Manager

Reported to the General Manager. Managed all aspects of accounting, finance, and logistics, as well as quality and support
services, including purchasing, production planning, quality assurance, and human resources.
- Served as a liaison for all information services and accounting/finance needs.
- Led successful migration from ISO 9002:1994 standard to the new ISO 9001:2000 standard. The company was the first producer to attain this quality certification.

GHI Ltd., Othertown   1993 – 1999
Manufacturer of fabrics, wall coverings, and decorative home furnishings with £45 million in annual revenue and 225 employees.

Manager, Accounting	1997 – 1999
Senior Cost Analyst	1995 – 1997
Manager, Financial Projects	1993 – 1995

(continued)

Managed all accounting functions, including issuance of financial
statements and coordinating cross-functional initiatives through 5 division.

- Determined criteria for new automated general ledger system. Evaluated several systems and determined the best option. Presented findings for executive approval and installed new system in record time, resulting in improving monthly closing cycle by 3 business days, providing better information, and reducing user complaints of inaccuracies by 65%.
- Realized £250,000 in productivity gains by evaluating, selecting, and installing an activity-based costing system that provided fast, accurate cost-per-data for tracking overhead expense, which improved processing time by 50% and transmission time by 75%.
- Coached, mentored, and rebuilt a cohesive and effective 6-person team of accounting professionals, effectively reversing a trend toward a collection of competitive individuals pulling in different directions. Fostered a collaborative and productive workplace environment and built solid business relationships.
- Major areas of work performed included monthly, quarterly, and year-end financial statements, monthly close process, special projects, and review of staff work (journal entries and account reconciliations).

Education

Master of Business Administration (MBA), University of Anytown
Bachelor of Business Administration (BBA), University of Anytown

Professional Certifications

Certified Business Manager (CBM)   2003
Certified Lead Auditor – ISO 9001:2000 Quality Systems
Certified Internal Auditor – ISO 9000:1994 Quality Systems

Hobbies & Interests

Golf and International Travel

Superior references available on request

Charles Chalmers

Linked **in** profile

Anytown AA0 0AA   GalleryDirector@earthlink.net   0123456 7890

Gallery Director/Curator

Performance Summary

My professional life is focused on art in all it embraces: drawing, painting, sculpture, photography, cinema, video, audio, performance and digital art, art history, and criticism.

My personal life is similarly committed. Recently relocated from Manhattan, I intend to make a contribution to the UK Arts community commensurate with my knowledge, enthusiasm, and sensibilities.

Professional Competencies

* Art History
* Art Theory
* Art Research
* Art Communities
* Alumni Networks
* Artist Networks
* Art Handlers

* Installation of Art
* Space Fluidity
* Hang/Light/Label
* Themed/Sequenced
* Space Reconfiguration
* Dynamic Dialogue
* Social Networking

* Recruitment & Selection
* Private Collectors
* Catering
* Graphics
* Photoshop
* PR
* Intercultural Exchanges

Professional Highlights

Art History

Thorough knowledge of art history from caves of Lascaux through current artists such as Bruce Nauman, Jessica Stockholder, and Luc Tuymans. Film history from Lumiere Brothers to Almodovar. Current with key critical art and film theory. Ongoing workshops and lectures with the likes of Matthew Barney, Louise Bourgeois, and Andy Goldsworthy.

Research New Artists

Connected to cutting-edge art and artists through involvement with the art communities and galleries of New York and Boston and the faculty, student, and alumni networks of RISD, Columbia, Boston Museum School, New England School of Art & Design, and now Mass Art. Twenty years of Manhattan gallery openings and networking with artists at MOMA, PS1, Guggenheim, Whitney, Metropolitan, and Film Forum. Attend International Centre for Photography workshops and lectures.

PR Materials

Energizing invitations, comprehensive press kits, illustrated press releases, and artist binder materials. Sensitive to placing art in historical/cultural context. Photoshop.

Management

Fourteen years' art staff management experience, including curriculum development. Responsible for art instructors, art handlers, and maintenance crews, as well as working with printers, catering, and graphic arts staff.

continued

Charles Chalmers	GalleryDirector@earthlink.net	0123456 7890

Professional Experience

1994-2005 Chair of Visual Arts, The Green Briar School
Curriculum development, portfolio preparation, internal and external monthly shows, theater sets, monthly video news show. Taught art history and all the studio arts, managed staff of three.

1989-2004 President, Art Workshops
Private art studio and art history curriculum, staff of four. Private groups to Manhattan museums and gallery tours.

1989-Present Freelance artist, photographer, and editor
Highlights from the *sublime* to the *ridiculous* include: Taught photography at Trinity School, Manhattan; photographer for the Ramones; editor of *Pioneer*, insurance industry trade magazine; assistant to Claudia Weill, documentary filmmaker, director of *Girlfriends*.

Education

MFA. Magna cum laude. Columbia University, 1988
Awards: Forman Prize for film criticism
Taught undergraduate Intro to Film, under Milos Forman and Andre Bazin.

Subscriptions
Art in America, Art News, Artforum, New York Times, Parkett, Sight & Sound, Film Comment, Modern Painters.

Memberships
MOMA/PS1, Whitney Museum of American Art, Guggenheim, Metropolitan Museum of Art, DIA.

Superior references available

Rem Koolhaus

11 Any Ave., Anytown AA0 0AA   0123456 7890   rkoolhaus@anyisp.com

Managing Director
Technology Industries - Global M&A Expertise

Performance Summary

Twenty-five-year track record of success in delivering legal, strategic, and business results for companies in technology industries. Encyclopedic knowledge of the international business and legal landscape. Corporate strategy & transactions expert with extensive global experience in M&A, JV, licensing, supplier agreements, public/private placements, divestitures, and other initiatives.

Business advisor to owners, and Board members.Strong general management and operational skills. Financially disciplined and focused on the company and stakeholders.Seasoned dealmaker and formidable negotiator — expert in handling complex financial, business, and cultural matters, including sixty M&A and divestures.

Core Skills

- IPO
- Patents
- Joint Ventures
- Licensing
- Shareholder Value
- Risk Management
- Divestitures
- JV

- M&A
- Litigation, Initiation
- Regulatory Compliance
- IP Management
- Operational
- Labour Law
- Board Advisory
- Investor Relations

- Growth and Exit Strategy
- Public & Private/Debt & Equity
- Startup Strategy & Capital
- Placements
- Pre/Post M&A
- Outside Management
- Executive Decision Support

Technologies

- Global Telecoms
- Connectivity
- Managed Networks
- Security

- IT
- Hosting
- Software Licenses
- Global Joint Ventures

- Internet
- Technology Transfers
- Network/Voice-based apps
- Technology Licensing

PROFESSIONAL EXPERIENCE

ABC, Anytown   2008 to Present
Specialists in Corporate Strategy and Development, Capital Raising, Corporate Governance, Growth Management, Transactions
MANAGING DIRECTOR

Executive in charge of all aspects of business operations – business development, P&L, contract negotiation, client deliverables, and engagement management. Competitively differentiated by early and continued collaboration with client executives in overall enterprise strategy to support legal structures for client growth initiatives.

Growth and Exit Strategies

- Partnered with executive team of £15 million software services company to deliver exit strategy and clear path toward strategic value enhancements.

(continued)

Rem Koolhaus	0123456 7890	Page 2

- Advised a £35 million business services firm on growth strategies and exit options.
- **Capital Raising** – Advised and participated in private equity fundraising for an early-stage Brazilian agro venture.
- **Startup Strategy & Capital Raising** – Delivered in-depth legal, growth, business, and corporate development support to start up "green" state-of-the-art European data center provider, leading negotiations with private equity participants and advising on acquisition strategy.

DEF Ltd., London, Chenmai, Beijing   1998 to 2008
– Internet Business Communications Provider in Connectivity,
Hosting, Security, Managed Networks, and Related Professional Services

Campany Director   1998 to 2008

Fifth employee hired and key member of the senior executive team – recruited to contribute business acumen, commercial insights, and general adviser related to startup operations, growth transactions, and exit strategy. Involved with all enterprise-level vision, strategy decisions. Managed department of 6 legal professionals supporting cross-functional business operations, corporate governance, legal affairs, transactions, and regulatory compliance in 15 countries.
IP portfolio, deal sourcing/corporate transactions, contracts/agreements, risk management, regulatory compliance.

Legal Services & Corporate Development Management – Strategies, Transactions, & Results

- **Capital Raising & IPO** – Directed private placement of £130 million equity investment. Principal in structure and execution of IPO – diligence, preparation of filings, dual listing on Nasdaq and Amsterdam stock exchanges – resulting in £330+ million in net proceeds to the company.
- **Corporate Governance** – Developed and rolled out corporate governance policies and annual compliance programme to business operations spanning 15 countries.
- **M&A, Divestiture, & Post M&A Transition/Integration** – Led due diligence, negotiations, and closing of 35 corporate acquisitions – Internet services providers and hosting companies – in 15 countries. Directed key aspects of post-close integration and transition, including realization of synergies, governance, brand, and culture. Managed bidding process, negotiations, and divestiture of non-value-added operations in 6 countries, enabling company to reduce quarterly cash burn by 80% and focus on core markets.
- **Investor Relations Strategy** Achieved strategic turnaround and growth strategy (2002 through 2004) while protecting investor confidence with a proactive outreach programme. Addressed potential de-listing by developing and presenting recuperative strategy first to Board, then to Nasdaq.
- **Exit Strategy Planning & Execution** – Called by Board to address liquidity crisis. Teamed with the CFO to formulate the exit strategy. Negotiated several auxiliary deals – including sale of non-core operating unit within 8 days – to produce operating revenues. Led ultimate auction process to optimize capital return to shareholders.

Distinctions

- Drove growth through international market penetration and strategic acquisitions to exceed objectives of £0 to £86 million in 24 months. Reduced cash burn rate by 80%, from £25+ million to less than £5 million per quarter. Decreased D&O/E&O premiums by £900,000 *p.a.*
- Served as the company's second-ranking officer in global business and legal matters 2003 to 2008.
- Assumed direct accountability for investor relations and corporate development functions.

GHI, Anytown   1994 to 1998
Global pioneer in Telecommunications Solutions, Equipment, and Services
DIRECTOR – VENTURES & ALLIANCES

Provided legal advice and business support to key areas of operations – IT systems/product development, marketing strategy, sales tools, software licensing, contracts – and advised senior-level management on transactional, IP, and regulatory matters.

- **M&A** – Managed project to identify and track synergy opportunities – valued at £1+ billion per year.
- **Global Joint Venture** – Managed GHI's interest in global telecom joint venture with XYZ Telecom. Team lead in negotiations to unwind complex alliance structure.
- **Intellectual Property** – Led legal team in analysis and resolution of key IP ownership issues between three global Telecom companies.
- **Technology Licensing** – Secured substantial reduction in desktop licensing fees through new £23 million multi-year agreement with A&E Tech.
- **Pre-/Post-Merger Business Transition & Integration** – Member of merger, transition, and implementation team dealing with organizational, financial, commercial, and regulatory issues. Collaborated in formulating post-merger internal trading programme and commercial model.

Distinctions

- Promoted within one year of employment.
- Winner of Excellence Award for contributions to GHI Mass Markets.
- Contributed critical legal and commercial support to new product launches – representing millions in annual sales revenue.
- Led policy formulation in addressing online copyright issues, software piracy, online hosting of pornography.
- Structured and negotiated long-term exclusive affiliation agreements with third parties.

LEGAL EXPERIENCE

JK & L, Anytown.   1988 to 1994
International Law Firm – Specialization in Corporate Transactions for Public &
Private Companies
SOLICITOR
Corporate transactional practice, including financing, acquisitions, dispositions, and mergers for private and publicly listed clients.

MN & O., Othertown   1985 to 1988
International Law Firm – Specialization European and South American Inbound
Investments and Domestic Legal Issues

SOLICITOR
TRAINEE SOLICITOR
Provided commercial , corporate and partnership, tax, litigation, immigration,and securities law advice, and M&A and private placement services. Early achievements include pursuing litigation appeal jury trial, and negotiating major commercial property agreements.

Rem Koolhaus	0123456 7890	Page 4

EDUCATION

University of Anytown   **1984**
Legal practice course

University of Othertown   **1983**
Graduate Diploma in Law

BA – Philosophy   **1981**
Othertown University

PROFESSIONAL AFFILIATIONS

Association for Corporate Growth (ACG)
Association of Corporate Counsel (ACC)

Superior references

Steven Christopher, PHR

11 Any Aven., Anytown AA0 0AA
01234 567890 | steve.christopher@anyisp.com

HUMAN RESOURCES MANAGEMENT • TALENT ACQUISITION
SUCCESSION PLANNING • CHANGE MANAGEMENT

Linked in profile

Professional Profile

Senior Human Resources Manager and Certified Professional in Human Resources (PHR) with 13+ years in the hospitality industry. Proven ability to structure HR strategy that aligns with corporate goals/objectives and provides tactical direction for the achievement of key initiatives to recruit, select, train, retain, and motivate top talent through the development of premier compensation programmes, improved onboarding, and employee training, coaching, and succession planning.

Professional Skills

Multisite Human Resources Management	Employment Law	Communications / Presentations
Strategic Planning & Budgeting	Regulatory Compliance	Managerial Training on HR Matters
HR Policies, Procedures, & Programme	Workforce Planning / Restructuring	Staff Training & Development
Organizational Development	HR Audits / Succession Planning	Employee Engagement & Motivation
Talent Acquisition & Retention	Online Recruiting / Social Media Recruiting	Employee Performance Evaluation
Compensation & Benefits Administration	Pre-Employment Screenings	Problem Solving
Employee Relationship Management	Employee Retention	Conflict Resolution & Teambuilding
Automated HR Records Management	Employee Developement	Special Events Coordination

Computer Skills

Applicant Tracking Systems | Talent Management Systems | Microsoft Office Suite: Word, Excel, PowerPoint, and Outlook Google+, Google Hangouts, Skype, GoToMeeting, Facebook, and LinkedIn

Performance Highlights

➢ **Trusted Adviser to Executive Leadership** with experience counselling/coaching business leaders and operations managers regarding employee relations issues. Demonstrated record of reducing labour cost while keeping HR functions running smoothly.

➢ **Senior HR Manager** with demonstrated success designing/implementing employee orientation programme and employee engagement survey processes (reporting results and developing action plans for improving employee engagement and productivity).

➢ **HR Programme Manager** who leads with purpose, genuinely cares about people, holds employees to high standards of performance, and influences positive outcomes for the company's success.

Professional Experience

ABC Restaurants Ltd,
Human Resources Manager

Anytown
2012 – Present

Employing 4,900 people nationwide with annual revenue of £75million.

- Advise executive leaders, senior managers, and general managers in the areas of employment laws, regulatory compliance, employee relations, workforce development, and succession planning.
- Manage human resources activities for 62 restaurants and 1,200 employees. Manage HR programme, including compensation, benefits, and staffing. Supervise 2 HR specialists/generalists and 1 administrative assistant.
- Partner with operations managers to recruit, train, and develop workforce.Guide and improve the employee performance management process, including job specs/requirements, employee appraisal process, staff ranking, individual development plans, compensation, promotions, and recognitions.
- Develop and guide the HR team to ensure overall effectiveness and achievement of departmental and company goals.
- Provide ongoing investigation of various HR issues to create a positive workplace environment. Administer compensation for employees.

Notable Achievements:
- Reduced hourly employee turnover by 25% by developing/implementing best practices in managerial coaching and employee relationship management.

(continued)

- Saved the company an estimated £577,000 by fighting compensation claims.
- Redesigned and implemented interviewing process resulting in employment of productive and loyal staff.
- Developed and implemented anti-harassment training programme.
- Rewrote all job descriptions.
- Conducted wage and salary survey for employees.

DEF CASINO   Anttown
Human Resources Supervisor   2007 – 2012
DEF is casino and hotel with 500 slot machines, 10 tables/games, and 200 hotel rooms.

- Facilitated employee relations programmes for all 600 employees, including mediating conversations between management and employees, investigating incidents, facilitating the peer review programme, overseeing the proper termination of employees, and scrutinizing all corrective disciplinary measures.
- Managed the Human Resources Training Department to ensure that new employees received training.
- Developed and implemented HR policies throughout. Designed and implemented the peer review board.
- Served as the Acting Director in the absence of the Human Resources Director.
- Planned, organized, and budgeted for employee-related events such as holiday parties and recognition ceremonies.
- Conducted wage and salary surveys.

Notable Achievements:

- Provided positive ongoing employee relationship management
- Reduced employee turnover by 50% over 4 years through various employee relations and employee engagement programme, such as designing and implementing an employee relations focus group for the General Manager.

GHI GROUP,   Anytown
Project Manager   2003 – 2007
A market research company.

- Oversaw daily management of 15+ separate marketing research projects and provided ongoing customer service for clients during market research studies.
- Managed a production staff creating questionnaires, reports, and various materials needed during the research study timeline.
- Designed employee and customer satisfaction questionnaires. Checked for fielding accuracy and monitored the daily progress of each study in the fielding process.
- Oversaw creation and launch of a website for client usage during a national automotive employee satisfaction survey.

JKL Ltd.,   Anytown
Visual/Advertising Associate   1997 – 2003
Clothing retailer.

- Implemented corporate advertising, marketing promotions, and season set-sell planners for all departments.
- Created an atmosphere conducive to shoppers. Organized all staff and customer VIP events.
- Set up showrooms in Anytown University
- Audited prices on a weekly basis to ensure correct sale pricing in the point-of-sale registers. Corrected any pricing errors.

Education
BA Business Administration, University of Anytown 1997

Certification & Professional Development

CIPD level 7
CIPD level 5
CIPD level 3

Professional Affiliations

Member of the Chartered Institute of Personal and Developement(CIPD)

Bonnie Cameron

11 Any Avenue., Anytown AA0 0AA

01234 56789

Purchasing Manager

PERFORMANCE SUMMARY

Twenty-five years' experience in business administration, marketing, and retail store operations with a history of professional growth and consistent achievement. Excellent management abilities, merchandising, inventory control, and purchasing skills. Demonstrates strong commitment to maintaining high levels of customer service while driving revenue growth through marketing and promotional strategies. Strong academic background with a BA in Business Administration and Accounting.

- Expertise in purchasing, inventory control, merchandising strategy, and customer service.
- Accurate in monitoring large inventory levels to maintain proper levels of inventory, establish reorder points, minimize lead times, set delivery dates, reduce stock-outs, and expedite the supply of critical items.
- Manages budgets and performs purchase planning/forecasting by analyzing sales data and market trends.
- Effectively communicates with all levels of the organization, vendors, and customers.
- Outstanding project planning and project management skills while meeting tight deadlines.
- Ability to adapt within fast-paced environments, learn new systems, and respond to shifting business strategies.
- Analytical with excellent decision-making, team-building, and leadership qualities.
- Technology: Excel, Microsoft Word, Management Outlook, Lotus Webmail, EDI, and JDA systems.

PROFESSIONAL COMPETENCIES

Purchasing Procedures & Techniques	Project Management	Electronic Data Interchange (EDI)
Inventory Control	Strategic Planning	Reduced Stock-outs & Inventory Turns
Establish Reorder Points	Purchase Orders	Invoice Payment & Processing
Vendor Relationship Management	Customer Service	Staff Leadership & Development
Forecasting	Business Strategies	Loss & Damage Claims
Delivery Schedules / Lead Time	Sales Reports	Merchandising Strategies
Budget and Profit/Loss Management	Sales/Profitability	Policies and Procedures
Analyze Sales Data and Market Trends	Negotiation Skills	Loss Prevention

PROFESSIONAL EXPERIENCE

ABC Ltd., Anytown

1999–Present

Store Manager

2002–Present

Multimillion-pound retail operation selling domestic merchandise and home furnishings. Tailors merchandise promotions and presentations for local market. Responsible for various tasks in the overall operation of the store, including measuring business trends, maximizing sales/profitability, expenses, payroll, shortages, customer service, loss prevention, safety, receiving, and all aspects of merchandising and inventory control. Supervised up to 40 employees. Progressed rapidly and promoted to positions with increasing responsibilities.

- Manages and purchases merchandise for annual inventory level of £3M+.
- Managed store inventory levels in 2010 and 2011 with an invisible waste of .38% of total store sales; store was chosen as best in the district.
- Increased sales by 12% in 2011 over companywide store sales of 5.9%.
- Coordinated and completed 2011 store remodelling project under budget.
- Monitors sales performance and merchandising strategy through the analysis of sales reports and comparison-shopping.
- Establish pricing on all custom orders for profit margin enhancement.

continued

Assistant Store Manager   2000–2001

Oversaw staff of sales associates, maintained schedules, conducted performance evaluations, and performed training sessions for employees. Merchandised store and developed unique presentations.

Department Manager   1999–2000

Responsible for customer service, displays, and marketing.

XYZ Ltd., Anytown   1985–1999

Store Manager   1997–1999

Responsible for management, supervision, and all store operations for a £12M Department store.

Progressed rapidly and promoted in positions with increasing responsibilities. Supervised up to 118 employees.

- Successfully directed and supervised store-remodeling project remaining under budget.
- Handled and resolved all escalated customer issues.
- Provided education and guidance to operations personnel for increased efficiency.
- Analyzed and developed long-range merchandise and operational strategies; store P&L responsibilities.
- Provided strong leadership skills to store employees faced with new competition in the area resulting in location remaining competitive.

Store Manager, Othertown   1995–1997

Developed and supervised store personnel and organization with a range of 65 to 115 employees. Responsible for sales and profitability of multimillion-pound operation. Analyzed and developed long-range merchandise and operations strategies.

Store Manager, Oldtown   1995

Directed and supervised store operations. Responsible for sales and expense controls in closing the store operation.

EDUCATION & PROFESSIONAL DEVELOPMENT

University of Anytown

BA in Business Administration and Accounting

Supervising People and Leading a Team

Sponsoring Organization: The ABC Group

Superior references available

11 Any Avenue
Anytown AA0 0AA

Jon Garibaldi

01234 567890
Jon.Garibaldi@gmail.com
Linked in profile

Sales Manager

Performance Summary

High-impact Sales Manager with more than 12 years of extensive experience in Marketing, Procurement, Sales, and Customer Relations. Deep knowledge across all sales and marketing disciplines, including project management, product launch, sales growth, business/product development, competitive research, and client communications.

Maintains a consistent focus on the bottom line; driving revenue growth, maximizing profitability, and capitalizing on all viable expansion opportunities. Creative, innovative, and forward thinking; adept at handling complex challenges with thoughtful, clearly-defined strategies that drive double-digit revenue growth.

Professional Skills

Outside Sales	Account Management	Territory Development	Strategic Planning
Customer Relationships	Proposal Development	Needs Identification	Product Management
Market Planning	Commodity Management	Supplier Management	Staff Training
Contract Negotiations	Sales Growth	Proposal Letters	Metrics Management
Financial Planning	Product Releases	Procurement	International Experience

——Professional Experience——

ABC Group, Anytown   2011 to Present

Gas turbines, steam turbines, and generators for power plants with £215.2M in revenue.
Marketing Specialist

Communicate with engineering to create comprehensive marketing plans and sales forecasts, build proposals, and negotiate contracts. Provide training to customers on products catalogue. Develop proposal letters for engineered parts for gas, steam, and generators. Collaborate with engineers on providing technical information to obtain quotes from supply management and to provide technical scope for customer proposals.

- Met and surpassed all financial goals and objectives, with £210 million in sales in one year.
- Established new marketing plans for product bulletins with £6 million target.
- Recognized with award for reducing quote response time from previously recorded metrics.
- Generated £5.3 million in sales by quoting customers on upcoming outages with appropriate project scope.
- Contributed to securing £75 million in new sales in one year by creating new customer proposals.

DEF., Anytown   2010 to 2011

Manufacturer of generators for power plants.
Sales and Marketing Specialist

Selected to drive revenue growth through establishment of long-term customer relationships. Reduced cost by domestically procuring parts previously manufactured in Japan. Created spare parts list for new equipment and maintained inventory for generator fleet.

- Exceeded sales targets by £1 million and increased margins by 5% in sales of generator spare parts.
- Increased spare parts margin 20% by sourcing domestically.
- Decreased customer response time by improving communication and streamlining the quoting process with Tokyo headquarters.
- Promoted Voltage Regulator service by creating new marketing materials.
- Generated 20% increase of marketing materials in promotion of Voltage Regulator service.

GHI Group, Anytown   2001 to 2010
Provider of gas turbines, steam turbines, and generators for power plants with £97M in revenue.
Sales Support Specialist   2008 – 2010

Established and cultivated strong customer relationships with new and potential customers. Reviewed customer data and trends for sales planning. Revitalized current customer relationships. Provided support and overview of all customer orders, including order entry, delivery, quality, and invoicing. Drove improvements in customer relationships. Created customer quotes for outage planning.

- Surpassed all sales targets by up to £750,000 in one year.
- Significantly reduced lead to proposal times for O&M and capital equipment.
- Reduced quote response lead time by focusing and prioritizing customer requests.

Procurement Specialist   2001 – 2003 & 2006 – 2008

Managed a £10 million inventory of raw material. Served as a liaison between Supply Management and Gas Turbine product line. Coordinated with Inventory Control group to reduce lot sizes and optimize stock purchases. Provided subject matter expertise on Six Sigma Project within the Inventory Department. Forecasted and procured raw materials for service spare part business.

- Spearheaded the automation of more than 1,000 items to supply base, saving company 10% in cost.
- Led the development of new strategic plans, successfully reducing raw materials inventory by £500,000.
- Recognized in 2003 for outstanding customer service.
- Reduced cost £150,000 in fibre optic cables.
- Saved 20% in cost by sourcing and qualifying new source for gaskets.

Marketing Specialist   2003 – 2005

Provided commercialization of product modifications for the Gas Turbine product line. Implemented business strategies for increasing sales of product modifications for Gas Turbine product line.

- Created new strategic business plans to enhance overall effectiveness of sales of services and product enhancements.
- Identified improvements to 12 product modifications to improve lead time from technical service communication.
- Drafted Product Bulletins to expedite the process of sending the communication to the customer.

—— **Education** ——

BA Business Administration University of Anytown   2003

Jake Bohannon

11 Any Avenue
Anytown AA0 0AA

 View my profile

0123456 7890
jake@Anyisp.com

Start-Up Construction Manager

PERFORMANCE PROFILE

Twenty years in construction management, with proven record of success in overseeing all phases of construction, infrastructure, and environmental projects. Experience includes full onsite construction management, estimating, budgeting, contracting, purchasing, scheduling, monitoring, and inspection of all work from start to finish. Responsible for initiatives and construction projects. Backed by a solid reputation in the industry, solid credentials,and a proven history of on-time and on-budget quality projects.

- Builds and nurtures relationships with clients, staff, suppliers, and construction inspectors.
- Promotes the successful execution of projects for owners.
- Project setup, subcontracting and staffing strategies, client relations, and contract changes.
- Delivers high-quality finished projects on time and within budget.
- Directs daily operations and problems that develop during projects.
- Assures all projects are built to specification.
- Optimum flexibility in contracting and procurement.
- Strong interpersonal skills, communication skills, and attention to detail.

PROFESSIONAL SKILLS

*Start-Up Specialist	*Safety and Regulatory Compliance	*Project Plan Execution
*Scheduling	*Contractor Coordination	*Bidding & Estimating
*Budgets and P&L	*Supplier & Client Negotiations	*Hazardous Waste Compliance
*Customer Relationships	*Manage, Train, and Mentor Employees	*Environmental Stewardship
*Certified Welding Inspector (CWI)	*Subcontractor Relations	*Fiscal Responsibility
*Equipment Installations	*Mechanical Inspector	*Fabrication
*Construction Management	*Residential & Commercial	*General Contractor
*Site Safety	*Health & Safety	*Cost Containment
*Crew & Subcontractor Supervision	*Project Management	*Sales
*Profit Margin Enhancement	*Construction Inspector Relationships	*Procurement

PROFESSIONAL EXPERIENCE

ABC Construction Services, Anytown   2005–Present
Construction Manager
General contractor specializing in construction management, including remodeling, installing, and start-up of mechanical equipment for residential, commercial, and industrial customers. Ensures profitability by accurate bidding, and by avoiding project delays, disputes, waste, accurate bidding, and customer overruns. Ensures workers have a productive and safe environment. Manages sales, contracts, production, finances, scheduling, subcontractors, resources,and customer relations.Supervises 15+ employees and subcontractors.

- Consistently sustains the company's profitability by effectively managing money and assets.

(continued)

(continued)
- Manages the company's profitability by implementing a cost control system to track expenses, supplier negotiations, on-time scheduling, reduced waste, and accurate bidding.
- Builds loyal clientele, as demonstrated by a 90% rate of current customers and up to 10% of new customers from referrals.
- Provides advice to the client on technical and construction concerns.
- Perfect safety record.
- Builds and nurtures loyal and productive relationships with subcontractors.

XYZ Construction Services Anytown   1996–2005
Owner/ Construction Manager
General contractor working with the Water Board, and private contacts.
Specialties include remodeling commercial and residential properties, structural steel and concrete work, building relocations, snagging and clearing waterways, custom signs, and wrought iron ornamentation.
Forecasted and created budgets, and built up loyal clientele.
- Negotiated contract to gut and remodel newly purchased office building.
- Achieved "high-quality firm" reputation due to innovative thinking and, effectively completing the job, resulting in an overflow of business proposals.
- Promoted a safe and productive working environment 24/7; perfect safety record with no lost time.
- Sustained the company's profitability by effectively managing money and assets.
- Managed sales, contracts, production, finances, scheduling, subcontractors, and customer relations.

PROFESSIONAL LICENCES

Construction Skills Certification Scheme (CSCS) Card

EUSR Utilities Excavation Support:
Categories 3,4&5
Asbestos Licensed Contractor
Hazardous Waste Removal Licence

PROFESSIONAL DEVELOPMENT & CERTIFICATES

Certified Welding Inspector (CWI #12879392),   2012
Institute of Welding Technology
Arc Welding Inspection and Quality Control Certificate,   2012
Institute of Welding Technology
Certified Pipeline Welding Inspector (CPWWI#63793695),   2012
National Pipeline Welding Inspector School
Preparation for AWS CWI Certified Welding Inspector Examination,   2012
Institute of Welding Technology
Arc Welding Inspection & Quality Control Certificate,   2012
Institute of Welding Technology
Certified Pipeline Welding Inspector (CWI #13268845),   2012
National Welding Inspection School

INDEX